RHAPSODY IN BLACK

RHAPSODY IN BLACK

THE LIFE AND MUSIC OF
ROY ORBISON

JOHN KRUTH

Backbeat
Books

An Imprint of Hal Leonard

Published in 2013 by Backbeat Books
An Imprint of Hal Leonard Corporation
7777 West Bluemound Road
Milwaukee, WI 53213

Trade Book Division Editorial Offices
33 Plymouth St., Montclair, NJ 07042

Illustrations by Glenn Wolff
Book Design by UB Communications

Printed in the United States of America

Library of Congress Cataloging-in-Publication Data is available upon request.

ISBN 978-1-47688-679-4

www.backbeatbooks.com

For Louie "Cannonball" Dupree
True Believer

The Papago [Indians] of southern Arizona said that a man who was humble and brave and persistent, would some night hear a song in his dream, brought by the birds that fly in from the Gulf of California; or a hawk, a cloud, the wind, or the red rain spider; and that song would be his— would add to his knowledge and power.

—Gary Snyder, *The Old Ways*

CONTENTS

INTRODUCTION

I stopped by to see my old friend Joel Dorn, a producer at Atlantic Records who had some hits years ago with Roberta Flack and Bette Midler, when I heard the news that Carl Perkins had passed away. It was a cold January day in 1998 and Joel sat slouched, deep in his chair, as his blue eyes gazed out the window at the gray winter sky, watching for signs of snow.

"Mac [Rebennack, better known as the New Orleans pianist Doctor John] once told me a story about how Carl drove from Nashville to Memphis to see this guy called Elvis Presley," Dorn recalled. "When he walked in, they were really tearing the joint apart, Elvis, Scotty [Moore], and Bill [Black]. When Carl finally got a good look at Presley, he went running to the bathroom, where he stood in front of the mirror like a teenage girl on the verge of a nervous breakdown, where he allegedly spoke these words: 'There stands Adonis and I have the face of a mule.' After just one look at Elvis, he knew it was a whole new ball game."

Other than Presley, nobody at Sun Records vaguely resembled a Greek god. Not the scrawny Perkins, or the rooster-coiffed, piano-pounding lunatic, Jerry Lee Lewis, or that square-jawed grinning hulk of the people, Johnny Cash, and, least of all, Roy Orbison, the skinny kid from Wink, Texas, with no chin and math-geek glasses. Sun's visionary producer Sam Phillips, whose unabashed truthfulness was as legendary as his razor-sharp musical instinct, was far from generous in his assessment of Roy's appearance: "I knew his voice was pure gold," Sam said, but then bluntly added, "I also knew if anyone got a look at him, he'd be dead inside a week."

Although Orbison's manager Wesley Rose appreciated Roy's voice, he, too, had serious doubts about the singer's star power. Rose, hoping to save some bread on a string section during a recording session with Orbison, confided to his producer Fred Foster, "He's not all that good-looking, especially when you compare him to guys like Fabian. I don't think he can compete."

Time has been less kind to the fleeting youth and talents of all the Fabians and Frankies we've known along the way than it has to Roy Orbison. Roy's singular voice and style—a campy vampire aesthetic comprised of jet-black hair (originally slicked back in a pompadour, then combed down into an unshakable Beatle-bowl helmet), pasty white complexion (thanks to a bout of childhood jaundice), and his trademark Ray-Ban Wayfarers—would be aped by future generations of punks and goth rockers.

Orbison was a true iconoclast. There was no mold. It's like Duke Ellington used to say: "There ain't but the one." Or as Roy's "half brother" Charlie T. Wilbury (better known as Tom Petty) put it: "No one could ever make a sound like that."

RHAPSODY IN BLACK

ONE

THE ROCKABILLY RIGOLETTO

The August afternoon sun had begun to sink, stretching the gangly kid's shadow into an elongated, abstract figure across the dry, parched earth. Grasping an empty pop bottle tightly in his hand, the boy began to sing into his make-believe microphone, warbling, uncertain at first, until something inside of him suddenly erupted, something strange, volcanic, burbling up from down below, something unearthly, startling, unknown even to himself, something Dwight Yoakam would describe years later as "the cry of an angel falling backward through an open window."

As the boy tilted his head back, facing the sky with his pale eyes shut tight, his voice began to soar with all the soul an eight-year-old could muster. In the distance oil rigs pinged and clanked in a steady four-four rhythm as the warm prairie wind sighed like violins behind his lonely song—one part opera, one part blue yodel. Excited, he barely slept that night, like a comic book superhero dying to tell someone about his newfound secret power.

A couple of days later, his father, Orbie Lee, asked Roy what he wanted to be when he grew up. Any other kid in town would have probably answered "sheriff," "roustabout," or maybe "taxidermist." But Roy Kelton Orbison replied without hesitation. He seemed to know what his earthly mission was destined to be pretty much from the get-go. "A singer," he told his father earnestly.

"Well, all the same, much as you love music, son, you'd better learn something about geology if you don't want to be stuck working in the oil fields for the rest your life," Orbie Lee advised knowingly.

Country music wasn't merely played on the radio around the Orbison household; it was an integral part of family life. Asked what he wanted for his sixth birthday, Roy replied, "A harmonica." Instead, Orbie Lee presented him with his first guitar, a Sears & Roebuck Gene Autry Singing Cowboy model, and showed him how to tune it, and how to strum and form his chords. His dad loved Jimmie Rodgers' blue yodels and hard-knock country ballads; and a couple of Roy's uncles, Orbie Lee's brother Charlie and Uncle Kenneth, on his mother Nadine's side, who sang from time to time on the local radio station in Vernon, would come around to pick and sing on the weekends. A pal of Orbie Lee's from work named Clois Russell stopped by the house to play old country favorites with him at Sunday afternoon fish fries.

Orbie Lee and Clois sounded pretty good together and performed occasionally around town at local dances. Roy was not only "blessed with his father's voice," as he recalled in an interview years later, but Orbie Lee fueled his ten-year-old son's love of country music by taking him to see Lefty Frizzell, whose Number One hit "If You've Got the Money, I've Got the Time" was one of Roy's favorites.

Orbison—now that's a name you don't hear every day. Irish in origin, from the north, about twenty miles outside of Belfast, in county Armagh, in the town of Lurgan, known as "The Long Ridge," a typical village lined with rows of small thatch-roofed cottages and a parish with a Protestant spire that looms over the town, tall and dark as a witch's hat. Lurgan was peopled, for the most part, by the British, who raised corn and manufactured and sold linen, both of which had begun to decline in profitability by the start of the 1700s.

Lurgan and neighboring villages of Portadown and Craigavon comprised what eventually became known as the dreaded "Murder Triangle," a region so named for the constant violent clashes between the Protestants and Catholics that continued all the way into the 1990s.

Roy's earliest known ancestor, Thomas Orbison, born in 1715, hailed from the land where "the Troubles" raged.

Sometime by the middle of the century, Thomas crossed the Atlantic to the New World and settled in Pennsylvania, where he raised his family. Both his son John and his grandson Thomas were born and lived in Cumberland County, a bucolic paradise settled by farmers and merchants from the British Isles and Germany. Samuel, born to Thomas and his wife, Jenny Moore, in 1815, was raised in Virginia and eventually migrated to the far southwest corner of Oklahoma, to the town of Olustee and there, in the barren plains, the family stayed until Orbie Lee—Roy's dad—was born on January 8, 1913. Orbie Lee had a twin brother (oddly enough also named Orby, spelled with a *y*) who died at birth.

Whatever legends and anecdotes have been told and retold around the family table over the years, it's pretty safe to say the Orbisons came from sturdy salt-of-the-earth working stock—merchants, farmers, and carpenters, who learned their trades and managed to look after their families despite whatever wars, disease, bank failures, and natural disasters came their way.

There was nobody like Roy in the Orbison clan, not before or since. Although his kin all loved, played, and sang country music with genuine feeling, it was Roy, the withdrawn, sensitive kid, who possessed the ability to tap directly into that deep turbulent/sometimes joyful river of song that flowed through his veins and one day would come thundering from the cathedral of his lungs.

Although Roy was raised in West Texas, under the spell of swing, C&W, and Mexican music, it was ultimately the echo of the ancient bard's song that resounded through his ballads. The deep sadness of his songs sprang from a faraway land torn apart for generations by the Troubles. Although his relatives fled Ireland centuries ago, the Celtic spirit that fueled Roy's soul never left him.

Orbie Lee and Nadine Orbison's story reads like a chapter in a John Steinbeck book. A couple of kids, married in the winter of 1933 at the tender age of nineteen, head west from Oklahoma into Texas searching for work, drifting through the dust and heat and relentless wind. Walking along the roadside one afternoon, they find a cigarette and share its precious, sumptuous smoke . . . a memory that would last a lifetime. Uncertain what tomorrow will bring, they never lose hope. She's sensitive, paints, writes poetry, has been married already once before. He can fix anything with his hands, is a passionate mechanic, blessed with the voice of a country singer. The Carter Family's penny-plain poetry reminded them to always "Keep on the Sunny Side" of life, while Blind Alfred Reed's "How Can a Poor Man Stand Such Times and Live" spelled out the plight so many folks faced at the time, posing a question that hounded Orbie Lee and the rest of his generation:

> When we pay our grocery bill
> We just feel like making our will
> How can a poor man stand such times and live?

As unforgiving as the elements were, the poverty and desolation of men's souls was that much greater. But through it all, the Orbisons kept their faith and kept on having babies. The first, Grady Lee, born in July 1933, came along just months after their marriage (and might have been the impetus for a shotgun wedding). Roy Kelton arrived three years later, in '36, followed, finally, by Sammy Keith, who was born ten years later, after World War II.

Everywhere Orbie Lee and Nadine turned they found nothing. Nothing but empty stares and weathered hands, open palms begging for a handout, scrounging in the dust or folded in prayer, their owners hoping that Franklin Delano Roosevelt, "The Poor Man's Friend" back in Washington, might pull some sort of miraculous hat trick and put the country back on track again. Migrant farmers stripped of their land and dignity knew all too well the meaning of that Depression-era ditty "You Get No Bread with One Meatball." The desperate "little man" needed somebody to come up with a plan, a fair deal for the average Joe trying to feed his family, clothe his children, and find some two-by-four they could call home, where his kids could go to school, make friends, and have a branch of stability to perch on in a world of constant change.

Meanwhile Hitler, the madman with the comedian's mustache, had pulled his tanks into Poland and was commanding his robotic army of Nazi tin men, wired on amphetamines and skewed ideology, to raze what remained of the Old World. Then, one winter day, the "Japs" bombed Pearl Harbor and suddenly everybody was back to work again, putting their shoulders to the wheel for the war effort—the Big One, the war that followed the war that was supposed "to end all wars."

With the sudden flood of defense plant workers pouring into Fort Worth, Texas, the region soon faced a polio epidemic. So Grady Lee and Roy were packed up and sent off to live with their grandma Schultz, Nadine's mother, a divorcée down in Vernon. Meanwhile, Orbie Lee and Nadine (along with their good friends "Double O" and Opal Harris) built B-24 and B-32 bombers, pounding sheet metal and riveting steel day after day on an assembly line, while the rank perfume of "Cowtown's" stockyards permeated their little railroad flat above a drugstore on the north side of town.

It was April Fools' Day 1945 when a nine-year-old Roy Orbison first mustered enough confidence to enter a talent contest sponsored by the local radio station in Vernon. Like a vision from a Norman Rockwell painting, the peculiar-looking kid with the Coke-bottle-thick glasses, jug-handle ears, and impish grin stood precariously on a footstool, holding his guitar, stretching his neck to reach the microphone. Roy strummed and sang Louisiana governor Jimmie Davis' "You Are My Sunshine" with everything he had, and in return KVWC granted him a slot every Saturday afternoon to sing a couple songs on the air. Young Roy's growing repertoire soon included heartfelt renditions of the coal miner's complaint "Sixteen Tons" and Red Foley's tearjerker "Old Shep," as well as a tune of his own called "A Vow of Love," which he composed one afternoon in his grandma's yard.

By summer's end, Harry Truman had nuked Japan and the Axis was in ruins. United once more, the family moved, along with their friends the Harrises, to Wink, near the New Mexico border, finding work in the oil fields now that warplanes were no longer needed. By the time the Orbisons arrived in Wink (a town named in honor of Colonel C. M. Winkler—a "wink" was about as long as it took to get from one end of town to the other), the former oil-boom town of 25,000 had shrunk to just a few thousand. There wasn't much to do in Wink other than cruise up and down Main Street in the summertime and listen to the sidewalks crack in the dead of winter.

"There was a lot of loneliness in West Texas where I grew up. We used to say it was the center of everything, five hundred miles away from anything," Roy once said.

Orbie Lee, like every other guy in town, worked as an oil rigger for the Olson Drilling Company, just over the state line in Jal, New Mexico. As his wages were slim, about $1.50 an hour, Nadine took a job working as a waitress at a local greasy spoon, while she studied nights to become a nurse.

While most boys played football for the Wink Wildcats' junior varsity team, the Kittens, the awkward, four-eyed Roy became obsessed with the country music he listened to broadcast over the radio out of Shreveport, Louisiana. He adored Ernest Tubb, who Orbie Lee took him to see pickin' and grinnin' on the back of a flatbed Ford. Roy watched, slack-jawed, as Tubb, with his white ten-gallon Stetson and blinding high-beam smile, sang his big hit song "Walking the Floor Over You."

But it was the plain-truth poetry and soulful vocals of the honky-tonk king William Orville "Lefty" Frizzell that knocked the young Orbison sideways (and would inspire his nickname "Lefty" years later, when he joined forces with George Harrison and Bob Dylan to form the short-lived supergroup the Traveling Wilburys).

Roy soon discovered the best way of making new friends in Wink was by strumming his guitar on the school steps or in the hallway between classes. Years later, Orbison recounted how he'd made his "first money" at the age of nine or ten, singing in a contest at an old-fashioned medicine show. Tying for first place, he split the cash prize of fifteen bucks with an older kid. Roy sang the Cajun waltz "Jole Blon," which, he explained, was "very difficult" as the lyrics were a jumble of "pidgin French [and] English." He'd learn the tune phonetically, one word at a time, by putting his "finger on the record and slow[ing] it down."

Along with "Jole Blon," Roy's respectable renditions of old jug-band numbers such as "Crawdad Hole," and Grandpa Jones' "Good Old

Mountain Dew" eventually caught the ear of fellow student James Morrow. Roy and "Jamie," who were both twelve at the time, started getting together after school at the Morrows' house to strum guitars together while Roy did most of the singing. Jamie, who also blew sax and clarinet, had a knack for making any instrument sing. His dad, who played fiddle, had an old mandolin that Jamie picked up and began to figure out. After Morrow taught his pal Charlie "Slob" Evans to thump an old neglected bass fiddle that had been lying around in the school's orchestra practice room, they formed a trio. Eventually they were joined by Richard "Head" West on piano and Billy Pat "Spider" Ellis, who, lacking a drum set, beat the stuffing out of the Morrows' sofa with a pair of drumsticks.

The aspiring combo remained unnamed until their junior high science teacher, Miss Hardin, cleverly christened them the Wink Westerners. Eventually, they built up an eclectic repertoire that included everything from raucous Dixieland tunes to Hank Williams' "Kaw-Liga" to Glenn Miller's "In the Mood" played in a Texas swing style.

Years later, the Wink Westerners' bassist Slob Evans defined their eclectic mix as "countrybilly." "We were trying to mesh these things together, because we didn't wanna be classified as country and western," he told *Mojo* magazine.

Roy soon wrote his second song, the tellingly titled "I Am Just a Dreamer," which he recorded on a small reel-to-reel tape deck at Dick West's house. Beyond his burgeoning keyboard skills, West had gained a local reputation as a "genius" when it came to tinkering with electronics.

Word of the young band started getting around, and soon the Wink Westerners were invited to play at a school assembly. Their first official gig took place at the Day Drug Store on Main Street. There, they serenaded a bunch of roustabouts who, impressed by the boy's earnest efforts, showered them with handfuls of spare change.

In 1949 a teenage band was virtually unheard of in West Texas. Just thirteen, Roy and the boys were still years from graduating high school, yet they were already performing at Wink Wildcat victory dances, the local pool hall, the VFW, and the Archway Club.

Ten miles down the road in Kermit, the local radio station, KERB, offered the Wink Westerners a regular early-morning spot to promote their music. After coercing their parents to take turns driving them down to the station, the boys would wake up at dawn, load the car with instruments, play a couple numbers live on the air, and head back to school just before the morning bell rang. But it was all in a day's work for the Wink Westerners, who, in their matching checked shirts and kerchiefs, resembled a crew of apple-cheeked volunteer firemen, ready to sing some forlorn kitten down from a tree.

The band's first real break in showbiz came one night at the Lions Club, when, much to their surprise, they were offered four hundred bucks to play a dance. Although Orbison later claimed the band only knew a handful of songs at the time, they immediately knuckled down and rehearsed every night to expand their repertoire. School superintendent R. A. Lipscomb found the boys' music impressive enough to hire them to serenade his crowd while he stumped for the post of Lions Club district governor.

That July, Lipscomb invited the Wink Westerners to accompany him to Chicago, where they stayed at the Hilton and performed in the lobby every day for a week while R. A. hobnobbed with his cronies at the Lions Club convention.

Photos of the combo portray a bunch of good-natured kids flashing "aw shucks" grins while their ringleader, Roy, stands front and center, resembling a scrawny Buck Henry with a kerchief tightly tied around his bulging Adam's apple, as he holds the premier guitar of its day, a Les Paul. The Wink Westerners were actually quite modern for their time. While Roy employed an Echoplex, which made his strings shimmer, Morrow, inspired by the father of the electric mandolin, Tiny Moore, of Bob Wills' Texas Playboys, plugged his axe into a portable reel-to-reel tape machine, which added a mercurial, ghostly tremolo to his nimble picking.

Roy Orbison's life growing up in Wink was basically an ugly-duckling story. Not that one day he would suddenly transform into a handsome swan, win the heart of the homecoming queen, and drive off happily ever after into the sunset in his two-tone '57 Chevy. But the peculiar kid eventually blossomed into something far beyond anything the small-town locals ever might have imagined.

The cruel teenage dramas that played out on the barren prairies of the Permian Basin had a powerful hand in molding Orbison's shy, withdrawn personality. Gawky and self-conscious, Roy watched from the sidelines as his older brother, Grady Lee, and his buddies built their local reputations muscling a pigskin downfield for the Wink Wildcats. Instead, the young outsider found a niche doing whimsical sketches for the high school yearbook and playing baritone horn in the school marching band. Roy's buddy Joe Ray Hammer (a name that sounds like a character from a Bruce Springsteen song) introduced him not only to the joys of blowing brass but to the zing of nicotine as well. In the long run, Orbison's relationship with tobacco turned out to have a much greater staying power than belching Sousa marches.

The fickle chicks who broke his gentle heart and the schoolyard bullies who goaded and pummeled him would never know the intense highs and lows of the human soul that Roy would experience and transform into breathtaking songs. The quiet, insecure boy was forced, for many of his formative years, to take refuge in the lonely attic of his mind, where he learned to dream bigger than them all. In his solitude, Roy mostly spent his time drawing and playing guitar. He also loved movies and regularly escaped into the black-and-white world, watching newsreels, war films, and cowboy movies—any human drama that allowed him to momentarily forget his own.

Although he wasn't sure of it at the time, Roy Orbison would eventually have his day, and the debonair football captain who once likened his homely face to his ass and branded him with the nasty nickname "Facetus" (a name that Roy, at a point of low self-esteem, referred to himself by when signing his friends' yearbooks) would have a lifetime supply of crow to chaw. Roy's revenge on the prissy, popular girls who taunted him with their beauty and cruel laughter would come years later in songs like "Pretty One."

For the young Roy Orbison, love was scarce as rain on the parched summer flatlands. Old friends reckoned he'd rather live in self-imposed exile than lower his extreme double standards. The "four-eyed" Roy actually refused to date any gal who wore glasses. Unable to score with the local girls, Orbison and his pals, including a dude known as Freako Gonzalez, allegedly drove nearly two hundred miles down to Mexico in the middle of the night to quench the thirst of their teenage lust with the buck-a-fuck whores of Ojinaga.

Wild as his Mexican sexcapades were rumored to have been, the most important rite of passage in Roy's young life would come on April 16, 1954, when Orbie Lee drove him up to Dallas to see Elvis play the Big D Jamboree.

The 6,000-seat Dallas Sportatorium was home to wrestling events on weeknights, but Saturday nights were reserved for the Jamboree, which presented a roster of regional country bands, along with a handful of stars from *Grand Ole Opry* and *Louisiana Hayride*. The shows, which were broadcast live over radio station KRLD, usually ran from eight until midnight and cost just sixty cents for adults and thirty for kids.

Roy witnessed a few impressive moments that spring night before Elvis took the stage to make his Dallas debut. There was the up-and-coming Sonny James, a suave, wavy-haired "Southern Gentleman," whose streak of hits dominated the country charts from the early '50s all the way through the early '80s, as well as the outrageous Charline Arthur, who prowled the stage playing guitar while singing in a sexy, throaty growl. If that wasn't provocative enough, the outrageous Miss Arthur was the first woman in country music brazen enough to wear slacks onstage. Also appearing that night was Hank Locklin, a country crooner heard regularly on the Hayride, whose tragic ballads and melodramatic rendition of "Danny Boy" would stick with Roy for years to come, influencing his recording of the song in 1972.

As good as these singers were, none of them could hold a candle to Presley. The former truck driver from Tupelo suddenly appeared, oily, dapper, and sneering at the astonished audience while thrashing at the acoustic guitar that balanced upon his gyrating hips. Meanwhile, Scotty Moore grinned, amused by the madness as he picked slippery country riffs on his Gibson ES-295 cutaway, while Floyd Cramer pumped the piano and Bill Black, known for some wild stage antics of his own, slapped his double bass, laying down a fat bottom while adding light rim-shot-like accents in lieu of the steady beat of a drummer, as D. J. Fontana had yet to join the fray.

Elvis was frenetic, playing a calculated game of give-and-take with his crowd, giving them a bit of hanky-panky with "That's All Right," then shifting into a percolating "Blue Moon of Kentucky" (with the sort of rhythm that the mother of the song's author, Bill Monroe, never would allow), and finally driving the girls over the edge with a revved-up rendition of Chuck Berry's "Maybellene."

While Orbie Lee found Elvis Presley a "greasy-haired" abomination, his son was transfixed, "dumbfounded" by the energy of "this punk kid . . . a real raw cat singing like a bird." Roy admitted later that he was taken aback by the shocking sight of Elvis spitting out his gum and telling "dumb off-color" jokes.

"There was just no reference point in the culture to compare it," Roy said in an interview years later, searching for a way to explain Elvis. To Roy, Presley was the phenomenon of his day. "Every so often the time is right and the circumstances are right, the talent is there, and everything just happens almost like it was planned. It wasn't planned," he told Penny Reel of England's *New Musical Express*. "Every once in awhile the world will push up an Elvis Presley or a Beatles. But that's really outside the realm of show business."

Looking at Roy's high school yearbook photo, no one would ever have guessed his hopes for the future (spelled out in trite rhyming verse) had a chance of coming true.

> To lead a Western band
> Is his after-school wish
> And of course to marry
> A beautiful dish

In June '54, Roy and his fellow bandmates Richard West and Billy Pat Ellis finally graduated from Wink High School, but before heading off to North Texas State College in Denton with Billy Pat and Joe Ray Hammer (Jamie and Charlie, who were both a year younger, had to stay behind to finish school), Orbison got a job shoveling tar on the interstate in the scorching summer sun. It didn't take long before he realized he wasn't cut out for the intense physical demands of manual labor. Returning home exhausted and grimy each night, Roy often collapsed on his bed, passing out in his sweat-drenched work clothes before managing to peel them off and stand, worn-out and numb, beneath a steaming shower. If he still had the energy left, he'd bolt down his dinner and then fall asleep for what felt like a few short hours before having to drag himself out of bed and do it all over again. But the experience wasn't lost on him. Years later the memory of that grueling job sparked a grinding chain-gang rocker called "Working for the Man," which turned his money green in 1962.

That fall Roy finally escaped Wink and headed up to Denton, where he later admitted to having "slept right through" his classes at North Texas State. Although bored with college, Orbison found inspiration in his music class. It was no surprise that he spent more time with his six-string, working out new chords and riffs, than on his studies. Drummer Billy Pat Ellis, who also enrolled in the class, soon discovered he'd been "doin' everything wrong."

When Roy wasn't up half the night playing guitar, he could be found down at the local pool hall trying to make a buck with a cue. Terry Widlake, Orbison's bass player/road manager from 1968 until the late '70s, recalled that "Roy was a real pool hustler back in his college days. That's how he made whatever extra money he had."

Despite his poor vision, Orbison apparently had no problem rocking the 8-ball into the corner pocket. But Minnesota Fats or Fast Eddie he was not. Shy and soft-spoken, Roy, no matter how great his skill, never had a chance against the mix of cutthroat pool sharks and small-time thugs he met hanging around in those neon-smoke-filled dens of iniquity.

More significant than his skill at billiards or his mediocre academic career was crossing paths with Pat Boone, who'd recently won a local talent contest and would soon make his national debut on *The Arthur Godfrey Show*. Pat's starched and ironed covers of Little Richard's "Tutti Frutti" and "Long Tall Sally" were just two of his thirty-eight Top Forty hits to come. The great-grandson of the legendary pioneer

Daniel Boone, Pat was on a mission to homogenize rock 'n' roll and make it good, clean fun for the entire family. Boone, with his wholesome smile and white bucks, advised Roy to cool the rockabilly jive and focus on writing radio-ready pop songs.

Returning home at the end of his first semester for the Christmas holidays, Roy had an epiphany one night while playing with the Wink Westerners at a New Year's Eve dance. In the long minutes before midnight, as the crowd waited anxiously for the ball to drop, the band found themselves stretching out on Bill Haley's clean-cut cover of Big Joe Turner's "Shake, Rattle and Roll." It was the day of the two-minute-and-spare-change pop single, built on tight, economic arrangements as determined by the commercial demands of the jukebox and AM radio, and the boys, until this point, had been blissfully ignorant of the joys (and pitfalls) of jamming. But after a few minutes, Billy Pat Ellis' slim backbeat turned fat and greasy as the primordial bump and grind of R&B began to seep into his playing, possessing the dancers and young lovers necking in the dark corners. The room soon grew steamy, falling under the sensual spell of the music. Slob Evans' bass throbbed slow and steady as a heartbeat while Morrow's fingers chased themselves up and down the fretboard of his electric mandolin. Roy's guitar growled and snarled, churning out chunky, rug-cutting rhythms as his pinky instinctively found that forbidden seventh, the bluest of blue notes.

Trying to "sound black" had worked wonders for Elvis, making him unique and exotic to some, dirty and taboo to others, but Roy had never been much of a fan of what was known around the South as "sepia" music. His heart, until that fateful night, had belonged to the lazy clip-clop of cowboy ballads and the lonesome boozy twang of the honky-tonk. But something strange and unexpected came over the Wink Westerners. Whether they knew it or not, they'd collectively fallen under that mystical spell that Lightnin' Hopkins, Muddy Waters, and John Lee Hooker often sang of. And now their "mojo" was apparently working, driving everyone in that small West Texas joint to the wall. There was no turning back. With the dawn of the

New Year, Roy Orbison became "fully converted" to power and glory of rock 'n' roll.

Pat Boone's career counseling aside, it was Roy's pledge as a member of Lambda Chi Alpha fraternity that turned out to be the apex of his brief academic stint. Amongst Orbison's fellow frat brothers were his old pals Billy Pat and Joe Ray Hammer as well as a pair of dudes named Wade Moore and Dick Penner. Around campus Wade and Dick were known as the College Kids, a duo who played and sang their own guitar-driven turbocharged rockabilly tunes, mostly about girls and how they looked and danced and kissed. In February 1955, Moore and Penner took their guitars and a six-pack of beer up to their frat house roof and within fifteen minutes wrote an infectious rocker called "Ooby Dooby." Built on a basic twelve-bar blues progression with a handful of stops thrown in for urgency's sake, the tune celebrates a young man's growing obsession with some girl who does a wild, sexy, rattlesnake dance known as the "Ooby Dooby."

Roy recalled seeing the College Kids live for the first time at a Saturday night school-sponsored variety show. "These two boys stepped out on the stage with a guitar and sang 'Ooby Dooby,' and they just knocked me flat," Orbison raved. "I was astounded, because they made more music than the whole orchestra."

By summer's end, Dick Penner would introduce Roy to engineer Jim Beck, who offered to cut a couple of demos for his group at his studio in Dallas. While impressed that Beck produced Billy Walker and Marty Robbins' records for Columbia, Roy was nearly beside himself after hearing Jim had worked with his honky-tonk hero, Lefty Frizzell.

After cranking out a suitably raucous rendition of "Ooby Dooby," the Wink Westerners took a shot at a cover of the Clovers' "Hey Miss Fannie" as the B-side of what would be their debut single—that was, if anyone at Columbia Records deemed them worthy, which, sadly, they did not.

But that didn't stop an opportunistic A&R man from delivering Moore and Penner's song to one of their own artists to take a shot at. Sid King and the Five Strings were a clutch of clean-cut rockabilly pioneers with a bouncy sound that revealed a strong Texas swing influence. Sid also had a penchant for zany novelty numbers like "Who Put the Turtle in Myrtle's Girdle."

The following March, King and the Strings recorded "Ooby Dooby" (their version was spelled "Oobie Doobie") in Dallas with an old-school Drifters-style vocal arrangement and a raspy honking tenor sax solo that was a throwback to the late-'40s/early-'50s jump records of Wynonie Harris. Their cover of "Ooby Dooby" ended with a big "doo-wah" that sounded more vaudevillian cornball than rockabilly slick.

In the meantime, Orbison continued struggling through his American history and English lit courses before dropping out of college for good after failing to show up for his final exams. With the end of his sophomore semester, Roy's college days were over, and he moved into a grubby bachelor pad with a couple of pals in Odessa. Out of school and out of work, he focused on getting his band together and scrounging up some gigs.

As Roy, Jamie, and Billy Pat played less and less C&W and more rock 'n' roll, they decided a new name for the band was in order. Hell, they didn't even live in Wink anymore—and besides, their name, the Wink Westerners, sounded old hat, like a bolo-wearing swing band from a bygone era.

A contest was held on a local weekly TV spot to name the band. Of the sixty-five or so suggestions that came rolling in, they didn't like any of them. While Little Roy and the Joy Boys was admittedly pretty awful, Roy Orbison and the Video Jambor-Jeans was simply out of the question. They needed something that brimmed with passion, something with an edge, something that would resonate with a young crowd, the kids who wanted to cut loose and dance and fall madly in love. The group eventually forged a handle of their own—the Teen Kings. It was simple, romantic. It sounded fast and dangerous, sort of like the name of a gang that James Dean or Sal Mineo might've belonged to and had their girlfriends stitch in big red letters on the backs of their black leather jackets.

Richard West was out of the picture now, and Jack Kennelly would soon replace Charles "Slob" Evans, who'd joined the navy. Slob was the first of the old Wink crew to find a girl and settle down and get married. He'd already had his fill of nightlife, having grown up in a bar where his mom worked as a cocktail waitress.

Kennelly, a former Wink native, who'd recently seen Roy and the boys playing a couple numbers on a local TV show, stopped by their duplex on Walnut Street one afternoon and, much to his surprise, was instantly corralled by Orbison to play bass in the band. Despite Jack's protests that he'd never touched a bass before in his life and had never even thought of playing the instrument, Roy steered him down to Armstrong's Music Store, put a bull fiddle in his hands, positioned his fingers on the neck, and showed him how to slap its fat steel strings. Kennelly had no money for the down payment (some three hundred bucks), but that didn't stop Roy from begging and cajoling a deal for him. Soon, Jack walked out the door, lugging the cumbersome instrument down the street, suddenly in debt but excited about his future as a Teen King.

Jack later admitted to faking his way through "the first dozen" shows. After just a few hours of feeling his way around, Kennelly found himself standing before a live television camera with a nervous grin on is face as his fingers fumbled up and down the neck of the instrument, as he desperately tried to keep up with the Teen Kings.

An hour or so later he was standing up onstage at the County Auditorium, opening for the legendary Chuck Berry. Whenever he found himself lost in the middle of a song, Jack, hoping to distract the crowd from noticing his musical ineptitude, would begin twirling his bass around like a chubby dance partner. The crowd, of course, ate it up, thinking it was all part of the act. Later that night, Jack went to bed happy, his fingers burning with blisters.

From that night on, Kennelly devoted nearly every waking hour to practicing the bass, learning to bump a hypnotic boogie or walk a slinky syncopated blues line. But Jack soon discovered the music business was just as unforgiving as his raw, aching fingertips after one particularly slow night at the Archway when the Teen Kings went home with the paltry sum of seventy-five cents each, along with a pack of chewing gum.

Even as stars of their local TV show, they weren't paid much better. Thanks to a sponsorship from the local Pontiac dealer, Roy and the boys were paid five dollars each for hosting their own weekly spot every Saturday afternoon from four thirty to five on KOSA TV, Channel 7, in Odessa. In addition to the Teen Kings' rowdy renditions of Little Richard's "Tutti Frutti" and the Platters' "The Great Pretender," viewers were treated to a guest appearance by whatever itinerant musician had just blown into town to perform at the Odessa Coliseum. Orbison's weekly show would include performances by that vulgar hip-shaking hillbilly bopper Elvis Presley and an up-and-coming leather-faced country crooner from Kingsland, Arkansas, named Johnny Cash.

The four Teen Kings were eventually rounded out by rhythm guitarist Johnny "Peanuts" Wilson, who Jack had met bagging groceries at the local market. Barely five foot two, Peanuts was "a little short guy with a big personality," as Billy Pat remembered him. Wilson, who also sang in the band, strummed a jumbo-bodied Martin acoustic guitar that was "dang near tall as he was," Kennelly recollected.

The following spring, the Teen Kings, with a pocket full of borrowed cash, thanks to Jamie's father, Henry, headed north to Norman Petty's studio in Clovis, New Mexico, where, on March 4, they once again laid down another loosey-goosey take of "Ooby Dooby." Shiny with tape echo, Roy's voice slipped and slid like mercury down a drainpipe as he kicked off the song, "Hey baby, jump over here. . . ."

Producer Petty would play a fleeting but important role in Orbison's early career. With its "modern" reverb chamber, Norman's studio was *the* destination and laboratory for many aspiring West Texas musicians, including Buddy Holly, Waylon Jennings, Buddy Knox, and '60s folksinger Carolyn Hester.

The lovely flaxen-haired chanteuse from Waco (and first wife of legendary folksinger/author Richard Fariña) recalled her first visit to Petty's studio in 1957: "My mom heard one of Norman Petty's acts, [the vocal group] the Roses, on Lubbock radio, so she wrote to Norman about her daughter, the folksinger. He phoned her and said he would be happy to give me a listen, so Mom and I drove over to Clovis on a very hot July afternoon, stopping once on the way for a nice, icy Dr.

Pepper. Norman's studio was brand-new at the time and squeaky clean. His wife, Vi, was there and Norma Jean Berry, their good friend and assistant in all their activities."

Taking her guitar out of the case, Carolyn nervously sang three or four songs for Petty. "Norman said 'I don't know much about folk music, but if you have enough songs to record an album, I think we could get you a record contract in New York.' He explained that one of his artists had made a big success and they'd be happy to record me right away," Hester said. Petty of course was referring the enormous popularity of Buddy Holly's "That'll Be the Day."

"I was in total awe of what was happening," Carolyn recalled. "Norman's Clovis sound was classic. The studio was built next door to his mom and dad's house, with the echo chambers built in the building next to his dad's car repair shop and gas station. The recording equipment was about the best you could find in that day. Norman's good friend Al Hamm was an engineer for Columbia Records. Norman and Vi were both very organized and kept things shipshape. Central to Norman and Vi's lives were their family, their pride in their musical abilities, and their Christian ethics. There was no alcohol, swearing, or dirty jokes around them at any time. You could have your family come to the studio if you wanted. I even met Buddy [Holly]'s parents there once. My dad played harmonica on one song, 'Wreck of the Old '97,' on my first album. George Atwood played bass on everything, and Jerry Allison [of the Crickets] played percussion on a cardboard box with brushes."

Petty soon secured a deal for Carolyn with Coral Records. Coral, along with Brunswick, the label that signed Buddy, was part of the Decca family. Although Norman Petty's approach to recording was no-nonsense, his business practices were somewhat questionable. For fledging regional bands, many of whom had no previous studio experience, Petty's deal seemed like a good one. Norman, an organist who briefly made the charts with a cover of Duke Ellington's sultry "Mood Indigo," which sold in the neighborhood of a half million copies, allowed bands and singers all the time they needed to record their songs. In return for his expertise, encouragement, and connections (Norman regularly secured record deals for the artists who walked through his door), he was known to take a share of the writing credit as well as a sizable percentage of the publishing royalties. Petty would appear as cowriter on many of Buddy Holly's greatest hits, including "Peggy Sue," "That'll Be the Day," and "Oh Boy," as well as a few songs written by Roy. To his credit, Norman pitched two of Orbison's tunes to Holly, who recorded tepid versions of "An Empty Cup (and a Broken Date)" and "You've Got Love" for his 1957 debut album, *The Chirping Crickets*. According to the Brunswick label on Johnny "Peanuts" Wilson's recording of the song, it was written by him, Norman Petty, and Roy, in that order. While "You've Got Love" was never a hit, the issue over writing credit for the song would trouble Wilson for years to come.

As the Crickets' manager, Norman claimed to protect the boys from flights of youthful folly by holding onto their money for them. But immediately following Holly's tragic death in 1959, large sums owed the doomed singer and his band mysteriously disappeared.

Two weeks after the Clovis session, on March 19, 1956, Je-Wel Records released the Teen Kings' debut single, a cover of the Clovers' "Trying to Get to You" backed with "Ooby Dooby."

But the miniscule Je-Wel label, based in Jal, New Mexico, was hardly what anyone might consider a professional outfit. Full of good intentions and with no experience to speak of, Jean Oliver, a singer/accordionist with a local group known as the Western Melodiers and a former girl-friend of James Morrow, sweet-talked her dad, Weldon Rogers, into funding the Teen Kings' first session at Petty's studio. From there they formed a record label they dubbed Je-Wel (a combination of Jean and Weldon), printed up a pile of 45s (with Orbison's name misspelled on the label), and distributed them around West Texas and New Mexico.

According to Weldon Rogers, the Teen Kings were "selling records galore." Nearly wearing the rubber off their tires, the folks at Je-Wel hauled trunk loads of "Ooby Dooby" to every record shop and radio station around the Southwest.

"Trying to Get to You," written by Charles Singleton and Rose Marie McCoy (who, after splitting with Singleton, went on to write a string of R&B hits for Big Maybelle, Louis Jordan, and Ike and Tina Turner), was originally recorded by the Eagles (no, not those Eagles, but a mid-'50s R&B group from Washington, DC) and released by Mercury Records in 1954. Roy had previously heard Elvis perform the song live, at the Big D Jamboree or when Presley was a guest on Orbison's TV show. (Recorded at Sun, in July 1955, Elvis' version of "Trying to Get to You" remained in the can until the following spring, when RCA released Presley's self-titled debut album one month after Roy cut the song in Clovis.) Although the Teen Kings' reputation was built on rave-up rockabilly numbers like "Ooby Dooby," "Trying to Get to You," was chosen as the A-side of the single. Its sad, romantic lyrics, (embroidered with flowing riffs from Morrow's plaintive clarinet) spoke not only to Orbison's benefactor Jean Oliver, but to the most "beautiful dish" in West Texas, Miss Claudette Frady.

Roy had seen Claudette around. There was no way he could miss her. She had it all as far as he was concerned—she was gorgeous and she liked music. At first Claudette dated the Teen Kings' butch-waxed, square-jawed bass player Jack Kennelly. They were hot and heavy for a couple months until Jack suddenly dumped her for some peculiar reason that Roy would eventually discover. Before the awkward and insecure Orbison (who, hoping to improve his image, began dying his lank, sandy hair black in the bathroom sink) could barely stammer the words he'd rehearsed to ask her out, she'd already started dating Peanuts on the rebound. Roy couldn't believe it! Claudette, the bewitching brunette with flashing dark eyes and perfect cheerleader curves, stood nearly half a foot taller than Little Johnny Wilson. Thinking about it only drove him crazy. He desperately wanted Claudette Frady for his own, but he knew he had no chance with her. Why in the world would she ever give old "Facetus" the time of day?

"I think she felt sorry for him because he was so poor," Terry Widlake said. "Roy was always broke. He never had any money. He'd spend whatever he had going to every movie in town. Claudette would bring him home-cooked food. Roy said he was particularly fond of the caraway seed cake she used to bake. But he would never eat it. He'd take it home to that terrible little shack where they all lived and share it with his mom and dad and brothers."

He might not have been much to look at, but Roy Orbison was the closest thing to a rock 'n' roll star that Claudette Frady was ever going to find in West Texas, unless she happened to cross paths with one of the Buddys (Knox or Holly). Besides, Roy was a real gentleman, kind, soft-spoken and mature—meaning he was older, which didn't please her mother, Geraldine, very much.

Alone in her room Claudette fell under the lilting spell of "Trying to Get to You," playing it over and over again, until she was nearly mesmerized. She, like lots of other girls, was certain that Roy was singing those sad, desperate lyrics directly to her. Dinky, Claudette's little sister, didn't think Roy Orbison was so hot. Meanwhile, Geraldine wanted to scream.

Pretty as she was, Claudette was by all accounts a lonely soul, a latchkey kid whose folks ran a popular barbecue joint while she was expected to look after her kid brother, Bill, and little sis every day after school. Roy Orbison's music spoke to her, quelled her fears, reassured her that somebody was there, someone who would listen to her troubles, somebody who cared. It's not hard to picture a beautiful melancholic teenage girl alone in her room, chain-smoking one cigarette after another, while primping before the mirror as she pined for her prince. It didn't matter if he was handsome or not—Claudette had more than enough gorgeous to go around.

She had fallen in love, like millions of girls would one day, with Roy's voice. As Tom Waits (who joined Orbison onstage years later, maniacally hammering away on a piano for the filming of *A Black and White Night*) put it, "He was a rockabilly Rigoletto. When you were trying to make a girl fall in love with you, it took roses, the Ferris wheel, and Roy Orbison."

Caught up in the drama of the lyrics, Claudette imagined herself as the longing of the reverb-drenched singer, who, after reading "her loving letter," desperately traversed distant "mountains and valleys" to wind up in her warm, waiting arms. Shakespeare it wasn't. But it did the job, along with a big slice of caraway seed cake, providing a burst of romantic high-test that kicked their new love into overdrive.

Years later, a young outsider from Freehold, New Jersey, named Bruce Springsteen would share an experience similar to Claudette

Frady's. Alone in his room, seeking refuge from the mixed-up, broken-hearted high school passion plays he later sang about, Bruce also surrendered his ears, heart, and soul to Roy Orbison, whom he would one day induct into the Rock and Roll Hall of Fame.

"Roy's ballads were always best when you were alone in the dark," Springsteen explained. "They were scary. His voice was unearthly." Bruce confessed he'd been "young and afraid to love" as a vulnerable teenager. Compared to any other singer of his day, Orbison sounded "like he'd dropped in from another planet." Weird as Springsteen found Roy and his music, he connected with his songs on an emotional level, claiming they got "right to the heart of what you were livin' . . . and that," Bruce explained, "was how he opened up your vision."

ALL RIGHT ... FOR A WHILE

Disappointed when the meager sales of "Ooby Dooby" failed to make him a star, Roy yearned more than ever to escape the small-town life of West Texas. When Johnny Cash made a guest appearance on his TV show, Orbison begged him for help. Always known to be a generous spirit, the Man in Black suggested Roy give his boss back in Memphis, Sam Phillips, a call in hopes of lining up an audition at Sun Records. But Mr. Phillips, famous for his fiery temperament, slammed the receiver down on the nervous kid, admonishing him that "Johnny Cash doesn't run my record company."

Over the years there have been more than a couple of versions of how Roy came to ink a deal with Sun. All agree that Sam Phillips first heard Orbison's irresistible "Ooby Dooby" over the phone, long distance, thanks to the persistence of Cecil "Pop" Hollifield, a record shop owner who booked gigs for Elvis in Midland and Odessa. What happened next remains somewhat vague, as the story has varied, depending upon it source. Some say Pop called Phillips in Memphis, to boast about Roy's new record that was "selling like hotcakes." Cecil then held the receiver up to the speaker of his Magnavox and played the song for Sam over the phone. Unable to hear the music due to static on the line, Phillips instructed Hollifield to mail him the record ASAP. In another version, Sam, thinking he might have another "Blue Suede Shoes" on his hands, urged Hollifield to find Roy and the boys and tell them to pack up their suitcases and equipment and floorboard it to Memphis on the double.

Phillips not only gave the Teen Kings their shot at the big time, he played hardball with Je-Wel, bringing their thriving little cottage industry to a grinding halt. Sam immediately signed an injunction to stop Je-Wel from distributing Roy's sonic hotcake. The judge also ordered Weldon Rogers to hand over the remaining stock, which he claimed amounted to about fifty records.

Just nineteen when he signed with Je-Wel, Orbison was released from his contract as he was underage (as Rogers would soon discover) and had no business making the deal in the first place. Aggravated by the contentious proceedings, Norman Petty retaliated by calling the pressing plant and ordering an extra 5,000 copies, which Je-Wel continued to sell after Roy and the boys hit the road for Memphis.

It was a Friday afternoon when Pop Hollifield made the fateful call to Sam Phillips. Whether the Teen Kings left the next morning or the following week is unclear. Either way, once Roy got word that Sam wanted to record his band, the Teen Kings shoved their amps and drums into the trunk and strapped their suitcases, along with Kennelly's bull fiddle, to the roof of Orbie Lee's borrowed Oldsmobile 88 and lit out for Sun Records on the double.

Apparently, none of them bothered to withdraw from their college courses; when they all flunked out later on, they couldn't have cared less. The Teen Kings were due in Tennessee in three days! Racing up the interstate to Abilene, past the wretched stench of Fort Worth's sprawling stockyards, they beat a mad path across Arkansas, stopping just long enough to gas up and get some chow at a greasy spoon outside of Little Rock. Then they rolled straight into Memphis, the Mecca of Hip, after twenty-four hours and nearly nine hundred miles, crammed together in the car, chain-smoking cigs, guzzling Cokes, cracking jokes, cutting farts, bragging about the girls they knew, and singing every damn song by Elvis and Hank. Arriving at 706 Union Avenue, the Teen Kings were bedraggled but stoked. They were actually going to record in the hallowed studio where rock 'n' roll was born!

Within a few short years, Sam Phillips' unbridled passion, curiosity, and sheer willpower had transformed a small radiator shop into the Memphis Recording Studio (as Sun Studio was originally known). Those cinder-block walls would reverberate with the some of the greatest music America, and the world, has ever known—from B. B. King's chain-lightning blues licks to the low-down strangled growl of Howlin' Wolf to Ike Turner and Jackie Brenston's boozy boogaloo, "Rocket 88."

Just a few years earlier, a twitchy, nervous teenager called Elvis Presley had come sauntering through the same door, looking to record a couple songs for his mama Gladys' birthday, even though his family was too poor to afford a Victrola of their own. Following in the King's wake came Carl Perkins, Johnny Cash, and Jerry Lee Lewis and a dozen of others lost to obscurity over the years. Yet Sam Phillips had seen or heard something unique in each of them, no matter how strange (there was Harmonica Frank Floyd, a middle-aged hobo who played guitar while blowing two harmonicas simultaneously) or just plain crazy (Jerry Lee Lewis) they were.

And now, finally, the Teen Kings stood in the inner sanctum, ready to make rock 'n' roll history. But by the time they arrived at Sun, on March, 27, 1956, Elvis was "real gone." Elvis had already left the radiator shop after Phillips sold Presley's contract to RCA the previous November for $35,000 (plus an extra five grand to cover Elvis' back royalties). That might not seem like a lot of money in retrospect, but Sam stuck by the controversial decision for the rest of his life, claiming he never once regretted making the deal. The sudden surplus of cash afforded him some extra breathing room, allowing Phillips to expand his roster of rockabilly stars to include the criminally underrated Charlie Rich, as well as Warren Smith, famous for his politically incorrect "Ubangi Stomp," and Billy Riley, whose band of Little Green Men laid down the nitty-gritty rockabilly hit "Flyin' Saucers Rock 'n' Roll."

Some of Sam's records, Roy quickly discovered, were pretty rough affairs. Rather than a finished product, they were more often an artifact of a performance, a moment of sonic glory, carved into in vinyl for posterity. Although proud to have been a part of the early chapter of rock 'n' roll history, Sonny Burgess later claimed the tracks he cut for Sun were loaded with mistakes and confessed that he ultimately felt "embarrassed by some of them."

"Sam had an ear for what sounded good," Burgess allowed. No matter how sloppily a band played, Phillips was ultimately after their raw energy and feel. Free-spirited and open to experimentation, Sam took a natural, organic approach to the studio. Following no particular recording etiquette, Phillips set up microphones intuitively, placing them wherever he thought they sounded best. Pianist/producer Jim Dickinson believed the Sun studio possessed a "special sound" due to its "old asbestos acoustic tile." As the room was a scant eighteen by thirty-three feet, there was little or no chance of isolating singers or instruments, and besides, nearly everything he recorded would ultimately bear the stamp of Sun's trademark "slapback" sound. Arguing with Sam Phillips over production values was a waste of time and breath, as Phillips claimed he had divine backup: "God," Sam was convinced, "gave me the best ears, I believe."

With Elvis' legendary (and most humble) producer at the console (originally a five-input Presto mixing board hooked up to a portable Presto PT900, which by 1954 Phillips would trade in for a pair of Ampex 350 recorders), the Teen Kings were understandably nervous. But, like a cool guy on campus who knew the score, Sam coached and coaxed Roy and the boys, prodding and goading them into delivering the best performance they could muster. And soon they knocked out another good but somewhat less inspired take of "Ooby Dooby."

Phillips decided to pass on recutting Claudette's personal favorite, "Trying to Get to You," as Elvis (from whom they originally heard it) had recorded the song shortly after their Je-Wel release. Looking for a track for the B-side to "Ooby Dooby," the Teen Kings fished through the endless piles of singles in Sam's office, searching for a catchy tune. Finding nothing inspiring, they began to kick around a rockabilly thing called "Down the Line," which had a real driving beat that immediately caught Phillips' ear.

The lyric, full of hepcat jive, tells the story of how Roy dumped his date, leaving her flat because she simply "ain't got the style." Then, to add insult to injury, he openly fantasizes about his ultimate dream girl, who he promises will "be cool and twice as gone."

As Sun had recently released a Johnny Cash number called "Cry! Cry! Cry!" the previous June, which was quickly followed by Carl Perkins' "Gone! Gone! Gone!" Sam, looking to complete the trilogy, renamed Roy and Billy Pat's rocker "Go! Go! Go!" Either way, the song (according author Ellis Amburn) was simply "a jazzed up" version of Hank Williams' "Kaw-Liga," the corny ode to a broken-hearted wooden Indian that Billy Pat and Roy had "changed it up a little bit."

Released on the first of May, the third recorded version of "Ooby Dooby," backed with "Go! Go! Go!"—now credited to Roy Orbison and the Teen Kings—was (finally) the charm. Initially selling roughly 20,000 copies, "Ooby Dooby" slowly scaled the charts, until it reached a respectable Number Fifty-Nine by early July.

When Carl Perkins first heard Roy, he was instantly impressed with the young Texan and claimed to hear strains of Bill Monroe's high lonesome pine echoing in Orbison's plaintive voice.

Sam Phillips' right-hand man, Cowboy Jack Clement, famous for writing Cash's "Ballad of a Teenage Queen" and engineering Jerry Lee's "Great Balls of Fire," "thought it was cute." And Malcolm Yelvington, who cut Sticks McGhee's "Drinkin' Wine-Spo-Dee-O-Dee" for Sun, thought "Ooby Dooby," was "the silliest thing I'd ever heard."

But there was no denying the damn thing was catchy. People found themselves taping their toes while mindlessly murmuring its dopey lyrics. Eventually the song moved a quarter of a million copies. After Elvis, Perkins, and Cash, Orbison's "Ooby Dooby" outsold everything else on Sun Records.

Music critic Greil Marcus considers the flip side, "Go! Go! Go!," amongst "the most thrilling rockabilly records ever made," and claimed the tune heavily influenced Buddy Holly's style, long before Jerry Lee Lewis hammered out his own version (which he called by its original title, "Down the Line") as the B-side to his 1957 hit "Breathless."

But right from the start Roy felt like the fifth wheel on Mr. Phillips' platinum Cadillac. Despite his immaculate jet-black pompadour and love of reverb, Orbison never comfortably fit the rockabilly mold. Combining the driving rhythm of bluegrass with a quavering country croon, Orbison had already been playing a similar style of music for the last ten years—they just hadn't called it "rockabilly" yet.

Levon Helm, drummer, vocalist, and mandolin picker for the Band, was in a high school group known as the Jungle Bush Beaters, dreaming of rock 'n' roll stardom, when he first saw Roy live with the Teen Kings at the Malco Theater in Helena, Arkansas. Helm adored Orbison's blend of rock 'n' roll and country, which featured Roy's electric guitar up front, as well as a second guitarist (most likely Johnny "Peanuts" Wilson) along with an "electric mandolin, drums, and doghouse bass," as he recollected. "They made a country sound, with a lot of good bottom to it," Helm wrote in his memoir, *This Wheel's on Fire*. "I saw that band and wanted to be up there with it."

By the time Orbison signed with Sun, he'd already begun searching for a way to express the pain and isolation that roiled the depths of his lonesome prairie soul. Rockabilly was all right, but there had to be something more beyond Brylcreem and twang. Besides, Roy was no hillbilly—he came from the flatlands. Unlike Sonny Burgess and most of the singers in Sun's stable who seemed like they'd fallen off a truck on their way to Sam Phillips' doorstep, Roy had actually finished high school and had even taken a couple of college courses. Orbison was certainly no wild and woolly "white nigger" who made an indecent spectacle of himself up onstage, as the country/gospel singer/mandolinist Ira Louvin would regrettably describe Elvis, claiming he was disgusted by Presley's outlandish gyrations.

In stark contrast to "Elvis the Pelvis," Roy barely moved a muscle onstage, standing like a deer, frozen in the white-hot glare of a pair of high beams. And unlike Jerry Lee, Orbison raised no hellfire. No high-octane mania fueled his performance. While Lewis sneered and howled like a sex-crazed satyr, Roy was either too self-conscious or too dignified to unleash the pent-up demons of his lust upon his audience. Yet at the same time, Orbison was hardly a eunuch, as the gravelly, feral-cat yowl (incredibly enough inspired by Bob Hope in *Son of Paleface*) that punctuated "Oh, Pretty Woman" later revealed.

While Orbison's early music bopped and surged with a youthful, naive enthusiasm, he lacked the two key ingredients essential to rock 'n' roll stardom—flash and vulgarity. Although ambitious careerwise, Roy possessed a tender heart. He wanted to warble weepers. Unimpressed with an early Orbison composition called "The Clown," Cowboy Jack Clement tried his best to dissuade Roy from singing ballads, telling him that he "simply didn't have the pipes," while Sam Phillips admonished the kid from Wink to sing in the style of the husky Mississippi blues growler Arthur "Big Boy" Crudup. Hell, it worked for Elvis and fulfilled Sam's million-dollar dream of finding "a white man who could sing the blues." Whether Sam Phillips realized it or not, with Roy Orbison he'd inadvertently found the Pavarotti of the prairie—a Texan who emoted like an Italian opera singer. And Roy's guitar picking was clean and precise. Unlike most singers of his day, Roy methodically worked out and played his own leads. He also possessed a rare hand-built amplifier that contained a custom echo unit designed by Ray Butts (revered by such top-notch guitar-slingers as Chet Atkins, Scotty Moore, and Carl Perkins). Perkins, who foolishly parted with his model, later explained that the Butts-built amp had "a sound of its own. It was the Sun sound in person."

Carl Perkins, having been on out on the road with Roy and seen him perform, immediately recognized Orbison's "raw greatness," long before his colleagues came around. As the rockabilly guitarist recalled in his autobiography, *Go Cat Go*, Orbison "absolutely warped" the crowd one night in Little Rock with his rendition of Slim Whitman's "Indian Love Call." "You could hear a mosquito in that building, it got so quiet," Carl recollected.

While Presley's hiccupping vocals (the loosey-goosey delivery of which brought to mind New Orleans pianist Professor Longhair's whiskey-oiled larynx) brimmed with abandon, Roy's brand of herky-jerky caused him to come off more like a jittery first-timer. Try as he might, Orbison's "whole lotta shakin'" lacked the steam of the Killer's lascivious bump and grind.

"We all loved Roy," Cowboy Jack reminisced. "He was a fun, silly kinda guy. But he was a hard-luck kinda guy just the same. Roy was the type of fellow who would fall out of a tree and land on a nail. We hung around a lot, became roommates, and lived for a while in a house on my father's property. I don't remember him ever takin' a drink, but we chased plenty of girls, until he fell in love with Claudette. Sam thought he was talented but he didn't know what to do with him. So he turned him over to me. Roy was a good guitar player. But he liked that semi-country pop sound and wanted to arrange the kind of stuff that we weren't equipped for at Sun. Memphis had a good symphony orchestra, but how were we gonna put a string section in that little studio? We experimented with and cut a lot of different stuff," Clement recollected. "He was having fun, but at the same time he was serious about it."

While intrigued by Roy's grandiose musical concepts, Cowboy Jack felt they were unrealistic and "taxed the capabilities of the musicians, and taxed the sound that we were able to deliver at that time. . . . He was a little bit out of place with what he was trying to do. . . . I did tell him he'd never make it as a ballad singer, and he never left me forget that," Clement admitted years later to British journalist Barney Hoskyns. "He did surprise me. I didn't see what a great singer he would become."

Although Roy initially felt that Sun was "a wonderful place," he soon came face-to-face with its limitations and learned "to make do." While the Teen Kings numbered five in all, Roy realized that even a big star like Johnny Cash only had the Tennessee Two. "He used Luther Perkins on guitar and Marshall Grant on bass. That's all he had. That's what Elvis started out with, just guitar and bass," Orbison told Penny Reel of *New Musical Express*.

In 1956 Roy barely squeaked out a second regional hit for Sun with a hard-driving number called "Rockhouse." The song's original inspiration was said to have come from an out-of-the-way nightclub where Roy once sang, about twenty miles from Wink, on old Highway 80 in Monahans, Texas. While the lyric followed Chuck Berry's surefire formula for radio play, celebrating the rock 'n' roll lifestyle, the song never seemed to get off the ground, despite Billy Pat's snappy snare, Jack Kennelly's surging bass line, and the elastic twang of Orbison's guitar. The problem was Roy's vocal, which sounds thin and shaky and ultimately unconvincing.

There was also the question of the song's authorship: According to Cowboy Jack, "Rockhouse" was actually written by Conway Twitty, whose mother still called him Harold Jenkins at the time. Apparently Roy nervously confessed that "he stole the song after hearing Twitty play it one night in Arkansas." Clement claimed that Twitty arrived for a recording date at Sun Studio; when "Roy saw him in the front office [he] immediately admitted to me that he stole it."

Despite his urgent confession, the writing credit for Conway's version of "Rockhouse" ultimately went to Jenkins, while Orbison's recording lists the song's authors as Jenkins and Phillips, after Roy was pushed to sign over most of his publishing to his boss in order to get out of his contract with Sun.

The B-side to "Rockhouse" was an edgy rockabilly number written by Johnny Cash with lyrics from a poem he'd originally written for his first wife, Vivian Liberto, called "You're My Baby."

While Elvis, Cash, Jerry Lee, and Perkins dominated the Top Ten, Sam Phillips, for the most part, remained unimpressed with Roy's efforts. Although he admired his voice, he seriously doubted Orbison's star power. Phillips feared Roy's fans would run the other way if they ever got a close look at him, with his limp hair, beady eyes, and weak chin. "He's not a good-lookin' boy at all," Sam confided to Carl. But looks never meant that much to Perkins, who claimed he didn't even like to walk past a mirror.

Orbison wasn't alone in that department. Bill Haley, with his bow tie, plaid dinner jacket, and spit curl falling down over his forehead, looked more like an over-the-hill maître d' than a rock 'n' roller. But that didn't stop a horde of British teenagers from mobbing Waterloo Station when Bill (who resembled J. Edgar Hoover in a baggy beige raincoat) and the Comets arrived in London for their first UK tour.

Image is a tricky thing. Once a pop star manages to carve his singular style into the public's consciousness, he is then expected to maintain it. Change is usually bad for business. Genius chameleons such as Bob Dylan, the Beatles, and David Bowie, who successfully reinvented themselves with each new album, are a rare breed. Cash's square-jawed Man in Black and Willie Nelson's braid-sporting, bandana-wearing stoned strummer, iconic as they might be, eventually became prisons for the men behind the performers. Orbison was trapped behind his perpetual Ray-Bans, like a bald man afraid to remove his hat. When Joan Rivers asked him, "Do you ever not wear your sunglasses?" Roy gently quipped, "Only when I don't want to be recognized."

Orbison's time at Sun barely lasted two years, from 1956 to 1958, but in that brief period he cut twenty sides, of which twelve remained in the can, unissued, until two years later, in 1961, when Sun compiled *Roy Orbison at the Rock House*, hoping to cash in on his future success at Monument Records. Roy, who was credited with writing just five songs in the batch, would drop most of his Sun material from his repertoire (as Elvis would) until the 1970s.

Although ultimately unfulfilling, Roy's association with Sun afforded him a near bulletproof cachet that would keep him afloat through the lean years to come. But the price he'd pay as a member of that exclusive gentlemen's club, he wouldn't know for another decade.

The fate of the five knights of Sam Phillips' rocking royal round table reads like a chapter from a cryptic fairy tale. In retaliation for having cast the rock 'n' roll scourge upon the unsuspecting youth of America, a tempest of biblical proportions would soon rain down upon each of them, as if they'd fallen under the vengeful hex cast by a diabolical sorcerer, fundamentalist preacher, or forest hag. Within four years following the 1954 release of Presley's "That's All Right," death, tragedy, and monumental buffoonery would become all of their faithful companions.

The United States Army leveled King Elvis in 1958, when they ceremoniously razed his pompadour and stripped him of his gold lamé swagger. The cocky crown prince of teen rebellion was then fitted into the ultimate straitjacket of conformity—khaki fatigues. Woeful beneath his buzz cut, Elvis solemnly sneered to do his patriotic duty and was shipped off out of harm's way to West Germany, where he entertained homesick American troops.

Once discharged, Buck Sergeant Presley, thanks to his manager, the notoriously exploitive Colonel Tom Parker (formerly known as Andreas

Cornelis van Kuijk, who was neither "Tom Parker" nor a "colonel" who served in any army, whether American or in his native Netherlands) was delivered into the waiting arms of that great Republican rock 'n' roll hater Frank Sinatra, who before millions of television viewers slipped Presley the keys to Sin City. Elvis, "a cretinous goon," as Sinatra once called him, would never attain Rat Pack status—after all, he was a damn hillbilly whose music, according to the Chairman of the Board, was "deplorable, a rancid-smelling aphrodisiac." Nonetheless, Presley, who was paid a record-breaking $125,000 for three songs and a few minutes of awkward chatter, from that point on found himself a card-carrying member of an elitist clique of undead Las Vegas lounge performers. However, the King's career was far from over. Although he'd occasionally rebound up the charts throughout the '60s, Elvis was pulverized by the British Invasion and put out like a rhinestone stud in a shag carpet pasture by the band who loved him most, the Beatles.

In the meantime, the piano pounding wild man of Ferriday, Louisiana, Jerry Lee Lewis, had usurped Presley's crown. Since his days as a Sunday school delinquent, the price of playing the devil's music had weighed heavily upon his troubled soul, and, certain that he was serving Satan, Lewis would beg, badger, and debate Sam Phillips not to release his new recording of "Great Balls of Fire." Although the singer ranted like a mad evangelist (fire and brimstone boiled in his family's blood, after all: His first cousin was the fallen Pentecostal preacher Jimmy Lee Swaggart), Phillips just scoffed and in the end, thank God, knew to turn a deaf ear to Lewis' skewed Baptist babble. The song immediately rocketed to Number Two on the *Billboard* charts, and "the Killer," who would outlive all of his peers at Sun Records, is still, to this day, waiting for Old Scratch to come calling to collect his due.

Jerry Lee soon found himself engulfed in another kind of fire when the news broke of his secret marriage to Myra Gale Brown, his thirteen-year-old cousin (once removed, if anybody was counting) and the daughter of his bass player, J. W. Brown, while he was still hitched to his second wife, Jane. The self-righteous rained ruin down upon him in biblical proportion, and the musical reprobate was immediately run out of the UK, abruptly aborting his tour in May 1958.

Returning on the first flight back to the States, Lewis found himself welcome as a leper as he stepped off the plane in New York. Scandal hounded him wherever he went, wreaking havoc on his life and career. Overnight, Jerry Lee had gone from making ten grand a show to begging old cronies for a bar gig. Nobody but Alan Freed would touch his records, and Freed, it turned out, was not long for this world. Having committed such monumental sins as "talking black" on the radio, proliferating such Negro slang terms as *rock 'n' roll*, and staging integrated shows, Alan Freed was a marked man. In November of '59 he was nailed by Congress on charges of accepting payola, (like everybody else in the business hadn't been on the take?), and friends like Jerry Lee Lewis were no help when it came to convincing the hanging judge of his integrity. Five years later Freed was gone, having drunk himself to death as he watched "America's Oldest Teenager," Dick Clark, inherit the musical empire he'd struggled to create.

Making a joke over Jerry Lee's immoral misadventures only made the situation worse, as Cowboy Jack Clement soon discovered. In what seemed like a clever attempt to rescue Lewis' nose-diving career and redeem his scandalous reputation, Cowboy Jack quickly cobbled together an "interview" record called "The Return of Jerry Lee," a sonic collage of questions from "reporters" smartly answered by snippets of the Killer's own songs along with bits of Billy Riley's "Flying Saucer." Nobody got the joke and, needless to say, Sun didn't bother shipping the disc over to England.

Lewis' business (with the exception of a couple sold-out shows in Alabama) was in the toilet. He had gone from five figures a night to scuffling for a couple of hundred, if he was lucky. After years of lying low, Jerry Lee would find forgiveness, not from his old rock 'n' roll fans but by singing songs of sin and redemption to the country crowd, everyday folks, who knew well the sort of temptations and conflicts of the soul with which Lewis grappled.

As "Blue Suede Shoes" bounded up the charts in March 1956, the car in which Carl Perkins was riding on his way to perform on *The Perry Como Show* in New York City rear-ended a pickup truck and plunged into a ditch in Dover, Delaware. While the driver, "Poor

Richard," better known to his mother as Stuart Pinkham, died instantly behind the wheel, Carl was miraculously spared, though he was found unconscious in the passenger seat with a concussion and broken collarbone. His brothers, bassist Buck and guitarist Jay, both survived the crash, although Jay would die two years later in 1958 from a brain tumor. In the wake of such overwhelming tragedy Carl bathed his battered soul in a river of liquor while collecting song royalties from Elvis (while the King for the time being was in the Fatherland) and, later, the Beatles. Eventually Perkins found his way back to the stage playing guitar and writing another hit, "Daddy Sang Bass," for his buddy Johnny Cash.

Cash's battle with pills was nearly as legendary as Presley's. Haunted since childhood by the memory of his older brother and hero, Jack, who was killed in a sawmill accident, Johnny cultivated a level of sensitivity for the human condition that was unique and unusual to both his geography and generation. Unlike most of his peers, who sang about the joys of malt shops, fast cars, and flirty girls, Cash wrote and sang anthems for the downtrodden, the dispossessed, and the forgotten. No songwriter since Hank Williams had portrayed life in the American South with such snapshot clarity and simplicity.

Johnny was soon saved from a life of depravity by "Mother" Maybelle Carter's doe-eyed daughter June, whose devotion to Christ led him through the shadowy valley of alcohol and addiction. (Elvis, on the other hand, stuck faithfully with his beloved pharmaceuticals no matter how Priscilla or Jesus wept.) But along with Johnny's rock 'n' roll lifestyle went nearly all trace of rock 'n' roll. Songs burdened with Christian morality and schmaltzy production soon replaced the rollicking joy of "Get Rhythm."

America loved Johnny Cash. He was no poser. He walked the walk. Having done time for various misdemeanors, Cash sang knowingly of life behind bars and would later tour American prisons, recording benchmark albums at such high-security joints as San Quentin and Folsom. After Johnny signed with Columbia Records in 1958 (whether paying off the debt owed Jesus or the Carter Family), he would sing more than his fare share of gospel over the next few years.

A surprisingly high percentage of rock 'n' roll's originators would meet with unmitigated disaster, whether self-inflicted or by fate. In 1957, Little Richard's career suddenly nose-dived. For much of his life, the irrepressibly flamboyant Richard Penniman was torn, as Delta bluesman Son House used to say, "between the Lord and that other fella." After experiencing a harrowing apocalyptic vision, Little Richard wholeheartedly denounced his homosexuality, got married (albeit for a brief time), and entered the seminary in a desperate attempt to get right with God. But very few of his fans were as ecstatic over Penniman's newfound redemption as he was.

With Buddy Holly dead and Chuck Berry doing time for "messin' 'round with jailbait" (as Mose Allison sang), it was enough to make rock 'n' roll fans everywhere believe in conspiracy theories years before the Kennedy assassinations took place.

Considering the overwhelming tragedies he'd face one day, Orbison, clad in black, understandably appeared shell-shocked and funereal for much of his life. The trademark Ray-Ban Wayfarers that loaned an air of mystery to a man who looked more like a substitute shop teacher than a rock 'n' roll star would eventually become a widower's veil. Roy's over-the-top delivery took simple verses of lost love and broken dreams far beyond the saccharine sentiments of '50s teen heartbreak tunes or the self-absorbed lyrics of '70s "confessional" singer-songwriters to come. Yet no matter how MGM or Mercury Records tried to slick up his songs with kitschy string arrangements, Orbison remained the genuine article. Like the bluesmen from the Mississippi Delta and Texas' Piney Woods, Roy had a passion that resounded with the authority and credibility of someone who had lived through and transcended personal tragedy and loss.

Ultimately Roy Orbison was an alchemist who transformed the overwhelming sorrow he faced in life into rhapsodic melodies that sold more than twenty-five million records and netted him fifty gold albums.

When Johnny Cash introduced Roy on his TV show in September 1969, he happened to mention that his neighbor was "the biggest record-selling artist on Earth and, y'know, that pretty well covers the market."

THREE

A CAT CALLED DOMINO

K icking off at a North Carolina schoolhouse, the Teen Kings' first official tour of the South was a humbling affair. For fifty bucks a day, Roy and the boys traveled the back roads of Dixie, playing a string of "unbelievable little towns," as Orbison later recalled, opening shows for their fellow Sun artists Sonny James; "the Singing Fisherman," Johnny Horton; and Johnny Cash. By the time they reached Memphis, Roy and the band had hit their stride. On June 1, 1956, the Teen Kings rocked the legendary Overton Park Shell, sharing the bill with Carl Perkins, Johnny Cash, Warren Smith, and Eddie Bond. But dissent had already begun brewing within the group.

With "Ooby Dooby" climbing the charts, the King himself stopped by to check out "the Big O." Elvis allegedly mumbled to Orbison that he was so "marvelous" that he (the "King" of rock 'n' roll) would never dare set foot on the same stage as him.

Years later, in an interview with *New Musical Express*, Roy searched for the words to express his love and respect for Elvis, praising him as "the firstest with mostest," "a wonderful fellow," and "a magnificent man, and a great raw talent."

The precious Polaroid of the pair became a talisman to Roy that he cherished for years, carrying with him on tour in the early days to bolster his spirit when he was miles from home, rolling down that long, lost highway.

Although it's well documented that Elvis put in an appearance that night at Overton Park to wish Roy all the best in his hometown, there has been some debate over whether Presley ever made the "marvelous" compliment or whether the photograph was ever actually taken. It seems odd that this rare, historical document has never appeared in print or on any of the dozens of compilations and reissues of Roy's music over the years. Whether the photo was Roy's personal souvenir or was eventually lost, it seems that Orbison's management would have wanted to exploit it to its fullest advantage. On the other hand, there's Billy Pat Ellis' testimony. According to the Teen Kings' disgruntled drummer, the only thing the King had to say backstage that night was to Jack Kennelly, praising him as "a damn good bass player."

Either way, Roy soon found himself invited into the King's inner circle, witnessing things he'd only previously imagined in dreams. One night Orbison rode shotgun as Elvis steered his purple Caddy through the streets of Memphis to pick up his date for the night. Dumbfounded, Roy watched as some prissy girl snubbed Presley after they arrived late. Whether stuck-up or trying to teach Elvis how to treat a lady, she had just turned down the biggest star in America. It meant nothing to Presley, who laughed and shrugged it off; there were plenty more where she came from. So Roy and the King spent the rest of the night hanging out together, guzzling soda pop and munching potato chips.

Roy quickly realized that if he wanted to ride with the King's posse of good ol' boys and good-time gals, he'd have to pony up—big-time. Upon receiving his first (and only) royalty check from Sun Records, Orbison immediately laid his money down on a brand-new white Cadillac and a sparkling diamond pinky ring, essential trappings amongst the rockabilly nouveau riche. According to Carl Perkins, Roy, who was notoriously slow when it came to reaching for his wallet, deemed such extravagances "foolish." But image has always been the name of the game in rock 'n' roll. You've got to look and play the part no matter how humble you might be on your own time. The public expects a rock 'n' roller to arrive in style, not in some old beat-up grocery-getter crammed full of drums, amps, and suitcases.

With the next tour, Roy took his rightful seat in Sun's pink Cadillac beside Cash, Perkins, and Sam Phillips' newest signing, the tempestuous Jerry Lee Lewis.

"Jerry Lee loved Roy's 'Mean Woman Blues' and cut his 'Down the Line.' That was big for him. Roy really admired Jerry Lee's style and pizzazz," Cowboy Jack Clement pointed out.

But once again, the tour, from Roy's perspective, was a disheartening affair. His pals the Teen Kings (particularly guitarist Johnny "Peanuts" Wilson, who'd been contemplating jumping ship for some time and forming his own group) were tired of being treated like second-class citizens. Meanwhile, Orbison's star was about to crash just as quickly as it had risen. He had careened headfirst into an invisible wall built by his fickle fans who, it turned out, were only interested in hearing "Ooby Dooby." Once Roy played his hit song, they seemed to turn a deaf ear to the rest of his set.

Recorded in the summer of 1956, "Rockhouse," no matter who wrote it, was going nowhere fast. In concert, Roy began to pander to his crowd with spirited covers of Bo Diddley, Fats Domino, and Chuck Berry hits. In his early days with the Teen Kings, Orbison claimed to be something of "a sensation-seeking fellow." Leaving all trace of self-consciousness behind in the dressing room, Roy put on a spectacle onstage, dressing wildly and moving, as he later claimed, "more than Elvis or anyone."

One fan recalled seeing Orbison in "a leopard-skin getup" literally leaping about in what Carl Perkins called "cat clothes." Just a kid at the time, journalist William Michael Smith, who'd grown up in Odessa, Texas, witnessed a young Roy Orbison play on the back of a flatbed truck (just as a young Roy had previously seen Ernest Tubb years before in Forth Worth). The evening's entertainment, sponsored by Otto's Ice Cream Shop, hoped to draw a large crowd by selling nickel cones. Smith recalled lapping grape sherbet while watching the "Wink Wildcat" pound out a rocking set that included "Ooby Dooby," "Tutti-Frutti," "Cat Called Domino," and "Down the Line." Smith would later describe Orbison's performance as "loud, sexy, and truly life-altering."

Eventually Roy abandoned such antics, dismissing them as "shallow." For him it seemed forced and unnatural, and besides, compared to the

Killer, who routinely inspired mad frenzy in his fans by just being himself—albeit with an untouchable savage fury—the Big O was beginning to feel more like a big zero.

Commercial radio in the 1950s was dominated by cover songs—middle-of-the-road remakes of popular black R&B tunes recorded by white artists. After cleaning up whatever lascivious lyrics that might offend (just how many folks in radio land ever figured out the double entendre of "a one-eyed Jack peepin' in a seafood store?"), Bill Haley would top the charts with Big Joe Turner's "Shake Rattle and Roll," while Pat Boone's pedestrian versions of Little Richard and Fats Domino songs regularly outsold the originals by four to one.

In Orbison's case, the argument of skin color was moot. He had that elusive quality that so many people in the early '60s were in search of: soul. Roy was as white as they come, yet just as much of a blues singer in his way, as Ray Charles, whose songs he regularly covered.

Whether you sing, or wail on a saxophone, or bend a guitar string, the blues is deeply personal, something you must ultimately work out for yourself. In doing so, it becomes a cathartic experience. Not only do you free yourself, you help others throw off whatever emotional shackles are weighing them down, drowning them in an ocean of guilt or regret. And, like a true bluesman, Method actor, or tribal shaman, Orbison dug deep, mining the depths of personal experience, transforming the misery that fell on him like a storm into transcendent melodies that yielded gold records. Roy not only healed himself in the process, he dressed the wounds of the lonely and lovelorn the world over, who bought his records and listened to his music as if their lives depended on it.

Orbison openly expressed his vulnerability unlike any other rock 'n' roller of his day. Cash, Lewis, and Perkins all flaunted a certain redneck machismo, while Elvis, whose mix of camp and sincerity (which rang true when he sang gospel) was more elusive. While Presley delivered the haunted lyrics of "Heartbreak Hotel" with herky-jerky reverb-drenched vocals and a sexy noir smirk, the King's take on lonely often came off like role-playing, a mask he conveniently donned to evoke the song's mood. Compared to Orbison, whose fans experienced emotional devastation when he sang "Crying," Elvis seemed unable or unwilling to connect to the deep pain and loneliness that lay beneath the shimmering rhinestone façade of his fame.

As long as Roy's music remained derivative, he would never know true success. It wasn't in the cards for him to prance about the stage, twanging his guitar as a rockabilly cat, a style he played as well as anyone but didn't invent. Rockabilly was all about rough edges and cool attitude, a sound and style that Orbison borrowed and tried on for size, but would never own. As Sam Phillips so bluntly pointed out, Roy had a serious image problem. Like most mortals, Orbison lacked the swagger and sex appeal of Elvis or the funky down-home charm of Carl Perkins, nor could he compete with the full-tilt lunacy of the maniacal Jerry Lee Lewis. And he didn't possess the smoldering lucky-sombitch charisma of Johnny Cash. Self-conscious and withdrawn, Roy would tag along in the backseat of rock 'n' roll's Cadillac until finally finding a way of expressing the depths of his Lone Star soul through the tragic romantic ballad.

The awkward kid from Wink with the nervous hiccup that both Buddy Holly and he picked up like a virus from the Tupelo truck driver would soon blossom into a singer of staggering power.

Not everyone who worked with Roy over the years felt they got a fair shake in the deal. Whether motivated by jealousy or the need to tell the truth from their point of view, many of his sidemen and collaborators to this day in interviews raise the issue of who contributed what to Roy's music. The first discrepancy over credit came back when Sam Phillips released "Ooby Dooby" in May 1956, giving Roy top billing over the band.

A showdown between Roy and the group had been festering for quite some time, and feelings of resentment finally came to a head on December 14, 1956, as they rehearsed "Sweet and Easy to Love" and "Devil Doll" at Sun Studios. Frustrated with their lackluster performance, Sam Phillips, who had never been terribly impressed with

Orbison's group to begin with, took Roy aside and suggested he bring in some seasoned session pros—guitarist Roland Janes, Stan Kessler on bass, and drummer J. M. Van Eaton to take care of business.

The Teen Kings were offended, angry, and disappointed. Since their early days in Texas they'd been a team, "a commonwealth," as James Morrow described the band, that bore all setbacks and expenses equally while sharing in whatever glory and cash came their way. Hell, they never would've made it to Memphis in the first place if Morrow's dad hadn't loaned them the money to record at Norman Petty's studio. They all lived, worked, and played together. A few of them had been friends since grade school.

Granted, Roy stood center stage and sang nearly all the songs and often sported a different jacket or kerchief, or went without a tie to distinguish himself from his bandmates in group promo shots. But things really began to change from the moment they arrived in Memphis. Sam Phillips knew who the star was, and according to Jack Kennelly, all the attention Sam and his crew lavished on Roy only made him "egomaniacal."

No one felt more jilted than James Morrow, the group's electric mandolin player, who began playing with Roy in after-school jam sessions back in 1948. Morrow's picking, for whatever reason, was frequently lost in the tracks they'd cut at Sun. It takes a good pair of headphones to decipher Morrow's presence on most of the records. Instead of mixing the mandolin, which gave the Teen Kings' live shows a unique sound (check out the live TV show recordings on *Lost & Found: The Unreleased 1956 Recordings* [Fuel 2000 Records]) to the fore, Phillips buried James' eight-string under Roy's reverb-drenched guitar and the relentless thwack of Billy Pat's snare drum.

It may have been a deliberate decision on Sam's part to obscure the mandolin, which by the mid-'50s was considered old hat, owing to its association with such out-of-style music as bluegrass and Western swing. But most likely this slight was due to the limitations of Phillips' small, primitive studio.

Even Jack Kennelly's bass, which was occasionally featured, walking lugubriously at the last moments of "Ooby Dooby" or driving "Cat Called Domino" with a punchy throb, tended to get lost in the mix.

"[The Teen Kings] were all right. But they were mean kinda guys," Jack Clement recalled. "One day we went out to lunch next door at Taylor's Café and they all just packed up and headed back to Texas without him."

Phillips, who rarely mentioned the subject over the years, shrugged off Orbison's breakup with his old buddies from Wink as "nothing more than their being extremely young."

By the time "Sweet and Easy to Love" and "Devil Doll" were released, in January 1957 (credited to Roy Orbison and the Roses, whose vocals bore a similar sound to Elvis's favorite harmonizers, the Jordanaires), the Teen Kings were back in Texas, trying to figure out their next move. While it would take Roy another three years before he hit the big time, his old friends would forever flounder in obscurity. Years later James Morrow described Orbison as "single-minded. . . . [But] his dream came true for him," he allowed.

"We always knew the talent was there in Roy," the Wink Westerners' bassist, Slob Evans, told *Mojo* magazine years later. "The rest of us were just going along for the ride."

Perhaps Roy's old pals found some cold comfort when his new record failed to chart, obscured by those of his labelmates: Billy Riley's frenetic "Flyin' Saucers Rock 'n' Roll" and Carl Perkins' jumpin' cover of "Match Box," a song he lifted from the legendary bluesman Blind Lemon Jefferson, who, in the 1920s, sang it for spare change on street corners. Thanks to Perkins' edgy rendition, it found its way into the Beatles' repertoire.

Eventually Johnny "Peanuts" Wilson would launch his solo career, returning to Norman Petty's studio in Clovis to record with his fellow Teen Kings, Kennelly and Ellis. Peanuts, whose songs were eventually recorded by the likes of Loretta Lynn, Conway Twitty, and Kenny Rogers, would cut "Paper Boy" at the May 1957 session, two years before it turned up as Roy's first Monument single.

But the real keeper from Wilson's Clovis sessions was a novelty number called "Cast Iron Arm" that Peanuts had written with Jim Scott and Roy, as well as the producer who never failed to get his share of the credit, Norman Petty. The song surges along, driven by a chunky rhythm guitar, a slapping snare, and a raunchy, sputtering sax, until it abruptly ends with a wobbly voice that sounded like it had been clobbered by the "Cast Iron Arm," crying, "That'll teach you to mess with me boy!"

Disappointed over the sales of his most recent single, Roy returned again to Texas shortly before his twenty-first birthday. With no band, his career appeared dead in the water. But that wasn't the only problem Orbison faced at the time. Bewitched by the "aggravating beauty" (as Hank Williams sang in "Lulu Walls") of Ms. Claudette Frady, Roy soon discovered why his old bass player Jack Kennelly had suddenly dumped her.

Although Claudette appeared to be a mature young woman of consenting age, Roy was shocked to find out she was only fourteen. But that didn't keep him from singing the praises of "Lawdy Miss Clawdy" night and day, although he knew if the relationship was ever consummated any time in the near future, he'd either wind up married or in jail. Faced with the option, Roy wisely chose door number one.

It seemed that Sam Phillips' gang of southern rockabilly rebels had a hankering for "Milk Shake Mademoiselles," those young, inexperienced (in other words—virgin) "Teenage Queens" whose names—Myra Gale, Priscilla, and Claudette—read like those on a dance card at a Confederate debutante ball. As the rest of America eventually came to learn, it was considered a "time-honored" tradition in the American South for an older, more successful, "worldly" man to pluck a young, impressionable lass from her humble circumstance and improve her lot by "schooling" her in the ways of life and love.

While Jerry Lee and Roy married their pubescent princesses, Elvis fell for Priscilla Ann Wagner in 1959, when she was also just fourteen years old. After promising her parents that she would be chaperoned around the clock, the King eventually spirited her away from her airforce-brat life in Germany to Graceland, where Priscilla rode the amphetamine/barbiturate roller coaster while attending an all-girls' Catholic school. Mother Mary had undoubtedly inspired all the forgiveness and forbearance that she needed to withstand the pernicious gossip surrounding Elvis' endless affairs.

And now Roy was following his father-in-law, Chester Frady, down the same primrose path, whisking away his lovely, lonely daughter, Claudette, determined to mold his child-bride into the ideal (complacent) woman, much to the chagrin of her mother, Geraldine, who'd recently been there herself and was far from thrilled at the prospect of a man of Roy Orbison's means and looks becoming her son-in-law. Hoping to talk some sense to her daughter, Gerry pleaded desperately with Claudette to reconsider her decision, certain she could "do better than that."

Despite Claudette's mother's trepidation, the pair were married on August 1, 1957, (although some conflicting sources claim the wedding took place on September 1) at the Church of Christ in Kermit, Texas, a house of worship that not only routinely warned its flock of the evils of rock 'n' roll, as did every other religious institution at the time, but refused the strains of music, of any persuasion, as part of their ceremonial worship. No apple-cheeked, blue-blazered, Brylcreemed boys' choir would set the rafters ringing that day with a joyous hallelujah. No silver-haired, humpbacked matron would rake the keys of the organ in praise of holy matrimony, no matter how awkward their age difference might've made the congregation feel (he was twenty-one; she, sixteen). Heaven was not alerted to their peculiar union with a blast of blasphemous harmony and rhythm. Roy's and Claudette's young lives had been lived to the beat of pounding oil rigs, car engines, hearts, and drums; their emotions fueled by romantic jukebox verse, words of yearning that spilled from their tongues between passionate kisses and late-night telephone calls. Yet they stood solemnly at the alter of silence, listening, perhaps blushing, eager to obey the minister's shopping list of vows as their blood coursed through their bodies in warm nervous rivers.

Old school chums sat nudging each other with bony elbows and sly grins, their eyes wide, dumbfounded that old "Facetus" had gone and robbed the most beautiful babe from West Texas' cradle. Chester Frady stood proud. He liked Roy and believed he was genuine in his love and commitment to both his daughter and music. Like Claudette, her father saw beyond whatever physical flaws his wife complained of.

Geraldine sighed, her eyes moist, certain she knew what the future held in store for her little girl. But no one did.

The following spring Roy returned to Memphis once more, eager to record a batch of new tunes he'd recently written. But he soon found himself stonewalled by Cowboy Jack and Bill Justis, who had a couple songs of their own they claimed were just perfect for him.

Justis, Sun's musical director/tenor saxophonist, who led his own big band around Memphis and released eight sides on Sun's subsidiary label, Flip, (including a slinky striptease number called "Raunchy" that George Harrison played for his audition with the Beatles), would foist an inane novelty number on Roy called "Chicken-Hearted."

Over a staccato guitar riff plucked by Roland Janes, Orbison delivered the self-damning testimony of a clueless rube while Martin Willis' raspy sax punctuated the song's lame humor like a bony finger repeatedly jabbing you in the ribs. Suddenly it seemed like old "Facetus" was back from the land of high school traumas, being forced to admit once more that he was a hopeless dork. This bit of knuckleheaded hokum didn't do Roy's career or image a lick of good.

To make it worse, the new single's B-side featured Jack Clement's insipid "I Like Love," in which Roy's "golly gee" falsetto sounded like a neutered Jerry Lee Lewis. Orbison later admitted that "Chicken-Hearted" backed with "I Like Love" added up to "a couple of the worst recordings in the history of the world." Distressed as he was over the garbage he'd been pushed into singing, Roy was either too "Chicken-Hearted" himself, or too nice for his own sake to stand up to Justis and Clement. He dreaded confrontation and regularly chose the path of least resistance whenever faced with difficult people and situations. Instead, Roy would quietly disappear, sometimes even when he was in the same room as you.

While the greatest rockabilly singers of the day sounded as if they might stop by to stick up a filling station on their way home from the recording studio, "I Like Love," had all the rebellion and sex appeal of a freckle-faced kid begging his mother for an ice-cold tumbler of milk and a big slice of chocolate cake. Was this really the best the Big O had to offer? It was 1957 and rock 'n' roll was raging.

The time had clearly come for Roy to move on. Self-conscious about his looks and growing more doubtful about the prospects of his own star power, Orbison decided he might be better off working behind the scenes as an in-house writer, cooking up pop confections for teen heart-throbs to sing. While Buddy Holly, Jerry Lee, Ricky Nelson, and Johnny Cash had all recently covered his songs with varying degrees of success, it wasn't until the spring of 1958 that Orbison got his big break as a tunesmith.

That March, Roy drove to Hammond, Indiana, to play a gig that Bob Neal booked for him, opening for the Everly Brothers. The Everlys were red-hot at the time, riding the nonstop rock 'n' roll roller coaster from coast to coast, playing an endless string of one-nighters across America with barely enough time to eat or sleep, let alone write another hit song. Instead, Don and Phil relied on the Nashville-based husband-and-wife songwriting team of Boudleaux and Felice Bryant, famous for the bluegrass standard "Rocky Top" and a slew of country crossover hits recorded over the years by everyone from Tony Bennett and Simon and Garfunkel to Sarah Vaughn and the Grateful Dead.

Backstage before the show, everyone was hanging out, smoking and joking, changing into their stage clothes, while standing one by one before the mirror to carefully slick their hair to perfection.

Shooting the breeze with Roy was not always an easy prospect, particularly if you didn't know him well. He could seem aloof, inscrutable, lost in a dreamworld. But the awkward silences that dampened the conversation were more often due to Orbison's habit of observation. Roy routinely took the time to think before he spoke, choosing simple, direct language to express himself.

Suddenly one of the Everlys broke through the cloud bank surrounding Roy to ask if he had any new tunes they might use. Orbison obliged, strumming a steady rocking rhythm on his guitar, over which he sang the praises of his "pretty little pet." To his surprise, Don and Phil immediately liked it, enough to ask him to jot the lyrics down. He scribbled them on the first thing within reach—a shoe box lid.

By June the Everly Brothers' new single, the Bryants' mellifluous "All I Have to Do Is Dream," shot to Number One, with the B-side, Roy's "Claudette," piggy-backing its way up the charts to a respectable Number Thirty.

Despite his recent success, Orbison remained below the radar, nearly forgotten. Soon after he returned to Texas, his prized Caddy was repossessed. Struggling to make ends meet, he wrestled with the grim prospect of hanging up his rock 'n' roll shoes for good and settling down and finding a steady job.

That July, Roy received a call from Wesley Rose's office in Nashville. Wes not only managed the Everlys at the time; his dad, Fred, had been partners with the raspy-throated star of the *Grand Ole Opry*, the diminutive but mighty Roy Acuff. Together they formed Acuff-Rose Publishing, the house that Patti Page built with her multimillion-selling postwar smash "The Tennessee Waltz." Wesley Rose had genuine power, the kind that could change Orbison's life with a single phone call, which he soon made to RCA Victor, to cut a deal with Roy.

Offered an advance by Acuff-Rose, Orbison took his best shot and boldly asked for five grand. He figured he could always back down, claiming it was only a joke. But nobody flinched and Wesley wrote the check. Rose assured Roy he needn't bother to worry about all the paperwork. Hell, Hank Williams never read a contract. And besides, if Roy was unhappy with anything he promised, Rose would gladly tear it up. Roy had his word.

With Wesley Rose now managing him, Orbison could finally kiss Sun Records good-bye, but not before signing over the lion's share of his songwriting credit to Sam Phillips. Some of Roy's best numbers, including "Cat Called Domino," "Sweet and Easy to Love," "Mean Little Mama," and "Devil Doll," were then credited to his producer.

Phillips rationalized taking credit for Orbison's early work as payback for the hours of free studio time Roy was allowed at Sun. Still, one has to wonder about what might have been had Sam bothered to nurture the Teen Kings as a band or Orbison's aspirations as ballad singer or even as a burgeoning rockabilly guitarist. Had Phillips taken more time and care to get better takes or a better sound on some of Roy's tracks, perhaps he might have had another "Blue Suede Shoes" on his hands—a killer track like "Cat Called Domino" certainly had a solid shot. Had Roy's portrait of total cool been released immediately after he recorded it and given a decent push by his label, "Cat Called Domino," with its driving rhythm and cocky lyrics, would undoubtedly have been a hit, not an afterthought.

Sun was limited by a small budget and a meager staff, who were improvising with a new music in an unproven market that few understood at the time. Although Sam was willing to take the ride with an unknown geeky kid from Wink, and Orbison—for the most part—was grateful to Mr. Phillips for his faith, generosity, and guidance, Roy's time at Sun was ultimately mismanaged, a lost opportunity. Rockabilly historian Colin Escott put it more bluntly, referring to Orbison's tenure at Sun as "one of the great comic horror stories" of rock 'n' roll.

Roy wasn't the only one of Sam Phillips' artists to feel ignored or short-changed. In the wake of Jerry Lee's meteoric success, Billy Riley, in a drunken rage, trashed the studio after discovering Sam had sunk his cash into promoting Lewis in lieu of printing up a second batch of his "Flyin' Saucers Rock 'n' Roll" after the first pressing sold out.

Roy didn't languish long. A session was lined up in Nashville for the end of September, at RCA's famous Studio B, with "Mr. Guitar" himself, the legendary Chet Atkins, at the console. But Roy quickly realized his new record company had even less of a clue as what to do with him than did his old pals back in Memphis.

At RCA, King Elvis's label, Orbison found himself once more low man on the totem pole, being offered a boatload of supper club slop that Presley's people had unequivocally turned down. No matter how "Mr. Guitar" and Nashville's A-team tried to breathe life into the innocuous "Seems to Me," "I'll Never Tell," and "Sweet and Innocent," they all came floating, belly-up, to the surface, like pale, puffy corpses drowned in lifeless, schmaltzy production. No one was surprised when these records quickly died on the vine.

Two months later, the week before Christmas, RCA gave Roy one last shot, to record Boudleaux and Felice Bryant's "Jolie," along with his own "Almost Eighteen" and a little ditty called "Happy Little Bluebird." Driven by a gently strummed acoustic guitar and plinky piano, "Almost Eighteen" was almost rock 'n' roll. RCA had clearly decided to play it safe with Roy, producing innocuous fluff with no trace of the danger and romance that was once essential to rock 'n' roll.

In his attempt to develop Orbison as a song stylist, Atkins unfortunately stripped him of his guitar. Roy's picking on his best rockabilly tracks for Sun was nowhere to be found on the RCA sessions. Not only did Orbison feel inhibited as a singer, tactfully wading his way through the schlock his producer and publisher had foisted on him, he was now surrounded by a crew of first-class guitarists, among them Hank "Sugarfoot" Garland, Harold Bradley, and Chet Atkins, who could play circles around him, albeit without Roy's edge.

Ever since Roy began to sing, the guitar had been the foundation of his music. Its rhythm, tone, and feel were essential to the way he delivered his lyrics. He felt naked and self-conscious without it. As a performer who stood stone-still onstage, Orbison desperately needed something to do with his hands. The only thing worse than leaving them slack, dangling by his sides, would have been to pantomime his sonic melodramas like the theatrical Johnny Ray, whose over-the-top emotional histrionics seemed to border on madness. Having a guitar slung over his shoulder was natural to Roy. Besides, the sleek, feminine curves of his favorite axe (a hybrid of a 1950's Gretsch Country Club customized with the neck off a Gibson Super 400 and pickups taken from a Sho-Bud steel guitar) went a long way toward enhancing his sullen presence. (Orbison's trademark guitar is currently on display in a museum in Germany; the one-of-a-kind instrument had disappeared years ago, after Orbison shipped it to a guitar builder in Japan in hopes of having it duplicated.)

Although he never achieved the technical ability of Chuck Berry or Carl Perkins, or wielded their sort of influence on the next generation of guitarists, Orbison had genuine chops on the instrument, playing solid, workmanlike leads on his early records.

Perkins considered his labelmate "a fabulous musician," calling him "a sly fox with that guitar." The king of rockabilly guitar admired Orbison's natural feel on the instrument, and the way he intuitively "dug those things out of his guitar neck."

Having recorded the likes of Carl Perkins and B. B. King, Sam Phillips knew a great guitarist when he heard one and was impressed with Orbison's timing, as well as his ability to effortlessly switch from bass lines to rhythm to lead. "He just hated to lay his guitar down," the producer claimed.

"Roy was a better guitar player than most people give him credit for," Harold Bradley said. "I didn't realize that because on the sessions he didn't play. He would come over and say, 'Harold, could you play this, or Grady [Martin], could you play that?' He usually had it all worked out in advance. The first thing a record producer used to do when an artist came in with a guitar was take it away from them. They didn't want the sound to leak into the vocal mic and affect the delivery of the songs. At the time, Roy had enough problems just delivering the songs as it was."

Sadly, Roy would become just another strummer. Unhappy about it as he was, Orbison was far too shy and unassuming to breathe a word about it to Chet Atkins, an industry giant who forged the music of Elvis, the Everly Brothers, and Eddy Arnold into platinum.

Veteran bassist and Roy's studio bandleader for over a decade Bob Moore, who'd backed Bill Monroe at the Grand Ole Opry and played sessions for the hilarious swing duo Homer & Jethro, never considered Orbison's picking anything particularly special. "As a guitar player, Roy was all right with it," Bob surmised. "He just needed something to hold while he was onstage."

Orbison's final session for RCA, held on this twenty-third birthday, April 23, 1959, was a washout. Neither song cut that day made the grade. Four uninspired takes of "Paper Boy" and five of with "With the Bug" (a.k.a. "The Well-Known Bug") would remain in the can.

"With the Bug" was a rough-and-tumble number from Roy's days with the Teen Kings, who, when bored and restless with the routine of the road, would toss invisible insects at each other for kicks. Once possessed by the bug, the infested person was expected to wriggle and shake until the invisible pest was thrown from his body and passed on to the next victim. Fun as it might've been for a pack of restless youth on tour, the spirit failed to make it onto tape. Within a year of signing with RCA, Orbison once more found himself a free agent.

The sad truth of the matter was that, though he'd had a few triumphs with Sun and sold a song to the Everlys, nobody at RCA gave a damn about Roy or his music. According to Bob Moore, Chet Atkins, the leader on the date, "didn't bother to turn the speakers on in the control room when that record was being cut. He just sat there practicing his guitar."

In the meantime, Sun Records had become a veritable ghost ship: Only singer/pianist Charlie Rich remained. Both Johnny Cash and Carl Perkins had deserted Sam Phillips and signed with Columbia Records in hopes of greater distribution and opportunity. But Perkins quickly found himself in a similar pickle as Orbison. Following his near fatal car crash, Carl turned to the bottle to ease his pain, only to become more disillusioned and disheartened when his music was drowned in the saccharine dross of Nashville production.

Cash, who never feared speaking the truth, spelled out the problem with Music City's practice of putting business above artistic integrity: "Carl is unique, and the music scene in Nashville was not then or is not now conducive to propagating his style of music. I don't know if Carl ever had the right producer; I don't know if he ever had the right record company behind him to understand and care what his talents were." Cash could just as easily have been talking about Roy's experience with Sam Phillips and Chet Atkins, but his luck in that respect was about to change.

Although they rarely performed on the same bills together anymore, Orbison and Perkins remained close friends throughout their lives. While shuffling between Texas and Tennessee, the Orbisons had become regular houseguests at the Perkins' home.

As far as Carl was concerned, Claudette was the Lone Star State's answer to Elizabeth Taylor and, like the gorgeous storm Liz was, the young Mrs. Orbison had her man coming and going every which way from Sunday. Unlike Jerry Lee and Elvis, who controlled nearly every aspect of their teen brides' lives, Roy was the "honeydew" in their relationship, as in "Honey, do this!" and "Honey, do that!" Perkins would later describe Roy's "pretty little pet" as "hard and lazy," and the day would eventually come when his wife, Valda, told Claudette and Roy to pack their suitcases and find a place of their own, as their welcome mat was officially worn out.

Perkins was far from the only man knocked out by Claudette's beauty. According to her brother Bill Frady, they had been walking down Hollywood Boulevard one afternoon when a movie studio agent approached Claudette to ask if she was an actress. When she said no, he handed her his card, hoping to persuade her to audition. After she politely declined, he scribbled his secretary's name on the back of her card just in case she happened to change her mind and need to get past the guard at the gate.

FOUR

DREAMSONGS OF THE GENTLE EMPEROR

On February 3, 1959, a single-engine Beechcraft Bonanza 35 took off from Mason City, Iowa, at two in the morning. When the plane crashed just a few minutes later in a snow-covered field in Clear Lake, the tour known as the "Winter Dance Party," along with the original wave of rock 'n' roll, would come to a sudden, jarring end. Roger Peterson, the twenty-one-year-old pilot, hadn't had much experience flying in severe weather conditions. Everyone aboard was instantly killed upon impact, including Buddy Holly, Ritchie Valens (famous for his irresistible Latin rocker "La Bamba") and the disc jockey turned pop star J. P. Richardson, better known as the Big Bopper. Also on the tour was "the Wanderer," Dion (Dimucci), who fatefully decided to ride the bus along with other band members, which included Buddy's bassist, Waylon Jennings, to their next gig, in Moorhead, Minnesota.

Although Holly and Orbison both hailed from West Texas, recorded with Norman Petty, and shared the image of the gawky but nice boy next door, the four-eyed disciples of the King were never all that tight. It seemed like life had once again consigned to Roy sidelines as he watched Buddy's meteoric rise to fame with a string of hit singles that rocked teenage America. With his horn-rimmed glasses and lumpy Adam's apple, Buddy was rock 'n' roll's original geek (an image aped years later by the other Elvis, Costello). While Orbison appeared moody and crestfallen, Buddy's awkwardness was a big part of his appeal.

Holly (although known within the industry for his hot temper) was cute, charming, and effervescent and, most important, nonthreatening compared to Presley, Jerry Lee, and Little Richard, who were unpredictable and seethed with lust.

With the exception of "Ooby Dooby," the portfolio of songs that Roy wrote and recorded during his time at Sun remained well beneath the radar while Buddy ruled the charts until "the Day the Music Died," as the fateful crash would become known in the annals of American pop culture. The catastrophe ended whatever competition once existed between them, and Roy, from that day on, swore off charter flights, although he'd make an exception from time to time.

"Buddy's death was a terrible, terrible tragedy, of course, and felt most personally by his family and friends due to the sweet soul that he was at heart," Carolyn Hester lamented. "The musical loss to the American scene cannot be calculated."

Dead at twenty-three, Holly had become a rock 'n' roll legend while Orbison languished in West Texas, punching it out in small bars and clubs, playing whatever gig he was able to scrounge.

Awake most nights until dawn, Roy regularly slept into the late afternoon, on an opposite schedule from Claudette and their new baby son, Roy Jr., who they called "R. D.," short for Roy DeWayne, named after his daddy, of course, and in honor of Orbison's pal, the surf guitar legend Duane Eddy. Living in a small, cramped apartment in Odessa, Roy would regularly saunter out to his car with his guitar in order to find the necessary solitude to compose. He was far from alone. The ritual is a well-known one for many songwriters. Over the years, hundreds of great songs have been written "in the back of the car, or in hotel rooms, in planes," Johnny Cash told *Time* magazine in 1959. Although Roy complained that songwriting was "a lonely experience," he understood the process demanded intense focus. And, in the end, alienation is a small price for a good tune.

Like most of rock 'n' roll's early producers, Fred Foster relied heavily on his instincts. Neither musician nor engineer, Fred had an innate sense for what sounded good. Somehow he managed to bring the best of country and pop together without winding up with the worst of both worlds. Growing up in western North Carolina, Fred had no real musical background to speak of beyond a Victrola and a pile of records in his family's living room.

"I never played an instrument well enough to upset anybody who really plays," Foster laughed. "I started with guitar and played a little bit of piano, but it only makes me upset 'cause I can't really play that well."

Moving to Washington, DC, in the early '50s, Fred, who wrote the lyrics to the McGuire Sisters' laconic 1953 hit "Picking Sweethearts," soon wound up producing the C&W sausage king, Jimmy Dean, and his band of Wildcats. Originally hired by Mercury Records, Foster quickly jumped to ABC/Paramount, where he produced George Hamilton IV's light 'n' easy "A Rose and a Baby Ruth," as well as Lloyd Price's tale of the badass gangster "Stagger Lee," boogalooed its way to the top of the R&B charts in the fall of 1958. "Go, go, Stagger Lee," cheered the backup singers while the horns wailed like police sirens as the song's hero repeatedly pumped the hapless Billy De Lyon full of lead in time to the drummer's fierce backbeat.

Sinking his entire savings ($600 of his own and $600 borrowed) into his new label, Monument Records, Fred recorded the catchy "Done Laid Around" by wavy-haired ex-Wildcat Billy Grammer. "Done Laid Around" quickly rose to Number Four on the pop charts. Thought to be a traditional song, "Done Laid Around" was actually written by folksinger/folklorist Paul Clayton, a little mix-up that cost Foster a bit of money and a lot of embarrassment, having to recall the first pressing and reprint the label with the song's original title, "Gotta Travel On."

Having started Monument Records in DC (hence the company's logo depicting the Washington Monument), Foster soon relocated to Nashville, where his fledgling label wasn't exactly welcomed with open arms by Music City's establishment. In no time an agitated posse of country music's biggest movers and shakers had gathered like a well-dressed lynch mob to run him out of town.

"Wes Rose invited me to a luncheon," Foster recalled. "He'd called a meeting of a whole bevy of the old pros to lunch. Then Wes stood up, tapped his spoon against his iced tea glass, looked right at me, and said, 'Why are you trying to destroy Nashville by making these pop shit nigger records?' I immediately got up and excused myself. I said, 'It seems I've lost my appetite.' Then I got outta there before they crucified me.

"Owen Bradley, who built the Quonset Hut studio and had recorded Ernest Tubb, Brenda Lee, Red Foley, and Patsy Cline, called me up and said, 'I heard you met the old guard. Don't let 'em scare ya, Fred. They're a bunch of tin-eared bastards who can't hear thunder! You can use my studio anytime.'"

Despite Foster's shocking encounter with Wesley Rose, Bob Moore, who owned one-third of Monument Records, had a different relationship with Rose. Bob considered Wes a friend and respected him. "Wesley was a hustler, a winner, the kind of guy who wasn't afraid slide into first base," Moore said.

In fact, Bob turned out to be the silver lining to Roy's problems at RCA Records: "I was the leader on that session," Moore explained. "Afterward, Roy was standing alone, in the corner, and I walked over and asked him if he was feeling bad or ill. He told me, 'I'm just fulfilling my contract, Bob, this is it. . . . After this, I'm through.' I told him not to worry, that I knew Wesley Rose and would tell him about Roy, so the next thing, Wesley went out to see Fred."

When Foster inked the deal with Rose in the spring of 1959, Orbison thought Foster had mistaken him for Warren Smith. For years Roy was convinced that Fred had confused "Ooby Dooby" with Smith's "Rock and Roll Ruby," which had been recorded and released by Sun in the same year.

Foster dismisses the story as nonsense, claiming he'd previously met Wes Rose and told him about his new label and asked him to keep him in mind if there were any new artists he was looking to sign. Fred said he was well aware of Orbison's singles on Sun, although he felt they "weren't the greatest records in the world." But he still found something compelling about Roy's "tender, wistful" nature, and was sure he might make something happen if he could line him up with the right song and musicians.

Roy's first session for Monument nearly got off on the wrong foot after he showed up late. It wasn't his fault. Apparently, no one had told him it had been booked. Upon returning to town, Roy walked into the Hawkins Street studio to say hello when he found his new producer Fred Foster and the notorious Nashville A-team sitting around, waiting for him in Studio B, wondering if the weirdo from Wink was going to show. Roy recorded three tunes that afternoon, including a knockoff he'd written with Cowboy Jack Clement called "Double Date," about a sad sack who goes home alone after both his gal and his pal dump their respective partners and take off without them.

As part of the deal with Monument, Wes Rose stipulated that Fred had to re-cut the pair of unreleased songs, "Paper Boy" and "With the Bug," from Roy's last go-round at RCA.

Back in Studio B again on June 3, with Fred Foster at the console, Roy and the band laid down an edgy take of "With the Bug," with Orbison's voice nearly as raspy as Boots Randolph's sax. The finished tracks didn't exactly make waves, and while the cute and corny "Paper Boy" failed to break the Top 100, it helped remind the public that Roy was still alive and in the game. Although "Ooby Dooby" by this time was ancient history, his name still managed to ring a few bells . . . if only faintly.

For whatever reason, Sam Phillips and Chet Atkins, both legendary figures in the music business who'd nurtured and produced smash hits by previously unknown artists, were still apparently clueless when it came to knowing what to do with Roy Orbison. With Fred Foster, Roy finally found the right fit—and the Monument house band, led by Bob Moore, was strictly top shelf. But there was still one last key member of the championship team missing.

Growing up in rural Gore, Oklahoma, Joe Melson embarked upon his musical odyssey as the leader of a local group called the Fannin County Boys that played occasional school dances and gigs in whatever small clubs they could find. After graduating high school, Joe moved down to Texas and enrolled at Odessa College, where he sang with a rockabilly band called the Cavaliers. Eventually Melson crossed paths with Ray Rush, a local impresario, who introduced him to Roy Orbison.

According to Melson, both Roy and Claudette adored his song "Raindrops" (a gentle waltz of lost love that Orbison later recorded on his first album, *Lonely and Blue*), while Joe was struck by the potential of Orbison's voice. As both of them were already capable of writing "a pretty good song," on their own, they reckoned they might come up with something extraordinary if they put their heads together. Joe claimed there was no set format to their organic approach to composing. For inspiration they'd cruise around together, carefully listening to and analyzing the latest sounds pouring from their dashboard speakers, grabbing catchy bits of lyrics and melodies that they'd later rework into their own first efforts.

As working at home with Claudette and the baby was out of the question, and the Caddy was too cramped for both of them, Roy and Joe rented adjacent rooms at the local Odessa Motel, holing up for hours at a time, working alone initially, coming up with a smattering of scraps and phrases, before sitting down together with their guitars to hash out and refine their ideas. Their original attempts were quickly abandoned, but after Melson played Roy a particularly hip guitar riff that he deemed "uptown," they agreed they'd found the hook for their first successful collaboration.

"Uptown," Roy's second single for Monument, was a snappy little number about a social-climbing bellhop with an eye for the girls and big plans for the future. Driven by Bob Moore's syncopated walking bass and Boots Randolph's raw gutbucket tenor sax, "Uptown" sounded more like something out of the Rat Pack's repertoire than the commercial country music coming out of Nashville at the time. To Joe Melson's ears it was "class rock."

The sense of elegance that Melson alluded to in his musical metaphor had its roots in big band–era swing. Bob Moore explained where the sound came from: "My buddies were the best musicians in town. We were all individuals but together, as a band we were known as 'the A-team.' For seventeen years we played with Owen Bradley on the weekends in a Count Basie–style big band at Belle Meade, the rich people's country club. Through my experience with the big band, I was hearing things in my head."

The A-team member perhaps most responsible for helping Moore materialize those sounds in his head was Homer Louis Randolph III, better known as "Boots." "I went up to Evansville, Indiana, with my first wife and we stopped into a club where Boots was playing," Moore recalled. "His personality and his playing just took over the stage. He'd already been to Nashville, so I wouldn't say that I brought him there. It was more like we played some golf together and I'd told Chet about him and the next thing he was 'in' and I got him on an Elvis session."

When Roy approached Fred with the idea of using a string section to give "Uptown" an extra schmear of sonic gloss, Foster replied, "'Good luck finding one in Nashville.' Nobody was using them at the time. Most folks were listening to fiddles on the *Grand Ole Opry*. The only thing that was holding the Nashville Symphony together in those days was violin rosin! But if that's what he wanted, I wasn't gonna stand in his way. Anita Kerr called me and said, 'I found four string players that I think will be all right.' Anita was a great artist and pianist in her own right. She kept cotton in her ears all the time. She said she couldn't stand the sound of traffic because it was out of tune. She had perfect pitch. She'd blow into a bottle of Heineken and tell you it was in E-flat. And she was right! She'd line us all up and conduct us singing 'On Top of Old Smoky.' She would meet and talk with the musicians and work very hard at the arrangements."

The glorious shimmer of a string section (no matter how humble its origin) on their song made Joe Melson ecstatic. Both he and Roy claimed it was "the most beautiful sound in the world." But Wesley Rose, the former accountant who fancied himself a record producer, considered the extra added expense self-indulgent and extravagant. Doubting his client's lack of star power, Wes would confide to Fred his fear that Roy could never make the big time because of his looks. Rose's callous remark would cause Foster to lose whatever dwindling respect he had left for him. "With friends like these," Fred said, "who needs enemies?"

Released in January 1960, "Uptown" was Orbison's first record since "Ooby Dooby" to hit the *Billboard* charts, hustling its way to Number Seventy-Two. Although it failed to turn the record industry on its ear, the modest success of "Uptown" assured Roy and Joe and the folks at Monument that they were, at the very least, barking up the right tree.

The B-side to "Uptown" was another story altogether. Anyone listening closely to Roy's songs was sure to discover a few sinister undercurrents running through his lyrics. Although disappointment, heartbreak, and betrayal were all common themes in Roy's music, "Pretty One," the second keeper of Orbison and Melson's partnership, was a particularly creepy portrait of a spurned stalker bent on revenge. Roy's breathy vocal is riveting, bone-chilling stuff, sung from the point of view of a jilted boyfriend warning the flirty girl (who he never refers to by name yet continues to call his "Pretty One" despite her wanting nothing more to do with him) that she will soon have her comeuppance one day when she discovers her youth and beauty have faded. The singer sounds disturbed yet oddly calm. But there's no need for him to stoop to the level of sadism with which Lee Marvin had recently shocked movie audiences when he threw scalding coffee in his girlfriend's lovely face, scarring her for life in *The Big Heat*—instead the singer confidently bides his time, taking pleasure in knowing that the ravages of time will pay his darling "Pretty One" back for all that she's done.

To Bruce Springsteen, Roy was "the true master of the romantic apocalypse you dreaded and knew was coming after the first night you whispered, 'I love you' to your new girlfriend. . . . He seemed to take joy in sticking his knife into the hot belly of your teenage insecurities," the Boss observed years later. "He sang about the tragic unknowabilty of women. He was tortured by soft skin, angora sweaters, beauty, and death. [But in the end] the wreckage and the ruin and the heartbreak was all worth it."

An angry young man himself, John Lennon was a big fan of Roy's music, and also wrote more than a few "stalker songs" early in his career, including "I'll Cry Instead," "You Can't Do That," and "Run for Your Life." Whether taking perverse pleasure in pushing his fans' buttons or revealing his dark side, John, in the bridge to Paul McCartney's chipper little Summer of Love ditty "Getting Better," casually sings of beating his woman and keeping her "apart from the things that she loved." One might argue that it's only a song, but beneath their cheery façade, the

Beatles as well as "the sweetest man in rock 'n' roll" (as *Rolling Stone's* Steve Pond later dubbed Roy) apparently had more than their fair share of demons with which to wrestle.

By March 1960, Orbison's all-star crew of writers, musicians, and arrangers were in place and working together to create a sound that would sell millions of records. Although it never made Number One, Roy's next single for Monument would make him a star.

"We approached things a little differently back then. At least I know I did," Fred Foster told journalist Rachel Di Gregorio. "I told Roy, 'Let's forget about gimmicks.' His first success had been this little teen thing called 'Ooby Dooby.' And I said, 'That's not going to endure. We need to make music that will last; that we can be proud of.' I always thought, 'Let's make every record as good as we can possibly make it, put it out, and just hope it sells enough so we can continue to do this.' Roy agreed with this mentality."

Bill Porter, who engineered all of Orbison's vintage Monument sides, greatly admired Fred Foster's "uncanny ability to pick the right kind of song, to pick the right people to do the arrangements and then [step] out of the picture and [leave] it alone."

"I have to give Fred Foster his due," Roy told Nick Kent in December 1988, shortly before his death. Orbison considered Fred more of "a perfect patron." "He didn't necessarily know much about music," Roy claimed. "It was mostly him letting me produce my own sessions."

Only a place as desolate as West Texas could have inspired a song like "Only the Lonely." No matter where you hear it, whether in a neon diner in New Mexico or a noisy, crowded Brooklyn bar, the song's moody brooding melody never fails to jolt your soul as Roy delivers the simple lyric which cuts to the heart of human alienation.

While Melson and Orbison argued over who came up with the title to "Only the Lonely," they had the sense not to break up their budding partnership over the rankling issue. Instead, they simply agreed to disagree.

Without a doubt the turn of phrase was a great hook for a song, but Roy and Joe would soon ironically discover that another tune by the same name had already been recorded, by Frank Sinatra, two years earlier, in May 1958. Sammy Cahn and Jimmy Van Heusen's introspective ballad "Only the Lonely" was the perfect vehicle for the Chairman of the Board's sensual blue croon, which sailed above Nelson Riddle's lush string arrangement.

Oblivious to the Sinatra album of the same title (although it must have been hard to miss at the time, as the record went gold and its cover featured an awful, kitschy portrait of Frankie in the guise of a weeping clown), Roy maintained he'd originally written the song with Elvis in mind. He even tried delivering it to the King early one morning when he pulled up to the custom wrought-iron gates of Graceland at the break of dawn in his Cadillac, with Melson riding shotgun. The guard soon returned with a note from Presley apologizing that he had a houseful of company who were still sleeping off last night's party. Whatever his condition, Elvis was unable to answer the door and blew Roy off, but promised to catch up with him again soon in Music City. He didn't.

According to Fred Foster, Elvis had always kept an ear open to whatever Roy was doing: "Whenever we released a new record, I'd get a call from Elvis's people. Sometimes it was Lamar Fike, a couple times it was Elvis himself, requesting a few boxes of the latest single, which he'd pass along to his friends."

Bob Moore, who played bass for both Orbison and Presley, recalled how Elvis would corner him in the studio while on break to find out, "What's Roy doin'?" "I'm not gonna tell ya," Bob answered the King incredulously. "I wouldn't tell him what you're doin'!"

Whether in party mode or deep in slumber, Presley had missed the boat with "Only the Lonely," as did the Everly Brothers, who also turned a deaf ear to the song when Roy tried to sell it to them before finally deciding to cut it himself.

While Orbison's gentleness was unique for his day, Johnny Ray's 1951 single "Cry" revealed a new level of vulnerability and sensitivity previously unimaginable from a male singer. Ray's live shows regularly climaxed when he rose from the piano and threw himself on the floor, as he tore his hair out and wept uncontrollably in an inconsolable fit. Considering that World War II vets were expected to silently suck up the devastating trauma they'd recently witnessed on the battlefield, such displays of unbridled emotionalism were unheard of from a man who wasn't considered deranged or insane. Ray's histrionics would soon earn him the dubious title of "the Prince of Wails." The kids ate it up, wholesale.

The pervading mood of melancholia in pop music soon shifted to one of morbidity, triggered by Nicholas Ray's benchmark 1955 film *Rebel Without a Cause*, which culminates in a deadly drag race scene, when Jim Stark, the new kid in town, (played by James Dean) bails from his car at the last moment before it flies over a cliff. His opponent isn't as lucky and dies senselessly over a macho game of chicken.

Teen tragedy sagas (the tackier the better) would reach their apex (or nadir, depending on your perspective) nearly a decade later, in 1964, with Jan and Dean's "Dead Man's Curve," which featured such campy production touches as screeching tires and angelic harp crescendos, all courtesy of the brilliant Beach Boy Brian Wilson. In a bizarre coincidence, Jan Berry would become partially paralyzed two years later, after crashing his Corvette just a few blocks from the deadly corner they'd immortalized.

Years before Berry's life was forever changed on that fateful night in Beverly Hills, Mark Dinning had soared to the top of the charts in 1959 with his masterpiece of macabre kitsch, "Teen Angel." Over a gently strummed acoustic guitar (undoubtedly inspired by the Kingston Trio, who sparked the burgeoning folk revival), Mark sang a maudlin ballad of a young girl squashed by a train one night after she returned to the tracks to fetch her high school ring.

Hoping to cash in on the fashionable mood of gloom, Roy and Joe struggled with writing "Come Back to Me My Love," which caused Fred Foster to wince at its obvious mimicry of Dinning's haunted hit. Foster wisely suggested they scrap the tune but hold onto Melson's backup vocal hook, a catchy, empty-headed string of nonsense syllables, and work it into a new number, which quickly became the countermelody to "Only the Lonely."

Recorded on March 25, 1960, "Only the Lonely" had more in common with the highly polished pop cranked out by New York's Brill Building writers than with the kind of music most folks associated with Nashville. Orbison's vocals, in style and spirit, were much closer to Neil Sedaka's than to those of any country singer of the day.

Released on May 1, 1960, "Only the Lonely" featured Orbison's smooth-as-glass voice wafting over a loping syncopated beat, accented by a plinky "Chopsticks" piano part and the luminescent chime of a xylophone (played by multi-instrumentalist Charlie McCoy), causing a spontaneous pandemic of goose bumps amongst the hopelessly insecure from coast to coast. Add to that a clutch of backup singers cooing Melson's countermelody that was so mellow and catchy, and "Only the Lonely" had most of America (and the rest of the world) singing along before they knew what they were doing or what the hell "dum dum dum dum-bee doo-wah" might have meant.

Engineer Bill Porter also played an integral role in the song's creation: "There's a story about 'Only the Lonely,' and I'm gonna sort of take credit for the Orbison sound, because as a result of what happened with that recording, he had a trademark," Bill told journalist Michael Fremer in 2009.

At first, Porter was perplexed over how to record a piece of music with such a wide dynamic range. He watched quizzically as Roy gently strummed his guitar while working out the vocals with a couple of guys Porter assumed were just hangers-on. According to Porter, they seemed to be "sort of like singing" at best. The next thing Bill knew, Roy turned to him and said, "'That's the sound I want.' These guys [were] whispering the words and I thought, 'My God! I'll never get that on the mix. If I opened the mic up that much, it would let everything else in.'"

Like most engineers, Porter traditionally built his mix from the ground up, starting with the rhythm section of guitar, piano, bass, and drums; then adding "the sweetening strings" and backup vocals; and finally putting "the artist on top," in "kind of like a pyramid." With "Only the Lonely," he was forced to throw out the map and take an uncharted route. Bill took Joe's gentle countermelody and "mixed down from that instead of mixing up [which allowed him to] get that on top of the mix fairly easy." That "dum dum" sound became Orbison's trademark. "That's what made that record," Porter pointed out, "that soft, breathy vocal."

"Only the Lonely" had a lot of angles to it, some of them unimagined by Roy and his crew, who all pooled their talents to make it happen. Rock journalist turned DJ Dave Marsh's take on the song was both surprising and undoubtedly shocking to Roy's fiercely devoted fans. Though the track was "not a song about masturbation," Marsh wrote years later, "masturbating may be the only solace for an artist whose persona is as desperately paranoiac as Roy Orbison's." Dave felt the singer's overwhelming sense of longing and isolation created "the perfect setting for the utter self-pity that so often accompanies wanking."

Sad and hilarious as Marsh's theory is, he has a point. Beyond the obvious lyrical metaphor, the song's gentle rhythm steadily bumps the melody along until it reaches a strenuous crescendo. As the song builds to its glorious climax, Roy hits an impossibly high note that, as Dave writes, "shrugs off all the agony." Perhaps Monument should have released "Only the Lonely" with a pair of cigarettes and a complimentary lighter.

Whether or not Orbison was aware of the subliminal messages encoded within his music, he appeared on *American Bandstand* on July 23, lip-synching his latest hit before a throng of awkward adolescents, under the auspices of their clean-cut host, Dick Clark.

Although Orbison originally believed "Only the Lonely" was "an exclusive statement," to his surprise he would quickly discover "the club is very big," much larger than he'd ever dreamed. Peaking at Number Two, "Only the Lonely" was unable to stop Connie Francis, Brenda Lee, and Elvis all from skipping ahead of him and capturing the top slot.

Meanwhile, Roy and his band toured relentlessly behind the song, ping-ponging across the continent according to an ill-conceived, haphazard schedule that not only drained him physically but managed to exclude some of the obvious and more lucrative venues. Oddly enough Roy, Orbison didn't perform in Chicago or L.A. until years later, in the 1980s.

Recorded on August 8, 1960, Orbison and Melson's follow-up was a dollop of commercial fluff compared to their last single. "Blue Angel" offered no haunted portraits or psychologically disturbed characters or dark tales of unrequited love. Lyrically it was rather sappy, a trite knock-off about teen love, all too typical of its time. Its power lay in its simple but insidious melody. Over a chorus of cascading sha-la-las and a string of silly yip-yip-yips that once more incited involuntary sing-alongs, Roy ended the tune with a stunning falsetto that was simultaneously loose and as controlled as a Zen master's brushstroke. "Blue Angel" ascended to Number Nine on the charts, and its B-side, an airtight production of Gene Pitney's "Today's Teardrops," featured Buddy Harman's snappy snare, a throaty sax solo from Boots Randolph, and a pack of giddy backup singers chanting, "Yeah, yeah, yeah," three years before a bunch of Liverpool longhairs would coin the phrase.

While many of Roy's B-side covers were considered throwaways by his standards, they regularly became hits for other artists. "Today's Teardrops" went nowhere for Orbison, but three years later it worked magic for Ricky Nelson.

Roy's next single for Monument was a twofer of Don Gibson songs released on December 1, 1960. The A-side, "I'm Hurtin'," borrowed the familiar refrain "whoa, whoa, whoa," made famous two years earlier when Dean Martin gargled the Italian pop hit "Volaré." "I'm Hurtin'" climbed to a respectable, but ultimately disappointing Number Twenty-Seven on the charts. Perhaps the arrangement was just too perky for Roy's crowd. In the overall scheme of things, the upbeat "Ooby Dooby" was a fluke—his fans might not have been morose to begin with, but Roy's mesmerizing delivery had a way of tapping into the deep reservoir of melancholia that lay just below the average teenager's party face. Meanwhile, the song's B-side featured Orbison demolishing another Gibson classic, "I Can't Stop Loving You."

First recorded by Don in 1957, the song swayed with a gentle lilt, like a lullaby for the legions of brokenhearted losers perched on bar stools in neon-lit cocktail lounges from coast to coast, crippled by regret and anesthetizing themselves over lost love. Both Kitty Wells' and Jim Reeves' versions brought a bit more country to the song, while Roy's rendition (released in 1961) was deeply haunted. The singer is wounded to the point of paralysis by the memory of a girl he pledges to continue to love for eternity, despite the fact that she's long gone. The string arrangement, in contrast to the emotional volcano that gushed from his mouth, is both sweeping and majestic. Roy moaned like a disembodied spirit.

One year later Ray Charles put his singular stamp on Don's blue valentine, taking "I Can't Stop Loving You," from the honky-tonk to church, giving it an earthy, gospel feel, as his gritty, bittersweet voice soared over a punchy piano vamp. But Don's brand of heartache was custom-made for Roy's blue and lonely persona. Throughout his career, Orbison depended on Gibson's economical verses and simple melodies to provide him with a solid repertoire whenever his own songwriting inspiration waned. After moving to MGM, Roy would release an entire album of Don's songs in January of 1967.

Among the dozen songs comprising *Blue and Lonely*, Roy's first LP for Monument, was a cover of the Everly Brothers' "Bye Bye Love," Gene Pitney's "22 Days," and another Don Gibson number, "(I'd Be) a Legend in My Own Time," which finds Roy adrift in some low-lit, lowlife cocktail bar where Boots Randolph's boozy tenor growls as neon champagne bubbles float and pop above a gallery of lost souls.

Upon taking one look at the album cover, a photo of Orbison, the loner, hovering behind the wheel of his convertible at the local drive-in, leering, nearly cross-eyed, at some distant object of desire, Fred Foster quipped that someone should "get some dark glasses on him." Although causing a couple of snickers, Fed's joke turned out to be more prophetic than anyone could imagine at the time.

The inspiration for Orbison's next single, the spellbinding "Running Scared," came from a most unlikely source—the French Impressionist composer Maurice Ravel.

Fred Foster recalled how he first turned Roy on to Ravel's mesmerizing "Bolero": "Roy took the record home and called me later on, saying, 'It's fantastic!' He took the feel and rhythm and used it for

'Running Scared.' But if you listen, you'll find that Ravel originally wrote the piece in 3/4 but Roy heard it in 4/4."

Orbison claimed the inspiration for the lyric came from a story he'd read in a newspaper on a transcontinental flight that made him think about the lingering attachments and unresolved emotions we often carry with us into new relationships.

The February 27 session (which produced "Running Scared," along with the B-side "Love Hurts," along with a funky foxtrot called "Night Life," released the following year) was clearly a milestone, not only in Orbison's career, but for the Nashville studio musicians who'd grown accustomed to cranking out three- and four-chord country hits in their sleep. For the first time, members of the A-team were forced to play outside of their comfort zone. Orbison's compositions were not only unorthodox in their structure but often challenging to play. Roy's latest song, built on the hypnotic dynamic of a bolero, also employed a rubato (free time) section that immediately struck the session players as ambiguous and counterintuitive to everything they knew about popular music. It didn't have a steady beat, and what was the point of a pop record if kids couldn't dance to it? According to Fred Foster, bassist Bob Moore tried to force the song into a concise, familiar format.

"Bob couldn't stand it. He wanted to play everything in meter. I felt I had to protect that. I told him that a meter was something you read for the electric bill," Fred said. "'Running Scared' had no set verse or chorus. It just started here and went to there. Bob said, 'We've got to change this!' I said, 'Don't you open your mouth! There's not gonna be any changes!'"

Although frustrations and tempers might occasionally reach a fever pitch at Monument, Bob, who Elvis dubbed "the King" before the crown became his sole property, was known to keep a cool head no matter what changes were thrown his way. The same went for Roy.

"I once told Roy that if Elvis was 'the King' then he must be 'the Emperor!'" Terry Widlake chuckled. Commanding as he was onstage, and inscrutable as he appeared behind his dark glasses, Roy, the Gentle Emperor, ruled his domain with equanimity.

"I never heard Roy raise his voice once. I never saw him mad," Harold Bradley pointed out. "At one of the sessions [for 'Running Scared'] he retreated into the control room while we tried to put his song in meter. Well, we couldn't do it, and he finally walked out and said, 'I think we should play it the way it was written.' He was always very positive."

"I didn't know Roy personally, but it seemed like he was very introverted. You get the feeling like he must have been asking himself, 'Why am I so successful?' But you don't write music like that with your ego hanging out on a limb," observed arranger/producer Charlie Calello (best known for his work with Sinatra, Barbra Streisand, and the Four Seasons). "He never lost his originality over the years. It came from such a different place. In some ways, I think the music was secondary. He used it to tell his story. It didn't always fit neatly into bars and measures. He must have faced some rejection with those songs," Calello said, referring to Orbison's unusual arrangements and time signatures. "Musicians are so opinionated and narrow-minded. Greatness is rarely recognized by the 'experts.' Usually it's too out there."

According to Foster, he and Roy routinely sat down in his office to pore over "every song, every line, and every note" prior to a recording session. After rehearsing the band, they would get together with Anita Kerr and kick around ideas for the string arrangement. Fred claimed that Anita not only had great instincts but possessed the uncanny knack of reading his mind. "She was always right!" he said.

"Fred and Roy would talk about the songs and which musicians to bring in," Harold Bradley explained. "Then they went to Studio B with Bill Porter and Fred would oversee the sessions. He'd monitor Roy's singing and just trim the ship as it went along. He never critiqued us. We were playing the songs just as they were written. Fred just wanted to get the best performance out of Roy that he could. They worked really well together. I know Roy had a lot of confidence in whatever Fred suggested to him."

But once everyone was in the studio, the session for "Running Scared" quickly hit a snag when Roy's voice, overpowered by the combined force of the strings, rhythm section, and backup singers. His vocal was getting lost in the mix as the song built to its carefully constructed climax.

"He'd hit a falsetto note that just wasn't able to cut through all the muscle we had behind him." Foster recalled. Faced with the limitations of a small studio and a band drowning out his singer, Fred told Roy he'd either have to "hit that note at full voice or [they'd] have to change the arrangement." Having put so much time and effort into the song, Roy felt that going back and changing anything would be "horrible."

Foster believed Orbison's problem delivering the song sprang from his overwhelming feelings of self-consciousness more than his lack of vocal ability. "I said to my engineer, Bill, 'Why can't we just stick him over in the corner with a bunch of blankets?'" Foster recalled.

"Bill Porter went and put up a coatrack with a bunch of coats because the band was bleeding into Roy's mic when he was trying to hit that high note," Harold Bradley recollected. The hastily constructed barrier not only gave Roy's voice a stronger presence on tape, minimizing the leakage from the drums and guitars, but it also provided a shield from the watchful gaze of his producer, the arranger, and anyone else who happened to be in the studio at the time. Once he felt safe and secure, Orbison shook off whatever shyness stood in his way and gave a stunning performance.

"I remember when Gene Vincent recorded at our studio and the engineer was having a terrible time because we just had a small room, before we built the Quonset Hut. The drummer was playing real loud and it was going into Gene's mic, so my brother Owen went out and backed him up and backed him up until he finally backed him out in the hallway. I think he sang 'Be-Bop-a-Lula' standing out in the hallway with just the mic cable propping the door open. So that might actually have been the first isolation booth." But Roy's coatrack was still a major leap at a time when bands recorded live, cutting the song in one take, with the singer in the same room.

Giving his vocalist one last shot, Foster told Roy that if he couldn't cut it, he'd "erase [the track] and no one will ever know about it but us." Roy's friend and neighbor Boudleaux Bryant, who was sitting at the console, gave it to him straight: "Roy, nothing ventured, nothing gained, you know—it won't hurt you to try."

With that, Foster began to roll the tape before filling the musicians in on the plan. As the song built to a majestic crescendo, Roy belted out the last line. "And those musicians," Fred recalled, "some of them while they were still playing, came right out of their chairs. They had no idea what they were hearing! After that, Roy didn't have any trouble hitting those notes at full voice."

Whether the isolation booth was first created by Fred Foster or Owen Bradley, every producer in Music City was soon building a version of their own. Fred recalled Chet Atkins stopping by the studio a few days later when he heard Orbison's voice, but the singer was nowhere in sight. "Where's Roy?" Chet asked. "In there," Foster replied, pointing to the patchwork of coats and blankets insulating Orbison from the outside world. "What the hell ya doin' that for?" Atkins said.

A couple weeks later Fred was "walking past RCA Studios where Chet was doing a session for Skeeter Davis but I didn't see her around anywhere, so I said to him, 'Where's Skeeter?' A minute later she poked her head out of the booth they got built for her and waved at me," Foster laughed.

Labeled everything from rockabilly and country to MOR, as well as disco at one particularly low point in his career, Roy's music continually defied all attempts to categorize it. His sonic cocktail blended every flavor of music he'd heard since childhood, from three-chord honky-tonk to morose Mexican love ballads, to whatever big-band jazz and classical music was broadcast over the radio in West Texas throughout the 1940s and '50s.

The Canadian singer k.d. lang not only adored Roy's voice but found his unconventional songwriting inspiring: "It showed a tremendous disregard for form," she told writer Barney Hoskyns. lang felt the "emotional crescendos and the movement" of Roy's songs made them unique at a time when most artists showed little originality and instead stuck safely to the typical Tin Pan Alley verse/chorus pop-song recipe.

As Lucky Wilbury (a.k.a. Bob Dylan), Roy's "half brother" and future partner in the Traveling Wilburys would later write in his memoir, *Chronicles*: "His stuff mixed all the styles and some that hadn't been invented yet. . . . You didn't know if you were listening to mariachi or opera."

Although officially a baritone, Roy confessed years later in an interview on Dutch TV that his remarkable range came to him naturally, resulting "from the fact that I didn't know what I was doing." As he told Joe Smith: "I didn't even know I could do that at the time. I didn't know there was a difference between full voice and falsetto. I could feel the difference, but I didn't understand the technical differences. Then the power of the voice came. It was a gradual thing, and it came with confidence."

Somewhere along the line a clever critic or young hotshot in the A&R department dreamed up the word *countrypolitan* to describe the blend of country, easy listening, and soft rock coming out of Nashville in the late '50s and early '60s. The term seemed to define the New South as it struggled to evolve beyond its rustic roots and antiquated prejudices.

Looking to break out of a small regional market, country music producers began slicking up their artists' old-style music with string sections instead of fiddles, electric organs and xylophones in lieu of the pedal steel guitar —which, just a few short years earlier, in Hank Williams' heyday, had been considered cutting-edge.

But while the term *countrypolitan* seemed to fit Patsy Cline's neon-blue torch songs tighter than a sequined polyester pantsuit—thanks to her cocktail piano trills and lazy behind-the-beat-phrasing—her music sounded downright jazzy. It didn't exactly capture Roy's eclectic musical mix.

To Fred Foster's ears, "Running Scared" had a "baroque classical" sound. Ultimately, most folks were not impressed by who or what influenced Roy's music, and cared even less what they called it. It just sounded good.

Beyond its lofty origins, exotic instrumental touches, and atmospheric back-up vocals, "Running Scared" unnerved people with its deeply paranoid lyrics, portraying a confrontation between two men over a much-desired woman. It's too soon for the protagonist to know exactly where he stands—their love is new and there is still an old score needing to be settled. The singer is no coward, and stands his ground quietly as his heart pounds louder and louder in rhythm with the building drums.

If this had been an Elvis Presley song (or movie), fists would've been flying by the end of the first verse. The song is also unusual in that it has no chorus. Instead, it simply unravels until it climaxes with Orbison's voice scaling the Everest of the final chord and with him (for a change) walking off triumphantly into the night, arm in arm with his new love. Rather than engage in a macho pissing contest, the song's protagonist quietly maintains his dignity and is rewarded for his gentleness. Unlike Sinatra, famous for calling the shots, Orbison wisely allows the woman to decide.

"The song went to Number One despite Wes Rose telling me that it was 'a piece of shit,'" Foster groused. "There were no gimmicks on any of those recordings. We just wanted to make music as timeless as we could. We didn't know what we were doing. We were just feeling our way along with a two-track machine." Monument may have been flying by the seat of their pants, but they were flying first class.

"Running Scared" would top the charts the first week of June 1961. Predictably, as the cash came rolling in, Roy began lavishing presents upon his family, to make up for all the lean years the poor kid from West Texas had known in his childhood and as a struggling songwriter. Yet despite all the new jewelry and sports cars that began to multiply in his driveway, Roy claimed he was fond of "the simple life," as he told *New Musical Express* in April 1963. Sure, the accoutrements of success were fine and dandy, but Orbison said he cherished whatever brief time he had off the road most of all.

Compared to likes of "Bye Bye Love," "Wake Up Little Susie," and "All I Have to Do Is Dream," Boudleaux and Felice Bryant's new song "Love Hurts" was dark, sexy stuff. Looking for another smash hit, the Bryants delivered their latest ode to teen love to the Everly Brothers, hoping the duo's tight harmonies would deliver their latest song directly to the top of the charts as they had before. But "Love Hurts" was a different sort of beast, a moralistic dirge that warned young lovers of the tragic fate that lay ahead if they messed around in passion's kitchen. Whether they were too innocent (doubtful), or their act too clean-cut, the Everly

Brothers' take on "Love Hurts" lacked genuine torment and came off as a tepid ode to puppy love gone wrong. It eventually wound up as filler on the B-side of their 1960 album, *A Date with the Everly Brothers*.

The following year, Roy took a stab at "Love Hurts," slaying anyone who came within earshot with the mournful, haunted requiem. No matter how schmaltzy the production or melodramatic the lyrics might get, the integrity of Roy's voice was never in doubt. He evoked the same level of authenticity as a bluesman or country singer who lived his songs. Like a weary veteran who had survived endless battles of the heart, Orbison sang knowingly of the price we pay for love. When he stood perfectly still onstage in a cold spotlight, moaning, "Love is like a stove, burns you when it's hot," nobody doubted for a minute that he sang from experience. It was obvious his heart had been charred in love's oven until it was hard and black as coal.

As the B-side to "Running Scared," "Love Hurts" would reach Number Five on the Australian charts. Yet Wesley Rose was unhappy. He'd originally wanted "Love Hurts" to be Roy's new hit single. Following a dispute with Rose over which song they would promote, Fred Foster directly delivered an acetate to Chicago DJ Howard Miller, who played both songs on the air and then opened up the phone lines for an audience opinion poll.

"It was no contest. It was an overwhelming majority—a hundred to one for 'Running Scared,'" Fred recalled.

It turned out that Rose had a secret agenda with "Love Hurts." As he was currently in a lawsuit following a falling-out with the Everly Brothers, Wesley hoped that Roy's version of the song would break while Don and Phil's recording, for the time being, sat on the shelf collecting dust.

In 1961, songwriter/producer and future member of the Atlanta Rhythm Section Buddy Buie began promoting concerts in Dothan, Alabama, better known as the Peanut Capital of the World. "I was an Orbison fanatic from early on in his career," Buddy boasted with a hot July drawl. "I brought him to the Houston County Farm Center, which had dirt floors and about 4,000 concrete seats. It was used for farm shows more than for music. When I booked him, they asked me if I got a band that reads music. I told 'em yes, which was a bunch of bullshit. For two months, every day they [a local group called the Webs, originally known as Spider (Griffin) & the Webs before their leader split for Texas and never returned] practiced, playin' Roy's songs 'til [they] sounded just like the record. When Roy first heard 'em he said, 'God almighty, these boys are good!'"

Bill Moody, a DJ on the Big BAM, "The Voice of the Deep South— 740 on the AM dial," emceed the show that night: "There was no air-conditioning in there and it must have been 120 degrees, but Roy sang his heart out for an hour and a half and I don't think he broke a sweat," Moody recalled.

"When he came back two years later Roy told me, 'I want that band. I want to take them on the road with me,'" Buie said. "I told him, 'Well, you can have 'em as long as I come along as the road manager.' That was our ticket out of town! [Rhythm guitarist] Bobby Goldsboro was with us at the time. He'd just gotten married and brought his wife along, so that made six of us altogether in the car."

"We were the only band in the area," Goldsboro explained. "Roy's promoter called and we were booked to back him up for four dates in the Southeast. It was during the summer of my second year at Auburn University. I wasn't as familiar with his Sun recordings as I was [with] the Monument records: "Blue Angel," "Crying," and "Only the Lonely." After the first concert I was in awe of his talent. By the second concert we were like old friends. He was a great guy to work for. In fact, after the first few weeks I started flying with Roy to the dates because we had become like brothers."

Bobby found the dynamic and structure of Orbison's songs "unique. . . . I've always played by ear and still do, so they weren't hard for me to learn. I remember commenting to Roy on a couple of occasions that there were too many beats after a line. He said that was the way he wanted to write it. I had never played some of the chords that I had to learn to back him up. I'm sure that had an influence on my writing."

Buddy Buie concurred: "My time with Roy helped me get my foot in the door as a songwriter. Roy was the sweetest human being I've ever known. He lived by that old adage 'If you can't say anything nice, don't say anything at all.' We had the best times on the road," Buie said, recalling years later going to the fights with Roy and feasting on Chinese food in Detroit. Coming from Dothan, Alabama, Buddy and the boys might as well have been on Mars.

The Webs, rechristened the Candymen in honor of Roy's 1961 hit "Candy Man," became Orbison's touring band but only recorded with him on only a few occasions, while Fred Foster relied on the bullet-proof pros of the Nashville A-team to cut most of Roy's records. The Candymen would later play on a handful of Orbison's MGM tracks, most notably "Crawling Back."

"For the tours, there were five of us in the band, plus Roy, his wife, his little brother Sammy Keith, and Orbie Lee—that made nine altogether in a Dodge motor home," recalled Rodney Justo, who handled backup vocals and played tambourine ("first chair," as he joked). "Sammy Keith was so young and inexperienced. I was always hoping that he would just get lost quick.

"I was twenty years old. We were all chasing a dream, gettin' fifty bucks a day, with no per diem. We had to pay all our own expenses. Roy was cheap, but at the same time he could be very generous. If you said, 'Hey, Roy, those are some nice cuff links.' He'd just take 'em off and hand 'em to you without thinking twice. He just didn't like to give you the money!" Rodney laughed. "Roy was a very loyal guy. There was this agent from the Midwest named Marlon Payne who booked him when nobody else would. And to show his gratitude we'd go out on tour in the middle of the winter from North Dakota to Vancouver. There was so much snow, we'd be driving through Regina [Saskatchewan] guessing where the streets were.

"Y'know how backup musicians are generally a bunch of yes-men? Well, the folks at Acuff-Rose used to call us Roy's 'No-Men,' because we thought we were the stars," Justo chuckled. "We'd open the show with a half-hour warm-up set and tell all of his corny jokes. Then Roy would get up and say, 'Good evening, ladies and gentlemen. I just flew in from out of town and boy, my arms sure are tired.' And they'd sit there still as Mount Rushmore, wondering what the hell he was he doing. Didn't they just say that ten minutes ago?"

Orbie Lee, who Rodney likened to the cowboy actor Slim Pickens, was very protective of his son. "He told me, 'The first time you steal a show from Roy you're fired.' Now how the hell do you steal a show from Roy Orbison?" Rodney mused.

"It wasn't long before Bobby got a record deal of his own and left," Buddy Buie said. "The band eventually wanted to do something more than back up Roy."

"He used to call me Rodno Justy," Justo said. "'Rodno,' he said, 'There ain't but three things that hurt me in my life: Claudette, my boys dying, and the Candymen leaving me.' I said, 'Roy, I don't think we belong in that category.'"

The following October, "Crying" (backed with "Candy Man") soared to Number Two on the *Billboard* charts, where it remained, unable to evict Ray Charles' "Hit the Road Jack," a slinky blues about a no-account gigolo, from the Number One slot.

"Crying" was emotionally devastating stuff. "I was all right . . . for a while . . ." Roy sobs, and in the space between the words, time seemed to stand still for a moment. You could just about feel the wind blow, whether across the Texas prairie, or down a desolate city street, or through the aching hole in his heart left by the old flame with whom he unexpectedly crosses paths again.

Whether or not Roy Orbison ever intended his music as therapy, his songs had a way of speaking to weary souls everywhere, be they on the brink of suicide, or staring at the void through the bottom of a bottle of whiskey or sleeping pills, or see-sawing precariously on a window ledge. His music also spoke to those less obviously in crisis, the great pretenders who go through the motions of their lives every day without speaking a word, while acting like everything is absolutely fine with their families and jobs.

Orbison was clearly a different kind of man, vulnerable, unafraid to wear his emotions on his sleeve. According to Roy, the song's intention was to show "that the act of crying, for a man, was a good thing." This was a bold statement, considering that "Crying" was released, as Roy told the *New Musical Express* in 1980, "in a real macho era when any act of sensitivity was frowned on."

With "Crying," Roy opened the door to a new paradigm. Surprisingly within Orbison's inner circle, there were a few people who still didn't get what he was all about. "Wes told us that 'Crying' was no good," Frank Foster chuckled. "He threatened to riot on me and sent the strings and male backup singers home. On the other hand, Sam Phillips said it was one of the best records he'd ever heard."

Flip the record over and Roy and the band could be heard jamming a down-home blues on the B-side, "Candy Man," the song that helped make harmonica wailer/multi-instrumentalist Charlie McCoy a Music City legend.

"Roy got another hit with that one and I got myself a career," Charlie recollected fondly. "I went to Nashville thinkin' I was a guitar player, but the first five guys I heard, I couldn't even hold their pick. When I heard all these guitar players I figured I had to do something else. It was the best thing in the world that happened to me, 'cause it pushed me back to my first instrument, the harmonica, which I started when I was eight.

"On my first session I played with an eighteen-year-old Ann-Margret, plus Nashville's legendary the A-team. You can imagine what my nerves were like that day," McCoy laughed. "On that session Bob Moore came over to me and said, 'Are you busy on Friday?' I said, 'Hey, I'm free the rest of my life!' He was recording with Roy Orbison and wanted me to play on it. I was a huge fan. I'll never forget driving around Atlanta when I heard 'Only the Lonely' for the first time. I had to stop the car, it was that impressive!"

The song that Bob Moore brought Charlie in to blow on turned out to be "Candy Man," written by Greenwich Village folksinger Fred Neil, who wrote "Come Back Baby" for Buddy Holly in 1958 and later penned Harry Nilsson's smash hit "Everybody's Talkin'," as well as the hippie anthem, "The Other Side of This Life" recorded by Jefferson Airplane. The gig paid forty-nine bucks. Not bad for a couple hours' work for a twenty year-old kid in the summer of 1961.

"Most folks don't realize that we also did 'Blue Bayou' during the same session as 'Candy Man.' We were recording direct to two-track then. There was no multitrack; the technology wasn't around yet. I was so high about 'Candy Man' that I really can't remember much about 'Blue Bayou,'" Charlie confessed.

"Fred Foster wanted 'Candy Man' to sound like Jimmy Reed's 'Big Boss Man'" (which was later covered by Elvis and would also feature Charlie's wailing blues harp). A huge fan of Jimmy Reed's laconic blues, McCoy had grown up listening to rhythm and blues on radio station WLAC out of Nashville, which from 10 P.M. on "played nothin' but the real blues—Little Walter, Sonny Boy Williamson, and Slim Harpo.

"They were running down the song when Roy said, 'We need some sort of an intro,'" Charlie recalled. "Of course, I was the new kid on the block, so I kept my mouth shut, but I walked over to Harold Bradley and whispered to him, 'I got an idea. I don't know. . . . What if I played this . . . and you guys come in and join me?' Harold jumped up and said, 'Hey! Charlie's got an intro. Listen to this!' I was shocked. It was the second session of my life and I was surrounded by all these heavyweight studio guys. That they used my suggestion just blew me away. After that, the record came out and was a hit and my phone never stopped ringin.' That was a key record for me. It was a mark of fate for a record like that to happen so early in your career."

"Charlie grabbed his harmonica, and the drummer on the session, Buddy Harman, taped his wallet onto the snare [giving it a muted, fat tone] and they cut the song in twenty minutes," Fred Foster added.

Bookended by a pair of hit singles (the title song and "Running Scared") *Crying*, Orbison's second LP for Monument, was filled out with a couple of B-sides and various tracks that had begun to pile up from his ongoing sessions. But a lyrical thread seemed to run through much of the album—Roy delves into feelings of overwhelming insecurity, in "The Great Pretender" and "Running Scared," which invariably lead to the agony of unrequited love, in "Crying," "Love Hurts," and the tragic "Wedding Day," which finds Orbison as the groom still waiting at the altar, watching helplessly as his dreams collapse, wondering if he should throw away the gold rings.

Between Orbison's odes to emotional devastation, a few moments of mirth were to be found on the record, from the pumping panther prowl of "Night Life," which finds Roy recklessly cruising the streets, to his airheaded valentine "Lana."

Stylistically, "Lana" was about as far from Nashville as Roy could get—a little twist number built on a punchy fuzz bass riff reminiscent of the kind of half-time brass lines that Roy probably huffed back in his Wink marching band days. Recorded on June 14, 1961 (before "Crying" or "Candy Man"), "Lana" wasn't released as a single until five years later, in June 1966, after Roy had left Monument for MGM Records. A lot had changed in that short time. The Beatles had gone from being a local Liverpool group playing gigs at the Cavern Club, to the mind-bending innovations of *Revolver*. By then, "Lana" sounded like a throwback to another time. Nonetheless, Orbison's voice remains fresh, effortlessly soaring, deliriously in love, under the spell of the beautiful L-A-N-A (whether inspired by Ms. Turner, the vivacious Hollywood starlet, or some fictitious vixen of the same name). Meanwhile the backup singers go zoom-zooming along, like something that would later ooze from Juan García Esquivel's quirky Space-Age Bachelor Pad music.

Orbison's string of hits just kept coming. Roy's sessions at RCA's Studio B on January 9 and 10, 1962, yielded seven new songs, including, "The Actress," "Evergreen," and Cindy Walker's easy-grooving fantasy, "Dream Baby."

"I had asked Cindy if she had any songs for Roy," Fred Foster recalled. "She said she might have something. The next morning she called and said she had two from her catalog, and a new song she tried to write the night before that was, in her words, 'pitiful.' That turned out to be 'Dream Baby.' When Roy heard it he said, 'Yes, sir, I think you found it!' Cindy wrote great stuff. [Walker's hits were recorded by everyone from Bob Wills and Gene Autry to Dean Martin and Ray Charles.] Later on, Willie Nelson recorded an entire album of her songs." (*You Don't Know Me: The Songs of Cindy Walker* was produced by Fred Foster and released in 2006, shortly before Walker's death.)

"Dream Baby" was a down-home porch rocker with Roy singing loose and bluesy over a gently strummed acoustic guitar. Floyd Cramer's funky-tonk piano kicks in, bumping the groove up a notch, while Boots Randolph blows some growling gutbucket baritone.

Released in June 1962, "Dream Baby" took England by surprise. Famous for his morose ballads, Orbison suddenly had scores of young Brits out on the dance floor swiveling their hips to his music. Backed by "The Actress," with its deceptively cheerful cha-cha rhythm, swooping strings, and backup vocals from a clutch of taunting sirens, the song's lyrics took dead aim at the more superficial aspects of Claudette's personality. Although wise to her games, Roy was all too willing to play the fool in exchange for her love.

RIGHT: A cat called "Domino"—Roy in the early days, looking slick. (Michael Ochs Archives/Getty Images)

BOTTOM: The Teen Kings in a Sun Records publicity shot, 1956. From left to right—Billy Pat "Spider" Ellis, Roy, James Morrow, Johnny "Peanuts" Wilson, and Jack Kennelly. (Photofest)

Roy recording at RCA Victor Studio in Nashville. (Michael Ochs Archives/ Getty Images)

Contract for "Crying" and "She Wears My Ring." Note Bob Moore as "Leader." (From the collection of Bob Moore)

The Monument imprint. (Author's collection)

Record sleeve for the single "It's Over." (Author's collection)

LEFT: R.O. on the move! At home in Hendersonville, Tennessee. (Michael Ochs Archives/Getty Images)

BOTTOM: Claudette and Roy. (Michael Ochs Archives/Getty Images)

RIGHT: Roy unmasked by
Marianne Faithfull, while on tour
in England, 1965. (GAB Archive/
Getty Images)

BOTTOM: Strange bedfellows—
Roy and the Rolling Stones, while
on tour Down Under, 1965. (A.
Short/Getty Images)

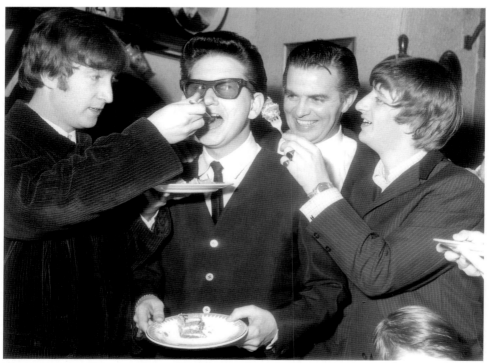

John Lennon and Ringo Starr make sure Roy gets plenty of cake on his birthday, April 23, 1964. (© Mirrorpix/Courtesy Everett Collection)

His pompadour was perfect, even while building model airplanes. (Courtesy Everett Collection)

Roy with his cherry-red ES 335 Gibson. (Redferns/Getty Images)

FIVE

OF CRICKETS AND BEATLES

Things were beginning to change fast in Roy Orbison's life. On June 29, 1962, Claudette gave birth to their second son, Anthony King, who they called Tony. Around this time songwriter Bill Dees reentered Roy's orbit again. A member of the Five Bops, Bill had previously recorded with Norman Petty, cutting a pair of songs at the Clovis studio, including a rave-up called "Jitterbugging," which they hoped would make some noise as the A-side of their single, along with a tune of his own called "Unforgotten Love," which featured the legendary producer on keyboards.

"We were from Amarillo, Texas, and had a Number One song in Wichita Falls, Kansas," Bill laughed. Playing dives from Wichita to Dallas, the Bops soon found themselves opening for Roy and the Teen Kings.

A year later Dees and Orbison crossed paths again when Bill's group, now known as the Whirlwinds, were scheduled to record. Unbeknownst to Bill and his band, the engineer had called in sick earlier, and when they arrived, they found Roy Orbison sitting behind the board. After the session Bill and Roy headed over to a local truck stop, where they sat drinking coffee, ruminating over their rock 'n' roll dreams until dawn.

Although the Whirlwinds fizzled out and none of the music recorded that night was heard again, Dees continued to write. In the meantime, Bill held down a series of blue-collar jobs to support his family. When

Orbison crossed paths with Dees again at a party in Borger, Texas, Bill sang him his latest tune, the ghostly "Borne on the Wind."

"I was fixin' to go onstage to play a show at a high school auditorium when somebody came up and told me that a friend of my family had dived in after his kids who were caught in an undertow. They managed to rescue one girl but didn't find him or two of the other girls," Dees said, recalling the inspiration for the song.

Overcome with emotion, Bill immediately disappeared into the bathroom, where he strummed his four-string tenor guitar. A melody was beginning to take shape when a torrent of words suddenly came flooding out.

Orbison was immediately struck by the power of Bill's tragic tale and the song's eerie melody. "When I got with Roy," Bill recollected, "he put that [syncopated] beat to it and wrote the lines, 'You don't love me, but you love for me to be in love with you.'"

Off the road briefly, Roy spent the Christmas holidays in Hendersonville with Claudette and the boys before returning to the studio again on January 4, 1963, to record "Borne on the Wind." Although Orbison's first collaboration with Dees ascended to the top of the charts in England, their remorseful requiem remained unreleased in the States until a year later, when it was tacked onto his first greatest-hits compilation.

Meanwhile, Roy phoned Bill, telling him to pack his bags and head for Nashville, where Roy would arrange a session for Bill at RCA Studio B, backed by Bob Moore's orchestra. But the three Orbison-produced tracks ("Blackie Daulton," "Summer Love," and "This Is Your Song") never saw the light of day.

Disappointed, Dees returned to Texas to scratch out a living for his wife and four kids, until early the following year, when he came boomeranging back to Music City. Practical enough not to rely on dreams when he had five mouths to feed, Bill held down a warehouse job in Nashville while tinkling the keys at the Palms nightclub on the weekends. Eventually he hooked up with Roy again, and the pair got down to the business of writing songs together.

Dees preferred composing on a four-string mahogany Martin tenor guitar, as he found the instrument's unusual tuning melodically more inspiring than the standard six. He usually worked out a song's concept and structure before showing it to Roy, who tinkered with it, customizing the tune to fit his dramatic vocal delivery.

"With Roy, we'd just sit down and go head-to-head, without a tape recorder or anything. I'd just do a lot of oohing and ahhhing," Dees explained. "Roy was very, very fast when he hopped on an idea. He was very quick-minded. He would say, 'When I get back from England I've got a recording session coming up on such 'n' such a date.' And he'd be working on some songs and I'd have little pieces of things, half written."

"In Dreams" was one of the few songs Orbison wrote on his own, without a collaborator. Recorded during the same session as "Borne on the Wind," this was Roy's masterpiece of romantic heartbreak, and its source was pure as it gets. Springing from the deep well of his subconscious, "In Dreams" came to Roy completely finished, while he was sound asleep. All he had to do was wake up and write it down just as he had heard it only moments before, echoing in his head.

Throughout his life, sleep had always been a good friend to Roy, a welcome refuge from the awkward, sometimes disturbing realities of his daily life. Yet the supernatural sandman in the song's soft-spoken introduction seemed oddly macabre. As the haunting strings begin to build methodically "the candy-colored clown" goes creeping into another bedroom, to cast his narcotic spell. While the "magic night" holds glorious visions for the singer/dreamer who finds himself reunited with his estranged lover, his joy only lasts as long as he remains unconscious. With the break of dawn he awakes to find all he has longed for was just an illusion and now he must face another day, filled with pain and disappointment.

Orbison's singles for Monument were meticulously crafted productions that reveal his lifelong passion for classical music. Like Phil Spector's "Wall of Sound," or Brian Wilson's "pocket symphonies" to come, Orbison's mini pop operas employed lush, over-the-top Wagnerian-style arrangements, filled with exotic rhythms and surprising tonalities. Nobody in Nashville but Roy would have added a xylophone to their mix at the time. This was years before Brian Jones' innovative use of mallet percussion on the Rolling Stones' songs "Under My Thumb" and

"Yesterday's Papers," or Bruce Springsteen's penchant for punctuating his verse with a chiming glockenspiel. Yet for all their divine excess, there was never a wasted note on Roy's Monument recordings.

Filmmaker David Lynch—master of the surreal and uncanny, whose portfolio of freaky flicks began with 1977's ghastly cult classic *Eraserhead* and includes the tender but unnerving *Elephant Man*, as well as the twisted '90s television drama *Twin Peaks*—would throw a peculiar light on Orbison's seemingly innocent verse when weaving "In Dreams" into his hallucinatory nightmare *Blue Velvet*.

Roy later claimed that he was "mortified" as he watched his beloved sandman become an accessory to "a dope deal." But in time, Orbison eventually came to appreciate Lynch's bizarre vision, which, as he said, "added a whole new dimension to 'In Dreams.'" Not only did *Blue Velvet* earn Lynch an Academy Award nomination for Best Director in 1986, it also managed to resuscitate Roy's floundering career at the time.

"In Dreams" managed to ignore every basic rule of songwriting, dispensing with the standard verse/chorus format. Roy deliberately molded his songs to fit his voice, instead of the other way around, employing unusual time signatures and adding unexpected extra measures whenever he felt the lyric or melody called for a deeper expression. That level of freedom was nothing new to such blues singers as John Lee Hooker and Lightnin' Hopkins, who doggedly held on to the same chord, building the rhythm while chanting some phrase over and over again like a shamanic incantation, watching, waiting until their crowd was near the point of frenzy, before finally changing the chord and releasing the rising tension.

Although Roy's best songs appear to flow seamlessly, they are in fact well-calculated affairs. Like a field commander in the war of love, Roy Orbison took no prisoners. Taking direct aim at his fans' emotions, he built the dynamics of his music with precise strategy and intention, leading to what author/historian Colin Escott termed the "Kleenex Klimax."

"His songs had songs within songs," Bob Dylan, who greatly admired Orbison, both as a singer and songwriter, wrote in *Chronicles*. "They shifted from major to minor key without any logic. There was nothing else like him on the radio. . . . Next to Roy the playlist was strictly dullsville . . . gutless and flabby." U2's lead singer, the man who'd named himself Bono Vox (Latin for "good voice"), claimed he was not only mesmerized by Roy's "angelic voice" but considered the laconic lullaby to be "probably the greatest pop song ever written," pointing to its unique structure, which allowed the melody to unfold without any repeating sections.

The flip side of "In Dreams" featured another Cindy Walker tune, "Shahdaroba," complete with an exotic, swirling Arabesque oboe riff that wafts like smoke from a hookah. Like "Blue Bayou," Walker's verse evoked a wistful paradise where Roy and his fans could escape the burden of their daily lives, even if only for two and a half minutes.

While *In Dreams*, Roy's third Monument long player, wasn't exactly a concept album, it could be considered a song cycle as it was comprised of set of tunes with repeating themes that ran through the lyrics from the album's title song to the Bryants' "All I Have to Do Is Dream," and Stephen Foster's classic waltz "Beautiful Dreamer." Although "Shahdaroba," "Blue Bayou," and the laconic "Lonely Wine" don't specifically mention dreams, the overall mood that permeates the album is of a desperate, pressing need to take refuge from reality. It's hard to cultivate a sense of nostalgia for a bleak land where nothing grows, where the dust just blows forward and back, and the air is hot and thick as grease. The songs of pure longing that Orbison wrote were most often for places he'd never seen and could only imagine in his dreams, like the idyllic "Blue Bayou." For a boy from Wink, Texas, the image of "fishing boats with their sails afloat" was akin to a mystical vision, while the "hurting inside" that he knew all too well could only be healed by "looking forward to happier times."

Back in the real world, Roy would soon lose another old friend. On March 5, 1963, Patsy Cline, who'd recently been banged up in a near fatal car crash, went down in small plane outside of Camden, Tennessee, along with *Grand Ole Opry* stars Hawkshaw Hawkins and Cowboy Copas. She was just twenty-nine.

Not only did Roy love the way Patsy torched a song, but he admired how she handled the crazy fame game. Cline always gave it her all, whether onstage or off, always making it a priority to sign autographs for fans, hoping, as she once said, "to mean something special to a whole bunch of strangers who suddenly become like family to you."

Orbison and Cline had become good friends while touring the South, playing a string of one-nighters together, along with teen idol Bobby Vee, who rode in the backseat of her old Cadillac. It had been three years since Patsy topped the charts with "Walkin' After Midnight." In the meantime, Roy's "Blue Angel" had shooby-dooed its way up to Number Nine earlier that summer. But it was actually Bobby Vee, the pretty boy from North Dakota, who was pulling in the crowds at that point with his sugarcoated cover of the Clovers' "Devil or Angel."

As Patsy's erratic driving had started to make a nervous wreck out of Roy, they decided to charter a plane to cut down on the extra stress and travel time between gigs. After landing in Dothan, Alabama, Orbison reached into his jacket pocket to discover he'd left his prescription glasses behind on the plane. Nearly blind without them, he was forced to play the show that evening wearing his sunglasses. Roy later confessed he felt "embarrassed" about going onstage with his shades on, but much to his surprise, the audience loved it. Those dark glasses instantly transformed his homely image, loaning an air of mystery to a nerd who suddenly transmogrified into a cool jazz daddy or enigmatic movie star. "It wasn't something I had designed or thought up," Orbison later explained. "It was a mistake."

He was never without his shades from then on. Day or night, inside or outside. Like Chaplin's moustache or Emmett Kelly's broom, they would become his trademark. From author Peter Lehman's perspective (whose book *Roy Orbison: The Invention of an Alternative Rock Masculinity* analyzes the singer's psychological state and the motives behind his songs, fashion, and performance style), Orbison's impenetrable Wayfarers "signified less that he was cool than that the man hidden behind them looked at the world darkly."

In the wake of the spectacular "In Dreams," Orbison's next single, "Falling," appeared formulaic on first hearing. The song had everything his fans had come to love and expect from Roy—his tremulous voice soared over a lush arrangement of cascading strings and angelic backup vocals, all buoyed by a syncopated backbeat and the snappy click of a pair of claves. But it was the lyric that bent the heads of those paying attention. Orbison slowly draws you into a skewed scenario where the singer finds himself unceremoniously caught by the lies he'd used to seduce the woman he desired. We never find out how his "baby" feels about his desperate apology. Now that he has confessed his love, she suddenly holds the reins in the relationship, while he appears weak and vulnerable, uncertain where he stands.

"Falling" is another powerful portrait of the lonely, tormented people who desperately seek love despite the inevitable disappointment and rejection they are certain will follow a fleeting moment of infatuation. The song is an ode to power, who's got it, and who is willing to give it up, a theme that Roy would revisit through-out his career, until his final Top Ten hit, "You Got It," in the spring of 1988.

The B-side of the new Orbison single featured an eerie take of Cindy Walker's "Distant Drums," a soldier's parting plea to marry his sweetheart before he's shipped off to war. Walker had originally written "Distant Drums" with country crooner Jim Reeves in mind. Although Reeves' gentle reading of the song clearly evoked bygone eras, from the Civil War to World War II, his producer, Chet Atkins, nixed its release, feeling it was too controversial if not in bad taste in light of the escalating conflict in Vietnam.

By 1963, the kids who'd grown up with Elvis, Jerry Lee, Buddy, and Chuck were no longer hanging around the malt shop with their hair slicked back in ducktails. Nor were they sporting blue suede shoes and bombing around town in souped-up Ford Fairlanes and Chevy Bel Airs. They'd either enrolled in college or found jobs, gotten married, settled down, and had kids of their own.

No matter what path the first rock 'n' roll generation chose, they, like most of America, were living under the threat of communism, from Capitol Hill to Moscow, from the shores of Cuba to the jungles of Vietnam. They built fallout shelters in their basements, stocked shelves with enough cans of Campbell's soup and franks and beans to last a radioactive half-life. There was also the nagging issue of civil rights demanding to be addressed. Old attitudes and prejudices of the past were questioned and dispensed with as a young, debonair president took office, replacing a weary, bald-headed general whose name had become synonymous with a decade of complacency and conformity.

The world was becoming an increasingly tumultuous place. For young people in search of answers, the burgeoning folk scene seemed to provide a few. Compared to the white-bread pop flooding the airwaves at the time, folk music had integrity. It inspired nostalgia for a past when life appeared (at least in hindsight) more simple and honest. Folk brought people together, not in fan clubs or on dance floors but on a broader scale, promoting such ideas as brotherhood and harmony in the heartwarming group sing-alongs (corny as they might have seemed) led by Pete Seeger, Odetta, and Peter, Paul and Mary. Bob Dylan, who'd begun his career as a champion of Woody Guthrie's songs and legend, soon found himself anointed as the golden boy of the new folk revival. His penny-plain anthem "Blowin' in the Wind" begged humanity to reconsider the lack of compassion and awareness in our everyday actions, while his unforgiving "Masters of War" took dead aim at the politicians and businessmen who instigate global conflict, causing death and destruction for their own profit. In light of such damning protest songs, Roy's cover of "Distant Drums" may have seemed trivial, yet it made a subtle but powerful statement about the emotional devastation that lovers face when torn apart by the sudden outbreak of war.

While the Big O rarely flexed any political muscle, four years later, in 1967, he would sing "There Won't Be Many Coming Home," a song whose righteous melody and marching rhythm evoked the "Battle Hymn of the Republic." Recorded for the soundtrack to *The Fastest Guitar Alive* (an inane movie in which he made his Hollywood debut), the song recalls the desperate days that followed the Civil War. The lyrics not only refer to the rising body count, they sympathize with draft dodgers wandering home in fear and trepidation as the haze lifts on the battlefield. Though the song was never officially banned, many radio stations quietly ignored Orbison's "There Won't Be Many Coming Home," despite the fact that the zeitgeist supported this kind of sentiment. It's curious, even laughable, that anyone could consider an old-school conservative family guy like Roy to be an antiwar agitator.

Perhaps Orbison was inspired by Bobby Darin's daring leap from slick lounge entertainer to "sincere" folksinger, when he decided to sing "Where Have All the Flowers Gone." Or maybe it was the Kingston Trio's heartfelt reading of Pete Seeger's famous protest song that moved him. Either way, Roy's rendition of "Flowers" was staggering, while bearing none of the self-righteous attitude that eventually sank the folk movement.

"Roy didn't usually get involved in political matters, but he was a staunch republican," Terry Widlake pointed out, recalling that Orbison and his band "played a private fundraiser on a boat in Boston harbor to reelect Gerry Ford, back in the mid-'70s." (It would be years before Orbison joined forces with longhairs such as Dylan and George Harrison, in the Traveling Wilburys, forging a pure pop album that interestingly enough bore no political statements. Nor was the record culturally revolutionary in any way, shape, or form, despite Dylan's and Harrison's pedigrees.)

Frustrated with his status in the States and inspired by Buddy Holly's success overseas, Orbison contemplated touring England. After all, Del Shannon had already paved a bit of road for him, introducing Roy's music to British audiences by singing "Crying" on his 1962 tour across the pond. Shannon had also met a bunch of charming lads from the north who played old-school rock 'n' roll with real commitment and passion for the music and the people who created it. Impressed with their Everly Brothers–style harmonies and hearing strains of Buddy Holly in their original songs, Del would record their perky valentine "From Me to You," making him the first Yank to sing a Beatles tune stateside.

With "Falling" ascending the British charts, Orbison flew to London to headline a twenty-date tour of the UK, from May 18 through June 9. His support acts included the Beatles and the dreadfully cheery Gerry and the Pacemakers.

On the opening night of his British tour, Orbison walked into the Adelphi Theatre in Slough and was taken aback by the sight of banners everywhere hailing the Beatles. Demanding their immediate removal, the lone Texan soon found himself confronted by the tag team of John Lennon and his debonair manager Brian Epstein, who, apparently wired on "Prellies" (a favorite amphetamine of the day), were determined to shake him down over the issue of the show's top billing.

Whether or not Roy was ready to admit it that night, the irrepressible madness the world would soon come to know as Beatlemania had already been ignited, and the band's frenetic set, which included a high-voltage cover of the Isley Brothers' "Twist and Shout," along with Chuck Berry's "Roll Over Beethoven," Barrett Strong's "Money," and Paul McCartney's latest wistful ode "All My Loving," written to Jane Asher, was clearly more than a moody, brooding ballad singer with an underrehearsed pickup band could compete with.

Back in the States, Roy had been stuck playing second fiddle to Elvis and Buddy Holly and the Crickets. Now, just a few years later and an ocean away, he'd come face-to-face with Holly's legacy, the Beatles. Orbison later claimed he was willing to concede the headlining spot and allow the lads from Liverpool to close the show since he was getting five times the amount money they were.

Devoted as the Beatles' fans were, their crowd unexpectedly went balmy over Roy on the first night of the tour. After Roy turned in nearly a dozen encores, John and Paul had had enough and apprehended Orbison. As the audience cheered wildly for another tear-jerking/panty-soaking ballad, Lennon and McCartney grabbed Roy by the arms and physically restrained him from returning to the stage while taunting him with jeers of "Yankee, go home!"

"It was pretty hard to keep up with that man," Lennon concurred. "He really put on a show."

According to Ringo Starr, following Orbison's mesmerizing set was a daunting task: "He'd slay them and they'd scream for more," Ringo recalled. While the Beatles gave it their all, shaking their carefully coiffed pudding-bowl hairdos as they mimicked Little Richard's ecstatic falsetto, Roy held the audience entranced "just doing it by his voice. Just standing there singing, not moving or anything." With his pompadour cresting in a perfect black wave above his pale, man-in-the-moon face, Roy may have appeared distant and unscathed on the outside, but the moment he opened his mouth his haunting bel canto revealed a raging wound that festered deep within, a living, breathing scar of all the pain and disappointment that life was certain to dish out to a young dreamer. He drove Beatles fans to the brink of madness.

"Roy hated it when the reviewers said he looked pasty-faced," Bill Dees said, "But the irony was you couldn't stop staring at him, standing up there so still."

In an interview with Radio Merseyside, Orbison confessed to DJ Spencer Leigh that he considered it "a big compliment" that the Beatles "were sort of frightened" by his performance. While Roy claimed he was having a good time, he was undoubtedly watching these boys usurp his and his entire generation's place in the cultural landscape.

What Orbison didn't know was that the Beatles had been big fans of his music all along. In March 1962, Paul sang a spirited cover of "Dream Baby" over the BBC radio, complete with a thuddy country bass part, as original drummer Pete Best whacked a fat backbeat on his snare and John and George cheerfully chanted the "sha-la-la" backup vocal bit. Then came "Please, Please Me," which hit Number One in UK in February '63, and clearly bore the influence of Roy's style.

In their early days, the Beatles banked on their cute image and lovey-dovey melodies, while Orbison's verse and voice delved into feelings of frustration, alienation, and rejection. With "In My Life" (the centerpiece of the Beatles' 1965 album, *Rubber Soul*), John Lennon would leave behind the cute and clever Jerry Leiber and Mike Stoller–style sonic "playlets" of adolescent love and express himself on a deeper, more personal level than ever before. Lennon suddenly began to take notice the people and aspects of life that held real meaning for him.

With both its lilting melody and nostalgic lyrics, "In My Life" bore more than a coincidental resemblance to Roy's "Blue Bayou."

Years later, Lennon joked that his schmaltzy '50s-style vocal on *Double Fantasy*'s hit single "Starting Over" had been inspired by "Elvis Orbison." For John, the song was a return to his rock 'n' roll roots. He compared it to "Dylan doing *Nashville Skyline*, except I don't have any Nashville, you know, being from Liverpool. So I go back to the records I know—Elvis and Roy Orbison and Gene Vincent and Jerry Lee Lewis," Lennon said in his last interview, just days before he was gunned down in cold blood outside of his New York apartment on December 8, 1980.

"It was February 11, 1964," Roy's onetime backup singer Rodney Justo recalled with a laugh, talking about the day Roy Orbison cut "Miss Brown" for Sound Stage 7, Monument Records' subsidiary label. "When we listened back to the song, Roy said, 'It's a smash!' But I knew I was doomed. I'd just seen the Beatles on *The Ed Sullivan Show*. They made everything obsolete overnight!"

The British Invasion had been an instant game-changer, not just musically but fashion-wise as well. Suddenly American girls by the thousands began taking a second look at their boyfriends. Struck by cloddishness of their dates whether they still clung to the trappings of the '50s greaser or had recently converted to the latest Ivy League trend (sporting corduroy blazers with suede elbow patches, Arrow shirts, crew cuts, and wing-tips), the girls delivered a unanimous response to their lack of aesthetic: "Eeew!"

Before the Beatles arrived at Idlewild Airport (as Kennedy International was previously known before the thirty-fifth president of the United States was shot in Dallas), a constant barrage of sonic dross flooded the airwaves, pouring from a million dashboards and transistor radios from coast to coast. With Elvis in the army, Little Richard in the seminary, and Jerry Lee in disgrace, mediocrity seized the day. It was as if rock 'n' roll had never happened. The battle was over and the good guys had lost. Alan Freed, the Cleveland disc jockey crucified for taking payola and "talking black," had apparently died in vain. Cheese ruled the day—thick and creamy and more than anyone could possibly swallow. The neutered had launched a cultural coup while America mourned the death of Buddy Holly and waited anxiously for the second coming of the King.

Beyond entertaining American troops stationed in Germany during his two-year mandatory military service, Elvis Presley would never perform in Europe again. As the Colonel held no valid passport, the King, who wasn't going anywhere without Parker getting his 50 percent, was left stranded on American shores to languish in the wretched excess of Hollywood and Las Vegas for most of the '60s. And with Jerry Lee Lewis persona non grata following his scandal, Orbison soon became celebrated by young Brits as the real deal.

Unlike Presley, Roy was no pretty boy, but his cool noir style was hip enough to be appreciated and adopted by a new subculture of fashionable pill-popping scooter boys known as the mods.

Kids in the UK were not only wild about rock 'n' roll; they voraciously dug into its mystical roots. In London, a blues scene was emerging, sparked by the old Chess recordings of Muddy Waters, Howlin' Wolf, and Sonny Boy Williamson. Art school dropouts like Keith Richards and Jimmy Page, who'd devoted their every waking hour to learning Chuck Berry riffs, soon fell under the spell of Mississippi Delta slide guitar masters—Son House, Robert Johnson, and Elmore James. The Brits seemed to know more, feel more, and, more important, buy more records than their somnambulant cousins back in the States.

Roy found England unlike anything he'd previously experienced in America. There was no quibbling over his authenticity. All you had to do was listen—the proof was right there in his voice. Whether owing to his newfound celebrity or to the freedom he found an ocean away from home, Roy felt happier in the UK than he'd ever been before in Texas or Tennessee. In a feature written for the *Record Mirror* in September 1963, journalist Norman Jopling recalled a freewheeling Orbison enjoying the dog races at Walthamstow Stadium. "He may well buy a greyhound to be kept and trained in Britain. If he does, he intends naming it 'In Dreams.'"

Returning to England again for a twenty-three-date tour, beginning on September 11, 1963, Orbison was paired this time with the Beatles' favorite band, the Searchers, who'd just hit Number One that August with "Sweets for My Sweet." Also on the bill was the most peculiar group the British Invasion had to offer—Freddie & the Dreamers.

The Dreamers' front man, Freddie Garrity, was a five-foot-three bespectacled former milkman from Manchester who flounced about the stage with his arms and legs akimbo, creating an unfortunate new dance craze called "The Freddie." Laugh at his spastic antics all you want, you had to admire Freddie and his Dreamers' pit-bull tenacity to make their mark in showbiz despite their "talentless idiocy" (as Lester Bangs deservedly bashed them).

"I'm Telling You Now," a song that announced the singer's unbridled intentions upon the object of his desire (whether requited or not) reached Number Two on the British charts that August and would eventually hit Number One on the *Billboard* charts in the States eleven months later, in July 1965. These dorks meant serious business. Even the Beatles had to play ball with them, inviting Garrity's gang to perform at their 1964 Christmas Show at London's Hammersmith Odeon. And from that night forth, rock 'n' roll's door was flung wide open for freaks and geeks of every stripe to come traipsing through, from Tiny Tim to Johnny Rotten. Freddie and his Dreamers had clearly lowered the bar on pop star standards, and whatever fears Sam Phillips and Wes Rose once projected about the weird kid from Wink with the weak chin were suddenly obliterated.

SIX

THE PRETTY WOMAN
AND A HOUSE
WITHOUT WINDOWS

Joe Melson had grown weary of living in Roy's shadow. As Orbison's partner, Joe had helped him break into the charts with his catchy refrains and poetic reveries. A fan of R&B and doo-wop, it was Melson who coached Roy in the vernacular of the style, teaching him to sing behind the beat, which took the square edges off his very white delivery. In return, Roy offered Joe a brief shot at the spotlight during his shows and helped him secure a solo record deal. But try as he might, Melson could never match Orbison's thunder.

Personality-wise, they were like night and day. While Orbison was laid-back and unassuming, Melson, as Terry Widlake recalled, was "always pumped up and preening in front of the mirror, until it nearly drove his wife insane. I think it constantly ate at him, that everybody was chasing after the four-eyed nerd who sang the songs instead of him."

"Roy was a star," recalled engineer Ronnie Gant, who began working at the "Acuff-Rose School of Music" in 1963. "But he was down to earth, very unpretentious. Gant described Melson as "an unbelievable egomaniac."

"Joe Melson wanted to be a star," Bob Moore concurred. "He had more hair than any guy I'd ever seen. He was a little strange but he had a lot of talent."

Signed to a publishing deal with Acuff-Rose Publishing, Joe would cut a total of seven singles for their in-house label, Hickory Records. Though they featured the A-team, the same crack band heard on Orbison's tracks, Melson's records didn't exactly jump right off the shelves.

Whatever notoriety Joe ultimately enjoyed, he'd eventually realize, came from his association with Orbison. Melson never exactly became a household name, but as Boudleaux Bryant wrote in his liner notes to Roy's first Monument album *Blue and Lonely*, it would be "an unpardonable oversight to overlook the contribution of Joe Melson to Roy's meteoric rise to stardom." Bryant pointed to the album's five songs on which they collaborated, including "Only the Lonely" and "Blue Angel." "Together," he wrote, their songwriting created "a perfect vehicle" for Orbison's voice. Bryant also admired how Roy and Joe transformed the innocuous "doo-wah"—a phrase routinely employed by 1950s backup singers—into "a pleasing little vocal gimmick" along with an entire vocabulary of "yea-yeas" and "dum de-dums." These were "artfully woven" in and out, throughout the songs, which, Boudleaux claimed, "when combined with Roy's vocal gymnastics made magic."

Frustrated in the role of Roy's junior partner, Melson knew he'd never make it big as long as he remained low man on Orbison's totem pole. And Roy, like many of his peers, began touring with pickup bands (whose members were increasingly younger and paid little in exchange for the rare opportunity to jam with a legend) in lieu of footing the bill for his whole entourage. Joe would soon find himself left behind on Roy's transatlantic tours.

With titles like "No One Really Cares," Melson's solo material belied a sense of hopelessness in his situation. Banking on his association with Roy, Joe tried on Orbison's mantle, that of the eternal loser (which Melson had helped to create). But Melson's slick pompadour and lucky-sombitch grin only backfired on him, making his brand of lonely sound simply bitter.

As their partnership fizzled out, Orbison began writing on his own before temporarily collaborating with Candyman/rhythm guitarist Bobby Goldsboro, who later scored a Number One hit with the cloyingly sweet but tragic tale of a young widower called "Honey."

Roy, along with his new songwriting partner Bill Dees, would soon hit the Top Ten in the states and Number One in England with "It's Over." According to Dees, their melodramatic opus wasn't inspired by any particular event in either of their lives but by "what we'd gone through with various girls, or how somebody played the fool for someone else and was being jerked around by this invisible chain."

"'It's Over'" is probably my favorite of Roy's songs," Fred Foster said, recounting the song's remarkable metamorphoses. Before the historic session on March 10, 1964, all of Orbison's Monument records had been cut at RCA's Studio B, which was also known as "Little Victor." "Then they built a larger studio and called it A, which made no sense since RCA Studio B was there before Studio A," Foster explained.

When Roy called to say he was leaving for Europe for the next two months, Fred urged him to do a session before hopping the plane so they'd have something in the can while he was gone. After asking Roy what he had in mind, Orbison pulverized him with "It's Over." "Well," Fred stammered, "I think that'll do. . . ." But Roy's stalwart producer was now faced with the dilemma of whether to return again to Little Victor or record at his new studio, which was considerably larger than their usual haunt. The new Fred Foster Sound Studio, constructed in the Cumberland Lodge Building on Seventh Avenue, formerly belonged to none other than Sam Phillips. But to Foster's surprise, he quickly discovered, "everything was wrong with it." Phillips had sold his new custom sound lab to Fred after a failed attempt at breaking into the Nashville scene: Music City was no Memphis. Sessions ran by the clock and studio musicians expected to be paid scale, not just a free lunch at Taylor's Café and whatever spare cash Sam could fork out of his wallet at the time.

When Fred called his old standby, Bill Porter, to engineer a session he'd booked for March 10, Bill told him he'd feel more comfortable in the new studio after he had a chance to test run it by cutting a couple of demos. Recording a few small groups first would give him the time he needed to work out all the bugs.

"Acoustically it was fantastic," Porter told journalist Michael Fremer in an interview years later. "It was in an old Masonic Lodge hall, all wood, big ceiling about twenty-five feet high. I mean you could put about one hundred musicians in it easy. But the console wasn't so good. The live echo chamber wasn't as good either."

Determined to get on with the session, Fred urged Bill to do his best under the circumstances. "Okay," Porter replied hesitantly. Then he asked how many pieces Foster had in mind. As Fred tried to recall everyone scheduled to play, Bill grew more apprehensive. "Well, you don't need to count. It's a demo session, right?" "Well, not exactly," Fred replied. "Man, I can't do a *real* session!" Porter complained. With that, Foster confessed that Roy Orbison was scheduled to record in just a few days with an unprecedented *forty-two musicians*. According to Fred, Porter lost it at that point and began to cry for help. Waiting for Bill to regain his cool, Foster listened as his engineer calmly stated his case: "I can't do it. There's no way. We don't have enough microphones," he griped. But Fred would not be deterred. "Buy them, borrow them, rent them, whatever you have to do, just get the equipment," he demanded. "We're doing the session on Thursday," which was just two days away.

After Porter got all forty-two musicians and singers situated and as comfortable as possible in the untested studio, "It's Over" demanded nearly as many takes before they arrived at the perfect performance.

Fred recalled Bill Porter frantically "running around like he's lost his mind completely. Sweat was pouring off of him. His shirt was soaked." Hoping to ease his anxiety, Foster tried to assure his friend; "Hey, it's going to be fine. You're a great engineer; there's nothing to worry about." "You just don't know what you're talking about," Porter snapped back.

"Poor Bill went completely white haired after that, and I've always blamed myself," Foster confessed to journalist Rachel DiGregorio. "But we did it, and sonically, it was one of the best-sounding Orbison records. It was certainly one of the best Bill Justis arrangements."

"'It's Over' was unbelievable," Harold Bradley said. "Fred had told Roy that he had to hit that note in a full voice to be heard over the band, because back then we weren't overdubbing anything. That's what makes those records so outstanding. We were all in the studio together at the same time. You don't see that anymore. There was an ambience and a room sound and a feeling that you just don't get when you stack tracks. That's the way we made all those hits. They were written arrangements, which was very different from most of the artists who were playing three-chord country songs. It was a challenge to walk in and play on Roy's stuff. Those songs were very unconventional. You'd have two or four bars just appearing in strange places, but the songs were very well constructed. He'd start off singing really low and wind up really high at the end. He didn't have the chance to go back and re-sing any of the vocals. What you hear now is exactly what he did."

One of the first gigs Bill Dees played with Roy was *The Ed Sullivan Show* on October 11, 1964. Sullivan, the deadpan impresario responsible for unleashing Beatlemania on a culturally dull America, introduced "the fella out of Odessa, Texas," as Orbison and the Candymen broke into a steady-rocking rendition of "Oh, Pretty Woman." With his hair black and shiny as a bowling ball, Roy stood before a pile of giant amps, while drummer Paul Garrison smacked his snare, smiling like he'd just won the lottery.

According to Dees, he and Roy wrote "Oh, Pretty Woman" on a Friday and recorded the song the following week. Seven days later it was rush-released by Monument. Preparing to hit the road again, Roy asked Bill if he "was still working at that warehouse?" When Dees replied, "Yeah," Orbison promised Bill that if he could get his hands on an electric piano over the weekend, he wouldn't be punching the clock the following Monday.

In short order Bill had gone from barely scraping out a living in the Texas Panhandle to cowriting and singing on both sides of the world's most popular record. Things began to move fast and furious as he found himself on tour with Roy for the better part of next year, flying to Europe twice and appearing on bills with the Beatles and the Rolling Stones.

"We were traveling all over the world," Dees recalled. "One minute you're playing poker on the plane and the next, there's a thousand teenagers waiting at the London airport to see him. It was like when the Beatles came over here. I toured with Roy across England [and the continent]. We were in a different country every day."

According to Harold Bradley "Oh, Pretty Woman" came about one summer afternoon when "Billy Dees was at Roy's house for a songwriting session when Roy's wife, Claudette, came in the room and said, 'I'm going shopping.' Roy reached in his pocket and asked her, 'Do you need any money?' and she said, 'No,' and started to walk away. That's when Billy said, 'Pretty women don't need any money!' And they started from there. They sat down and knocked out most of the new song before Claudette returned."

"Yeah, pretty women never need money," Bill laughed. "From there, the rest was easy." But according to Dees, Fred Foster wasn't satisfied with the song's original ending. Although the song virtually popped out after the original burst of inspiration, taking only "a matter of minutes," to write, Bill and Roy spent the best part the next day and a half trying to resolve the song's story line, once the seemingly unattainable object of desire suddenly turns around and comes "walking back." Unlike the untouchable goddess of Antonio Carlos Jobim's sultry bossa nova, "Girl from Ipanema" (which climbed to Number Five the same year as "Oh, Pretty Woman"), Roy's dream babe, undoubtedly under the spell of his feral mating growl, immediately pulls a U-turn in the song's final moments, when all seems hopeless.

Perhaps Bruce Springsteen best summed up the appeal of "Oh, Pretty Woman" when he dubbed it "the best girl-watching rock 'n' roll song ever."

"It was the first of August, a Saturday, in 1964," Fred said, recalling the historic session. "It was lightning perfect, a killer performance . . . unbelievable. It made you come right out of your chair. We had three electrics and three acoustics on that song. That was Roy on the twelve-string guitar. He could certainly play well enough," Foster said. "That was Boots Randolph on sax. There were actually two saxophones in there but you can barely hear them, as they're buried in the mix."

"Back in those days, people would call up me, Boots, and Ray Stevens, not even knowing what they wanted us to play. They'd say come down to the session and find something," Charlie McCoy reminisced. "They started playing that guitar riff and Boots said, 'This is in a weird key for the sax [A] but I think I can play it.' I went over to Fred and said, 'Do you hear the harmonica on this?' He said, 'No, not really. . . .' Boots was playing tenor and he said, 'Hey, my baritone's over there. Why don't you grab it and play a couple notes?' All I did was go, 'Bah-bahh!'" Charlie laughed.

McCoy's diversity as a multi-instrumentalist is truly unique. Beyond picking a variety of strings (that's his guitar accompanying Bob Dylan on "Desolation Row," doing "a bad Grady Martin imitation," he joked, as well as his bass laying down the bottom on Dylan's *John Wesley Harding* and *Nashville Skyline* albums), Charlie can cover embouchures on both reed and brass, playing trumpet, tuba, and saxophone, which is a rare skill. McCoy's drunken trumpet blares away on Dylan's "Rainy Day Women #12 & 35." "Hey, I don't play 'em very well," Charlie later confessed, referring to the slop he played on the song better known as "Everybody Must Get Stoned." "They said they wanted it to sound like a Salvation Army band. I said, 'If you mean you don't want it too good, then I'm your man!'

"When you do sessions today you never see another musician, and that's sad," McCoy pointed out. "Everything [on Roy's Monument sessions] was done live. It was so much more satisfying when everyone was there together. It was like you were playing on a 'record' then. You knew you were on to something big. I had that feeling with 'Oh, Pretty Woman.' It was magic."

Over the years, there's been plenty of conjecture and dispute over who concocted the famous guitar hook that catapulted "Oh, Pretty Woman" to Number One. Orbison's son Roy Kelton believed it was solely his father's invention and vehemently denied Jerry Kennedy's role in forging the infectious riff, calling the Nashville session guitarist's claim to authorship "a flat-out lie."

"Billy Sanford, who was in Roy's road band at the time, said that he came up with it, with Roy," Bob Moore explained. "Billy's a great player, a joy to have on the session," the bassist/bandleader added.

Sanford recalled cutting the song with Roy's road band, in hopes of capturing the energy and edgier sound that people heard at Orbison's shows, instead of the homogenized string sections and vocal arrangements they'd come to expect on his records. To confuse matters further, Sanford didn't recall Bob Moore being in the studio that day, while Bill Dees remembers Bob standing in front of Roy at the microphone, counting him in. While Jerry Kennedy claimed to have been at the session, Bob Moore's workbook/diary reveals that he and Jerry had flown to Dallas that day. "Oh, Pretty Woman" was also unique as it was one of the few Orbison tracks (up through his tenure at MGM) that Moore—or Harold Bradley—didn't play on. Filling in for Bob that day was Henry Strzelecki.

No matter how it all went down, "'Oh, Pretty Woman' sold 1.3 million copies," Fred Foster pointed out. "The whole country got the fever with that one. It's one of the most played records of all time. Ray Charles, Aretha Franklin, Frank Sinatra, and Elvis have all recorded versions of it."

Topping the *Billboard* charts on September 26, 1964, "Oh, Pretty Woman" finally bumped the Animals' "House of the Rising Sun" out of the top slot after the song had enjoyed a long, leisurely three weeks "of sin and misery." At a time when pop music had become the exclusive domain of British Invasion bands, Roy was the only American to break into the UK charts. But "Oh, Pretty Woman" would prove to be his last hit in a streak of nine Top Ten singles.

Wesley Rose, whose instincts as a producer were not always spot-on, felt that Roy should maintain his status as a ballad singer and steer clear of recording rock 'n' roll. "Oh, Pretty Woman," as far as Rose was concerned, should have been cut without drums, a bit of advice to which Fred Foster thankfully turned a deaf ear.

There was another small detail that helped cement the song in America's (and the world's) consciousness, which quickly became almost as iconic as Roy's Ray-Bans—his declaration of "Mercy!"

"He turned to me with the guitar lick and said, 'I feel like I need to say something while they're playing,'" Bill Dees recalled. "I said, 'Every time you see a pretty girl you say, "Mercy!"'"

But with such enormous success often comes a few sour grapes. Bill Dees, a fine singer in his own right, whose voice reveals a bit more country pine and blues bark than Roy's, provided a high Everly Brothers style harmony to a number of Roy's songs, yet his vocal contribution to "Oh, Pretty Woman" as he pointed out, went uncredited, a bone of contention that still haunts him to this day.

"That was my harmony. I sang it on the same mic with Roy Orbison," Dees told me, sounding more bewildered than bitter. "I had joined the musicians' union, but the union rep didn't show up that night and I didn't know what the deal was."

Later on, after a friend asked him later how much he was paid for the session, Bill returned to Monument Records to ask the same question. "They kept me standing around waiting for a while. I don't think Fred cared for me all that much. Maybe I was too happy, I think," Dees laughed. "He didn't bother to come out of the office. The secretary returned with a check for eighty dollars and said, 'Don't tell anybody.' I suppose they would've been slightly embarrassed and the union would've been pissed off if he turned in the papers without my name. I would've thought they would have had contracts for something like that. I sang harmony on both sides of that record [including mariachi-flavored B-side 'Yo Te Amo Maria,' in which Orbison and Dees switch vocal parts, with Bill taking the lead on the chorus] and there is no published credit that I did that. I wrote with Roy for four and a half years and was a gofer for him at times, got him his razor or whatever. . . . Roy Orbison recorded sixty-eight songs that we wrote together. I had the Number One song in twenty-two countries at the same time and nobody even knows my name."

"How did Roy react to the success?" Fred Foster asked rhetorically. "You know, he suffered terrible tragedies in his life. When I asked him how he was bearing up, he said, 'I learned along the way to go down the middle. I don't want be on top of the mountain or down in the valley.'"

With Orbison's meteoric rise, Wesley Rose began demanding more and more control over his career. Now at the top of his game, Roy would cut just two more singles for Monument, "Goodnight" and "(Say) You're My Girl," but with Wes Rose now usurping Fred in the role of producer.

"'Oh, Pretty Woman' was at Number One at the time. We had every pressing plant in America printing them," Foster groused. "Then he did his next record with Wes. It shipped at 200,000 copies and we got 100,000 back. The next one after that shipped at 100,000 copies and we got 50,000 back. That was writing on the wall that even Ray Charles could've seen!"

Foster made no bones about his feelings for Wesley Rose. Rose may have initially rescued Roy from RCA and the cloying production of a clueless Chet Atkins and delivered the floundering singer to Foster's door, but in Fred's estimation Rose was second only to Colonel Tom Parker, who, he claimed "killed Elvis, just as sure as putting a gun to his head.

"Wes was always jealous of everybody else's relationships. He always had to be Number One. He had no talent. None! He hired Bill Justis to do the arrangements for him. After the sessions I asked Bill, 'How'd it go?' and he told me it was 'a bunch of shit.'"

The overall feeling of animosity amongst the Nashville musicians and producers toward Rose is understandable. They perceived him as a bean counter who tried to impose his self-important attitudes and bland aesthetics on something he knew little about—music.

"Wes was important to Roy when he got to Nashville with 'Only the Lonely' because he told him, 'Why don't you do it yourself?'" Terry Widlake pointed out. "But Wes had the business handed to him. He and [Orbison's booking agent] Harvey Forester were the problem. Roy used to tell me he wanted me to be his manager. I said, 'But Roy, you already *have* a manager!' I was powerless to help him," Widlake sighed. "I couldn't breathe a word or Wes would dress me down. By the early '70s [Roy] was playing shopping malls in Joliet, Illinois. But I did handle him in Canada."

"Hands down he was the worst-managed act in America!" Buddy Buie grumbled. "Wesley Rose loved Roy like a son and got him a good record deal, but they booked him as a country singer. They didn't know how to handle him. They didn't understand that he was a superstar."

"Roy's management had no clue what to do with him," Rodney Justo agreed, recalling a three-day tour of Texas Roy did with Webb Pierce, Stonewall Jackson, and Jeannie C. Riley in 1965 that nearly turned into a full-scale brawl. "When we walked in with our long hair they all started with that 'are you a boy or a girl?' shit. Everybody wanted to fight us!"

Bobby Goldsboro related a similar tale when Roy found himself before a throng of rednecks: "The only time I remember him being a little nervous about performing was at a concert in front of a crowd of rowdy, loud cowboys. They were hollering for Roy and he said, 'They're gonna kill me!' I said, 'Aw, Roy, they're gonna *love* you.' Inside I thought, 'They're gonna kill him!' But he went out and sang great . . . and they loved him."

Although Rose was certain Monument Records couldn't possibly fulfill the demands of Roy's new contract, he ceremoniously offered Fred Foster the first shot.

"Wes came to see me and said he submitted an offer to MGM in writing. He wanted one million dollars for Roy, which was no problem. I was figuring on giving that to him anyway. Then he said they wanted to book Roy on twenty prime-time television shows. I said, 'Well, a seven-year-old could handle that!' Who in their right mind was gonna turn down Roy Orbison at that time? The problem came with shooting a motion picture. They wanted to put Roy in the movies and I didn't have a studio. So I had to let him go. Wes Rose told me, 'I don't want you stockpiling any tracks. You can only do four more.'"

Once Rose began dictating the what, how, and when of Roy's career, it quickly became clear to Fred that his friend's days at Monument were numbered. It was no coincidence that Orbison's best records were made with Fred Foster at the board. "Fred let him do what he wanted," Cowboy Jack Clement explained. "I couldn't get into it. It wasn't where we were headed at the time with Sun. We didn't have a studio that could handle that sort of production."

Although disappointed with the records Roy would make at MGM, Bob Moore stood firmly beside his friend Wesley Rose in the end. Moore and Foster clearly had their issues. While Foster's production is most often credited for Orbison's hits at Monument, Bob had been Roy's bandleader on all of his sessions since he began recording at RCA.

"Fred couldn't pat his foot in time," Moore groused. "I knew who did what and called all the musicians in. If I had known then what I know now, I probably wouldn't have brought Roy to Monument in the first place. Wesley and Fred had gotten into it and the shit was hittin' the fan. Then Fred paid me off with my own money. I didn't want any lawsuits or a bad reputation around Nashville. So I got my money and got out."

Broadcast across England over the BBC on August 5, 1964, *The Roy Orbison Show* opened with Roy clad in a mod collarless jacket and skinny tie, standing awkwardly on a sterile set amongst glowing white triangles. In some shots you can actually see the nails used to build the shabbily constructed shapes. Roy tapped his foot gently in time to "Oh, Pretty Woman" as some good-looking bird in a miniskirt slinked toward him in pumps, with her hair piled high and her pear-shaped bottom swaying to the grinding rhythm. Orbison seemed quite happy to play the game, grinning through it all, enjoying himself. For a moment they "danced" together. Actually, there was very little dancing going on, particularly on Roy's part. Mostly they let their wrists do a bit of twisting. She smiles at him, beaming right on cue with the song's lyric as an extra dollop of brass kicks in and a handful of "birds" come hully-gullying up to the stage. Beyond his remarkable voice, Roy's stage presence, even with his perfectly coiffed, shiny black pompadour and trendy togs, which now included mandatory Beatle boots, was ephemeral at best.

The bird gazed at Orbison like he was Cary Grant. But this was the '60s, an era when the right aftershave, if we were to believe TV commercials, had an such an intoxicating effect on females, they were willing to throw themselves at whatever man was savvy enough to splash a dash of Aqua Velva on his neck, no matter what he looked like or what he did for a living.

As Orbison strapped on his custom Gretsch/Gibson/Sho-Bud hybrid, the drums gently pounded the familiar palpitating heartbeat to "Crying." The British arrangement featured a marmalade of flutes and accordion, with a luscious choir of oohs and ahhs. The television studio lights bounced off Roy's Ray-Bans, giving him a strange alien aura as the orchestra reached a dramatic crescendo and the backdrop suddenly shifted perfectly on cue. Of course he hit the high note effortlessly.

It was staggering. In his own gentle way, Roy Orbison had just conquered Britain, much the same way the Beatles had America only six months ago. Roy appeared bemused, as if he wasn't quite sure it was actually happening or if it was just another dream. He gently bid the television audience "good evening," polite as a maître d' running down the list of the evening's specials. There is no trace of the danger that rock 'n' roll once posed to churches, schools, or society at large.

On camera Roy moved and spoke gently, thoughtfully, gnawing self-consciously at his bottom lip as he introduced "Pretty Paper," Willie Nelson's sentimental saga of a homeless and forgotten soul. This is a rare, striking moment in which we find Orbison "unplugged," softly strumming an acoustic archtop guitar, singing of a poor social outcast, forgotten amongst holiday shoppers, the sort of morality play we'd come to expect from Johnny Cash.

Willie admired Roy since the first time he saw him back in the day at the Dallas Sportatorium. Two years after opening a show for Orbison at Atlanta's Fox Theatre, Fred Foster signed Willie to a three-year contract at Monument. In October '64, Nelson played Fred a new holiday song he'd just written, inspired by the sight of a legless street beggar selling pencils and paper outside of a Fort Worth department store. Foster was floored and immediately called Roy, who was in London at the time. Bill Justis was summoned to whip up a lush arrangement and the demo was immediately sent overseas. A few days later, while in thrall of a fever, Roy walked into London's Pye Studios (home of the

Who, the Kinks, the Animals, and Petula Clark, to name a few) and delivered the song in one take, along with the B-side "Almost." Rush-released that November, "Pretty Paper" still had enough time to jerk plenty of tears for the Christmas season.

Nelson would eventually jump from Monument to RCA as well, but unlike Roy, the Red Headed Stranger found a home there for much of his career. His first release was his own version of "Pretty Paper." Although Willie's vocal was nowhere near as dramatic as Roy's, his gritty delivery gave the song's lyric an immediate, earthy impact.

Orbison, as his British television audience could see, may have been odd, a bit of misfit, but he was hardly a rebel. There was no trace of swagger in his performance, beyond the lascivious growl that punctuated "Mean Woman Blues" and his new hit, "Oh, Pretty Woman." Yet one had to wonder what was going on behind those Ray-Bans. Half of Britain must have assumed he was blind. Why else, in polite society, would a chap don his sunglasses indoors? Roy Orbison was truly an enigma, "a house without windows," as he would later sing.

Roy's "Mean Woman Blues" was anything but mean. With its gospel vamp and tongue-in-cheek lyrics, Claude Demetrius' twelve-bar blues, essentially a knock-off of Ray Charles' "I Got a Woman," was just good clean fun for the whole family. But what would Mum and Dad say if they knew that Roy, like his old Sun labelmate Jerry Lee Lewis, had also married a fourteen-year-old girl? At the very least Orbison, unlike Jerry Lee, had the sense not to flaunt his teen queen in public.

While the bodacious cradle-robbing Lewis took his licks for marrying Myra Gale, Chuck Berry was arrested in 1959 under the Mann Act for transporting an underage girl across state lines to have sex. Although Berry wound up doing eighteen months in prison, the courting and marrying of teenage girls was still an accepted tradition throughout most of the American South, as long as nobody raised Cain over it. After all, even a drugged-up Elvis Presley, who was later deputized by Richard Nixon, had managed to float above the law by the grace of his infectious Southern charm, while Roy Orbison's reputation as a gentle-man remained as spotless as Pat Boone's white bucks.

SEVEN

ROLLING WITH THE STONES AND OTHER PUNCHES

Following his 1964 tour of Australia with the Beach Boys, Roy returned Down Under once more in late January 1965, with five young long-haired louts known as the Rolling Stones. Unlike the moody, broody crew of SoCal surfers and the perky Mersey beat bands Roy had previously toured with, the Stones were an altogether different beast. Led in their early days by multi-instrumentalist Brian Jones, they were devotees of the devil's music who took their name from a Muddy Waters song. Their first hit was an ominous cover of Howlin' Wolf's "Little Red Rooster." And now the lightning crack of Charlie Watts' snare propelled the onslaught of Jones' and Keith Richards' snarling guitars to the top of the charts with a nasty three-chord rocker called "The Last Time." The Stones, as Roy described them, were "a wild bunch." Gone were the cheerful demeanor, careful grooming, and nice, neat matching stage outfits of the Beatles and Gerry and the Pacemakers. Coming out of the nitty-gritty London blues scene, the Stones were the antithesis of wholesome bands like the Searchers. They wanted to break Freddie and his Dreamers' legs, punch the living daylights out of Herman and his Hermits (especially after the latter's insipid little sing-along "I'm Henery VIII, I Am" ended the Stones' one-month reign over the charts with "(I Can't Get No) Satisfaction" in the summer of

'65). Their singer, a grimacing misanthrope named Mick Jagger, didn't even wear a tie! Even that gnarly Newcastle band the Animals could fashion a Windsor knot!

Jagger prowled the stage in a T-shirt, taunting the crowd with a series of effeminate dance moves he'd copped from Tina Turner, while Jones, a flaxen-haired dandy, dressed like a pimp on the back nine of a golf course in his red velvet pants and white shoes. Keith Richards (who the gravel-throated singer Tom Waits once likened to "a killer at a gas station") bore a sinister sneer as he wrenched jagged, reverb-drenched riffs from his guitar, while Watts and the zombie-eyed bass player Bill Wyman looked so sullen they might mug you after the show, if you were stupid enough to ask for their autograph.

Splitting the bill with Roy and the Stones for the fifteen-date tour were a clutch of opening bands that included a vocal trio called the Newbeats, whose Sta-Prest suits and searing falsettos still didn't manage to add up to three-fourths of the Four Seasons. Orbison and company played five shows in two days for crowds of 5,200 at the Agricultural Hall in Sydney. According to Bill Wyman, the shows were "terrific," with "girls swarming toward the stage." The next day the Aussie press slagged the Stones for their lurid music and unkempt appearance while Roy was praised for his "family-type image." As journalist Norman Jopling wrote a couple years earlier in the *Record Mirror*: "Roy himself is one of the few performers who sells discs purely on the sound and not on the person. For Roy is the complete antithesis of the pop singer, being a bespectacled un-hip-looking gent in his thirties."

Next stop on the Big Beat '65 tour were two shows in Christchurch, New Zealand, "a dump," as Wyman described it in his diary. At one point during the four-hour flight, their charter plane hit a nasty patch of turbulence and began to reel and rock. To make things worse, Mick Jagger allegedly leapt from his seat, grabbed the stewardess' microphone, and began invoking the ghosts of Buddy Holly, the Big Bopper, Ritchie Valens, and Patsy Cline, all of whom had previously perished in plane crashes. Then the thick-lipped imp brazenly dared God to "knock us out of the sky."

Orbison found little humor in Jagger's twisted jokes. After safely touching down, he calmly warned Jagger to keep his distance. "You'll never ride in an airplane with me again," he told Mick. "Don't speak to me."

"It was only because we were with Roy Orbison that we were there at all," Keith Richards recalled years later in his memoir, *Life*. He considered Roy, who initially had top billing on the tour, "a beacon in the southernmost gloom."

Richards was mystified by Roy's "incredible talent for blowing himself up" from the introverted, lobster-red, sunburned bloke he saw playing cards backstage to the commanding figure who took the stage following their raucous warm-up. Orbison seemed to inexplicably transform before his eyes "from five-foot-six to six-foot-nine." Keith not only found inspiration in Roy's larger-than-life stage persona, he dug the solid backbeat and infectious guitar hook to "Oh, Pretty Woman," which can be heard reverberating through the Stones' "(I Can't Get No) Satisfaction," which shot up the charts shortly after their tour together ended.

Keeping up a grinding pace, Roy was back in the UK again by the middle of February for a thirty-date tour with opening acts the Rockin' Berries, a lightweight pop group given to breezy harmonies and cute comedy routines, which featured Christine Perfect (later Christine McVie, of Fleetwood Mac) along with Cliff Bennett and the Rebel Rousers, a British R&B band whose most memorable member was not their lead singer but the Rolling Stones' future pianist Nicky Hopkins. Also on the bill was Marianne Faithfull, Mick's chick, who'd hit it big with Jagger/Richards' first songwriting effort, the "drippy" ballad (as she described it) "As Tears Go By."

Marianne, who told *Melody Maker* she'd "always wanted to see what he really looked like," sweet-talked Roy into removing his shades and posing, unveiled for the camera, as she coyly peered over the top of the famous impenetrable lenses. It's a curious image. Other than his perfect black pompadour, Roy appears so completely normal, perhaps a bit bashful standing beside Swinging London's perfect bird.

Marianne described Roy as a "large and strange and mournful, looking like a prodigal mole in Tony Lama boots." She found him oddly detached, "curiously removed," as she put it, as if he'd sent "a cardboard cutout [of himself] on the road" to play the tour while "the real Roy" relaxed at home, reading and building model airplanes.

But when she discovered him knocking on her hotel door late one night after the show, she wasn't sure what the mystery man had in mind. Marianne admitted she was suddenly taken aback when Roy "actually took off his glasses. I don't even know what that meant," she told *Mojo* magazine years later. "It's possible that he was making a pass. He must have liked me. He used to twinkle at me, but if he was making a pass, it went right by me. With me he was an absolute perfect gentleman, and it didn't slip for one minute."

Following that tour of England, Roy would play France, Holland, Belgium, and Sweden before finally flying back home on March 30.

On May 23, Claudette gave birth to their third son, Wesley, in Jacinto City, Texas. It was a difficult time, to say the least. There was little joy between the estranged couple, and the delivery was further complicated by a breech birth. After meeting his new son, Orbison headed back to Hendersonville alone, to hole up in his "loveless mansion," as Hank Williams once sang.

The cover photo of Roy on his first MGM album, *There Is Only One Roy Orbison*, (released July 1965) portrays the Big O looking confident and movie-star cool behind his famous shades, facing the future with nothing but blue skies ahead. Although the record offered nothing new or improved since his days at Monument, Roy, in the liner notes, curiously celebrated "a new climate of freedom" at MGM.

The album featured a stripped-down, solid-rocking remake of "Claudette." But the timing of the song's release was odd to say the least. Coming seven years after the Everly Brothers' edgy skiffle version, a rehash of "Claudette" at this point seemed like an afterthought, an obvious ploy to get back on the charts again after the enormous silence in the wake of "Oh, Pretty Woman." But there might have been something more draconian going down—Orbison had recently divorced his "pretty little pet" six months earlier after learning of her brief affair with Braxton Dixon, the builder of their Hendersonville dream house. Perhaps as he did years before with "Pretty One," the Big O may have been waging an icy game of revenge. How bittersweet would it have been for Roy to top the charts with a song that glorified their storied romantic past? Undoubtedly Claudette and their friends must have heard the song in a whole new light as Roy sang once again of his uncontrollable urge "to squeeze her to death."

"Ride Away," the loping ballad of a free-loving motorcycle rebel who finds on the open road momentary escape from the overwhelming heartache and misery in his life, would one day sound eerie in retrospect. It was Roy's biggest hit for MGM, reaching Number Twenty-Five on the *Billboard* charts in the states and coming in just a few points lower in the UK.

Of the latest album's batch of songs, "Sugar and Honey" was the real surprise, a low-down boogie number with a slippery blues guitar riff and honey-coated backup vocals that stood in contrast to the most low-down, lascivious growling of Roy's career.

Written by Buddy Buie and Bill Gilmore, bassist in the Candymen, "Afraid to Sleep" brims with premonition and an undercurrent of doom that permeates much of Roy's best music. From the moment the singer switches off the light and closes his eyes, he is haunted by his lover's lingering memory.

"It never got heard and it was never was a hit, but it's my prized possession," said Buddy Buie, who would go on to become known for cowriting the Classics IV's "kinda groovy" hit song, "Spooky."

Back at his Hendersonville hacienda, Roy was suddenly confronted by the grim realities of his shattered home life. Their deserted house now felt more like a mausoleum. Off the road briefly, and with Claudette and the kids back in Texas, Orbison finally had a moment to catch his breath and take stock of his life. Perhaps he'd taken her for granted—Claudette was so young, and he'd left her on her own to raise the boys while he traveled the world. She'd felt isolated, abandoned, heating up frozen dinners for her sons in their fabulous mansion. Each night, before the pale light of the TV screen, she sat, frustrated, smoking cigarette after cigarette as her soul was slowly devoured by fear and loneliness. It wasn't long before she fell into the arms of Braxton Dixon, the man she saw and spoke to more often than her own husband.

To fend off the blues, Roy rented an apartment in town, hoping the buzz of Music City nightlife might distract him for a while, before boarding a 707 back to his home away from home, England.

Sonically, "Crawling Back," the leadoff number on Roy's second album for MGM, *The Orbison Way* (released in January 1966), strongly resembled Elvis's "I Can't Help Falling in Love with You." While both songs portray a man deeply devoted to his beloved, in Presley's case, that eternal emotion brought him strength, reaffirming his faith in life, where with Orbison, love is an unhealthy obsession that borders on the parasitic. Opening with gentle triplets plucked on a nylon-string guitar, reminiscent of Presley's 1961 hit, Roy regretfully recalls the saga of a groveling clown of a man who seems all too willing to sacrifice every-thing, including his pride, to please his beautifully aloof tormentor. Despite the hopelessness of their dysfunctional relationship, he returns home again (emphasized by pulse-quickening tom-toms) to the only woman who truly understands him. A strange and interesting twist comes in the song's bridge when we discover that in her loneliness she, too, is equally dependent on him and might love him as much as he does her. If the psychic carnage of "Crawling Back," was any sort of reflection on the inner dynamic of Roy and Claudette's unraveling relationship, perhaps it's best that no one know the details of what went on between them behind closed doors.

Riding on the throbbing pulse of Bob Moore's bass, "Breaking Up Is Breaking My Heart" is an adrenaline-spiked anthem to yet another crumbling love affair. The strings soar as Orbison desperately yearns for reconciliation. With each modulation the passion continues to rise. This Orbison-Dees cowrite was undoubtedly a blueprint for Bruce

Springsteen when writing such songs as "Born to Run" and "Thunder Road." Hitting Number Thirty-One on the *Billboard* Hot 100, "Breaking Up Is Breaking My Heart" climbed to Twenty-Two in the UK and Australia, while racing to Number Two in Canada.

Roy's second release of 1966, *The Classic Roy Orbison*, featured the rockin' "Twinkle Toes," recorded "live" at a party, complete with a bunch of friends chatting and clapping along. "Fake live" recordings had suddenly became a craze after Dylan released "Rainy Day Women #12 & 35" in April 1966, followed that October by the groovy atmosphere of Donovan's "Mellow Yellow." But in this instance Orbison had beat them both to the punch with "Twinkle Toes."

Over a gritty fuzz guitar riff and a beat built to twist to, Roy sings the praises of a go-go dancer who, although perky on the outside, is (not surprisingly) heart-broken within. "Yeah, yeah, yeah," Roy chants while the crowd whistles, hoots, and hollers. But Orbison knows the score all too well. Like "Twinkle Toes," he, too, is just playing the game until real love finally comes his way. While a great piece of '60s pop, "Twinkle Toes" barely made it past the velvet rope of the *Billboard* Top Forty.

With "Pantomime," Roy offers a glimpse of a lost, lonely weekend without Claudette and the boys. Wired on "black coffee and electric sunshine," he's all too willing to throw away his time and money in hopes of filling the gaping void he's come face-to-face with since their parting. As he sings, "I cry inside, I die inside," in the song's bridge, Orbison's voice dances on a precarious tightrope between control and a banshee wail.

Yet perhaps the most striking aspect of *The Classic Roy Orbison* was not the music but the album cover photo depicting Roy standing beside one of his prized roadsters. Resembling the son of Dracula, Orbison, clad in black, skinny and pale in the midday sun, poses besides his car like a Southern gothic aristocrat politely beckoning you to take a ride from which you're certain never to return. As author Peter Lehman observed, "This no longer looks like a living man."

While on his following tour of England, Roy put in a surprise appearance at Hawkstone Park, waving to an adoring crowd as he set out to take a celebrity lap around the track on a borrowed motorcycle. A fine mist and an oil slick were all it took, and a moment later Orbison's wheels spun out of control. Rolling the bike, he shattered his ankle. Feeling foolish and hoping to not make a big deal out of his crack-up, Roy managed to smile as he calmly straightened out his Ray-Bans and mounted the motorcycle. Although battered and in excruciating pain, he managed to cross the finish line. Keeping up appearances at all costs, Orbison winced as he signed dozens of autographs before heading off to the hospital for medical attention.

For the rest of the tour, Roy performed sitting on a stool with his foot in a cast, strumming his guitar as he sang. Upon hearing the news of her husband's accident, Claudette, whose sad, sore heart still yearned for Roy, immediately caught the next plane across the Atlantic to be by his side.

Their reconciliation came quickly. He forgave her for the affair. She'd been alone while he was always on the road, month after month, flying here and there. And yeah, although he'd never admit it, there had been more than a few girls on the side over the years. . . . But damn it, she'd been a virgin when they got married. Claudette, as far as Roy knew, never had another man except him . . . and Braxton, that son of a bitch.

Claudette and Roy remarried that August, and they got the family back together again. "It was a hush-hush affair," Orbison told a reporter from the *Daily Sketch*. Things were gonna be different this time around. He was going to spend more time at home, with his wife and the boys. But their joy was short-lived.

EIGHT

LOVE, DEATH, AND B MOVIES

Art most often imitates life, but in Roy Orbison's case it turned out the other way around. The disturbing dramas that lay at the heart of his songs eventually came home to roost like a cruel joke. One day it seemed as if all the years of heartbreak and ghosts of the dark emotions he conjured in his music suddenly became flesh and, like a terrible monster, hunted him down, wreaking havoc on him and his family.

Something unforeseen and unexpected was destined to happen on the sixth day of the sixth month of 1966, a bit of spooky numerology that evokes the lyrics to some old hoodoo blues song, or a one-in-a-million lottery ticket. Undoubtedly there were plenty of preachers stirring up the fire and brimstone and placing bets on Armageddon that day, but the doom they predicted, while not exactly world-ending, managed to fall like a storm on Claudette as she and Roy were on their way back from the National Drag Races in Bristol, Tennessee.

"Me and my brother [Don] rode out to Bristol with them on our bikes," recalled Ronnie Gant. "Our wives doubled up with us while Claudette had her own bike, a 450 Honda. Roy rode a Harley. They hadn't made any arrangements for a hotel room and when we got out there everything was booked. We all wound up staying in the worst fleabag motel you ever saw. But they didn't complain a bit or say, 'Let's get out of here.' The next day we were coming back when Claudette had a flat tire in Knoxville. It was Sunday, so they had to stay overnight to get it fixed the next day. So we went back without them."

Nearly home after the two-hundred-mile trek, the pair were pulling into Gallatin at dusk when Roy, on the spur of the moment, gunned his engine and raced ahead to show Claudette a shortcut around Old Hickory Lake back to Hendersonville. He waited for her headlight to come slicing through the twilight, for the sound of her motor to rumble through the cedar and hickory trees, but the stillness seemed to last too long and suddenly his blood ran cold. Turning his bike around, Roy shot back to the intersection, where he found Claudette laid out, unconscious on the asphalt in front of York's Grocery Store. A pickup truck had pulled out in front of her motorcycle and sideswiped her.

No one can turn back the hands of the clock, no matter how hard they pray or how much they can pay. Time keeps rushing forward like that black ribbon of pavement below our wheels, as we hurtle down life's highway toward our ultimate destiny. Fate whisked Claudette Orbison from this world that June evening, for whatever reason, whether due to cosmic plan or plain old human clumsiness.

A local woman named Aline Hampton happened upon the scene and gently draped her sweater over Claudette's pale, broken body. She recalled seeing Roy, a total stranger, hovering over his beautiful, lifeless wife, "paralyzed" with grief. The ambulance soon arrived, its siren wailing like a banshee in his skull. Numb, as if in a dream he desperately tried to wake from, Roy climbed in alongside Claudette and rode down to Sumner County Memorial Hospital. But no one at the hospital could save her. She was already gone, DOA. It wasn't long before gruesome rumors began to spread, some claiming the beautiful Claudette had been decapitated.

Charged with manslaughter and freed on $750 bail, the man behind the wheel, a contractor named Kenneth Herald, headed back to the motel room he called home and switched on the TV set, awaiting his trial in shock and grief. There was no sense in seeking revenge. There was no justice to be wrested from the situation. Roy understood it was an accident, plain and simple. He could only feel pity for the man, suffering alone within the four walls of his own private hell for many years to come.

Six weeks earlier (there's that number again), Anna Dixon had leveled a pox upon Claudette in retribution for her illicit affair with her husband, Braxton, assuring the rock star's lovely young wife that one day soon the swift boomerang of karma would come flying back to whack her for all the heartache and misery her selfishness caused. Dixon's prophecy, "The Lord will take care of you," now seems downright diabolical in retrospect. If it had been another century, Anna might have been burned at the stake for sorcery.

There is no handbook for catastrophe, no dependable manual filled with directions on how to successfully manage a disaster of this magnitude. Shock freezes the mind. Words fail when they're most needed, sounding superficial at best. And Roy, who'd been on the road for most of his three sons' short lives, now fumbled, trying to find the language in his lungs to explain the Lord's unknowable reasons behind such a devastating event. Whatever he finally managed to gently whisper to the boys he hoped might provide a branch of stability in a world that appeared to be collapsing all around them. One day their lives had been filled with fun and rekindled love, and now suddenly it all seemed strange and cruel.

Orbison would later explain to the London *Daily Sketch* that his eldest, Roy DeWayne, who was just eight at the time of Claudette's death, "seemed to understand." This comment was typical of Roy, a guy who could make 3,000 people in a theater cry, yet he had difficulty expressing himself emotionally whether with his children or to a journalist.

Claudette's father, Chester Frady, a man's man from all accounts, couldn't bring himself to tell his wife, Geraldine, the awful truth. All they knew was that there had been a terrible accident, and the family immediately packed their bags to fly from Texas to Tennessee to be by their ailing daughter's side. But when they arrived at Claudette and Roy's Hendersonville home instead of heading directly to the hospital, Gerry's confusion quickly gave way to hysteria as her son Bill confirmed her worst suspicions.

Claudette had once confessed that her greatest fear in life was to be lowered down into the brown earth while her casket was stained with raindrops and the tears of her loved ones hovering above. Perhaps worse than all the mud and misery was the fact that there was no mass performed at her funeral. Although she had recently converted to Catholicism, through which act she simultaneously managed to rebel against both the conservative Baptist community of Nashville and the growing women's liberation movement of the day, the sacred rituals of Claudette's newly adopted faith went quietly and purposefully ignored. Instead there was a private service for the bereaved at the Phillips-Robinson Funeral Home. She was just twenty-five.

Years later, Bill Frady took to the internet to give his account of the mournful day: "It had been either misting, drizzling, or raining since we had left Texas when we were going to Tennessee for Claudette's funeral. As my cousin Ronnie, myself, and the rest of the pallbearers were taking Claudette's casket out of the hearse at the gravesite, the drizzle stopped and rays of sunlight started to break through the clouds. So Claudette did get her wish."

"Claudette was a damn good lookin' woman, hard to keep your eyes off of," Buddy Buie said. "It was hard for Roy to lose her. He'd already lost her once."

Any ordinary man would have been traumatized beyond hope by the sight of his lover dying on the road. Music had always nurtured Roy's soul. He needed it like an alcoholic needs booze. He depended on it to help him transcend the painful, awkward moments in everyday life. But now he began to crave something else: *speed*. Not the little diet pills that kept him hot-wired on the road during those long, lonely tours, but the sheer velocity that scoured his mind, leaving nothing for his anxieties to cling to. Only speed could throw him headfirst into the present, where the past and future no longer mattered, where, just for a fleeting moment, he felt fearless and free.

Roy's garages were filled with fabulous time machines with such evocative names as Excalibur, Ferrari, Corvette, and Jaguar, shiny beasts that uncorked an intoxicating brew of exhilaration at a moment's notice. Amongst Orbison's ever-growing vintage car collection were a handful of Triumphs and MGs, along with the 1925 Studebaker that Claudette had given him for his last birthday. There were so many, in fact, that he once considered opening a museum in Houston.

"Sometimes he'd trade cars twice a day," Ronnie Gant chuckled. "He'd drive around in a new Grand Prix he just got that morning and then decide he didn't like the color and take it back."

The oddest of the lot was a vintage Mercedes limousine that had formerly belonged to the executed war criminal Joachim von Ribbentrop, one of Hitler's most maniacally devoted lapdogs, who allegedly memorized and quoted Der Führer's *Mein Kampf* at will. One has to shake his head in wonder over Roy's decision to possess such a highly tainted relic. His enthusiasm for the Fatherland (evident in his second marriage, to a German industrialist's daughter; the Iron Cross that dangled at his throat; and his recording "Mama" in Deutsch) puzzled many fans and caused more than a few rumors to fly over the years.

"Roy collected Nazi memorabilia. He was a huge historian and knew everything there was to know about World War I and II. He could have taught college courses on the subject," Terry Widlake explained. "The prize of his collection was a piece of the wooden propeller blade from the Red Baron's triplane that had been shot down. Barbara bought it for him at an auction. When they brought Hitler's Mercedes to the RiverGate Mall in Nashville, Roy wanted to go see it. He figured it was a counterfeit. But he didn't enjoy going out in public. It turned out to be the genuine article, and he was very disappointed afterward."

It was in the XKE ragtop that Roy roared south, steering that sleek torpedo down Mexico way with his old boyhood buddy Bobby Blackburn riding shotgun beside him, looking for action. With their makeup-caked faces and laughing, lipstick-smeared mouths, the hot local "cucarachas" eased Roy's pain in the delirium of the tropical night, helping him to forget, at least momentarily, the strange dream he'd been living north of the border.

Rodney Justo recalled going to see Roy shortly after Claudette's death and was shocked by the harrowing vision his friend laid before him. "He told me, 'Well, y'know, I can't help but thinking about her in that box, down in the ground, with the worms eating her body and maggots eating her eyeballs. . . .' It was terrible. I wondered how was he ever going to get over it. Then, to make things worse, they started to criticize 'Too Soon to Know' over in England."

Recorded just a few weeks before Claudette's death, Don Gibson's haunting hymn "Too Soon to Know" was (understandably) misunderstood by many of Roy's fans as a maudlin tribute to his late "Pretty Woman." Like most of Gibson's chart-topping repertoire (which included "I Can't Stop Loving You" and "Oh Lonesome Me"), "Too Soon to Know" was a litany of doubt and regret sung by a proud man faced with the daunting task of pulling himself from the emotional wreckage of devastating heartbreak, while desperately hoping all the while not to "let it show." While "Too Soon" barely made it to Number Sixty-Eight on the charts in America, the news of Claudette's fatal accident spiked the song's airplay in the UK, sending it to Number Three.

Released in December 1966, *Roy Orbison Sings Don Gibson* was painfully out of step with the heady psychedelic trends percolating in London and San Francisco at the time. The album cover illustration by Jim Pearsall depicts Roy resembling a square-jawed star from some TV cop show, with Don, reflected in the hard glare of his aviator shades, looking like an extra on *Perry Mason*.

Beyond being a smart business deal for Wesley Rose (both Roy and Don were signed to MGM and Acuff-Rose Publishing), the project seemed like a natural pairing. Roy greatly admired Gibson, who was ten years his senior, and had been a fan and interpreter of Gibson's songs since first recording "I Can't Stop Loving You" and "(I'd Be) A Legend In My Time" on *Lonely and Blue*. Ironically, his version of "Legend in My Time" went virtually ignored until eight years later, when Ronnie Milsap topped the country charts with the song.

While Gibson's melancholic lyrics perfectly fit Roy's persona, musically, his songs, with their down-home rootsy feel, were limiting in their traditional structure. Ultimately, the album offered very few, if any, unexpected twists or turns or the occasional odd measures that made Roy's earlier recordings so unique. Strip away a couple layers of the production—the string section and backup vocals—and the album foreshadowed the funky, plunky country aesthetic of Bob Dylan's *Nashville Skyline*. And unlike his coproducer, Wes Rose, Jim Vienneau (who'd previously recorded Conway Twitty and Connie Francis) wasn't afraid of a little rock 'n' roll, as the punchy keyboard fills in "Big Hearted Me" and the big beat of "Lonesome Number One" attest.

"Vinny was the most unassuming guy," Ronnie Gant recalled. "He was not a real hands-on kind of producer. He stayed out of the way for the most part and let the musicians do their thing, where Wesley would make a few suggestions. . . ."

"Wes was not the most musical guy who ever lived," engineer David McKinley said about his former boss. "His father possessed the talent. He would sit there and slate the takes and keep them in sequence. That seemed to be the most important factor at a Wes Rose recording session."

Despite Roy's solid vocals and Bill McElhiney's sometimes groovy, sometimes gooey arrangements, Wesley Rose and Vienneau's production comes off somewhat cold and distant at times. Although featuring Bob Moore, Charlie McCoy, and a number of the A-team pros, Orbison's MGM records all too often lacked the rarified atmosphere that made his Monument recordings so timeless.

With the development of multitrack recording—the mode jumped from three to four to eight tracks—producers and engineers began cutting everything as clean as possible, isolating vocals and instruments and overdubbing performances separately, which inadvertently gave the music a sense of complacency. Technological advances couldn't sustain Orbison's former magic. It was clear he'd hit a creative plateau. Some tracks on *Roy Orbison Sings Don Gibson* sounded like they'd been recorded on any given Tuesday afternoon in Music City with everyone phoning in his part.

Something was clearly missing in Orbison's new music. He'd undoubtedly been through hell. And gone was the unique creative atmosphere he'd found at Monument (strained as things may have been at times between Fred Foster and Bob Moore). He certainly wasn't writing like he used to, but Roy always had a way of making a good song his own, whether it was written by him or the Bryants, Don Gibson, or Cindy Walker.

"I believe they used a three-track machine at Monument, and there was very little or no overdubbing on Roy's earlier records. They would just keep cutting until he got it right," Ronnie Gant said. "In Nashville we'd usually cut three songs in a three-hour session. Roy was the first to record just one song in that amount of time. It might've been the talk of the town, but it didn't matter, if it was a hit song.

"Nashville had the best musicians in the world," Gant said. "Over-dubbing took a lot of the feel out of the music, once everybody started going for perfection. But actually, most of his recording was all done at the same time, the rhythm section, and strings—I think he was just trying to fulfill that MGM contract."

Perhaps the most miraculous aspect of Roy's new album was that it ever got made at all, considering what he was going through at the time. With his move to MGM, Orbison's string of hits seemed to dry up overnight.

"I backed away from some of the MGM stuff," Bob Moore said. Moore, who wasn't very fond of the tone or feel of an electric bass, was asked to play it on Roy's MGM tracks in lieu of his Italian upright, which had given a deep, warm presence to many of Orbison's vintage Monument sides.

"They changed the studio and I didn't agree with that," Moore said. "Bill Porter had been the engineer on every session until then, and they replaced him. That hit me in the heart. Bill and I went to the same grammar school together."

Asked why he didn't make the move along with Roy to MGM, Bill Porter replied: "I never could figure that out. Orbison never, as far as I'm concerned—and I'm not saying anything bad about the guy, because I really like him—but he never understood the engineer's contribution. It's as simple as that."

Roy, who avoided confrontation at all cost, never broached the subject with Bill. "All he ever gave me was a steak dinner one time. That's all," Porter groused.

"[When] the combination's working, don't change it. With Orbison, the change occurred basically because of Wesley Rose. He wanted that contract with Roy. He was doing his job as a manager. I'm not faulting Wesley," Bill said, "but he didn't know that much about the music, and Roy listened to him. . . . Monument initially took the risks with Orbison. Their concept of how to record Roy was what made it work."

Calamitous as the events in his personal life were, the rumblings of a professional landslide that was to last well over the next two decades were just beginning. As part of Orbison's million-dollar contract with MGM, Wesley Rose had originally stipulated that his client be offered a multimovie deal to sweeten the pot. But it came as no surprise, particularly to those close to him, that Roy Orbison couldn't act. Apart from wielding the majesty of his voice, Roy rarely, if ever, expressed himself with the level of emotion that most actors regularly bring to their craft. Quirky and striking as Roy's image was, he was far from Hollywood handsome and lacked the kind of charisma needed to fill the big screen. In truth, he failed miserably as a movie star. *Life* magazine even went so far to describe him as "an anonymous celebrity." At best, his movie debut, *The Fastest Guitar Alive*, evoked a bad episode of *Bonanza*. Stripped of his trademark Ray-Bans, Roy appeared as wooden as Hank Williams' brokenhearted cigar store Indian, Kaw-Liga.

Following the formula of the worst Elvis Presley films (in fact, the King's handlers flatly turned down *The Fastest Guitar Alive* before it was pawned off on Roy), the flimsy plot featured Orbison cast as "Johnny," along with his sidekick "Steve," played by Sammy (not Samuel) Jackson, as a pair of young rebels disguised as medicine show hucksters, who rambled around from town to town, toting a wagon behind them filled with vivacious dancing girls (one of whom was Joan Freeman, Presley's former flame in *Roustabout*). Not only were Johnny and Steve uncertain what their future would bring, they seemed unsure of their motivation, not knowing if they were acting in a Western or a comedy. Either way, the pair managed to divest every fool Yankee they met of his gold in their mission to help restore their beloved, bedraggled Confederacy. Predictably, the more often dull than droll dialogue was designed to lead up to the moment when Roy finally broke into song.

Inspired by the sleek gadgetry popularized by James Bond films and the TV series *The Wild, Wild West*, Roy was issued a custom six-string that transformed into a deadly weapon. With just a quick flip of a switch, a rifle barrel suddenly protruded from his guitar, and the instrument he'd strummed just moments before to serenade a series of comely barroom maids instantly transformed into a deadly weapon that could blast a hole through a man the size of a pie tin. Sadly, Roy's best line of the film, "I could kill you with this *and* play your funeral march at the same time," fell flat.

Some of the movies' songs didn't fare much better. While "Medicine Man" found Orbison sitting onstage cross-legged "Injun" style, pounding on a tom-tom, laying down a steady rhythm for a clutch of blonde go-go-dancing squaws, "Pistolero," the film's best number, featured Roy dressed in a tacky Zorro getup with his hat cocked to one side, strumming his instrument/weapon as a pair of mariachis blared away on their trumpets.

Universally panned by the critics, *The Fastest Guitar Alive* has gained a better appreciation in recent years from a new generation of hipsters both for Roy's painfully awkward performance and for the movie's ridiculously kitsch production values. One Hollywood reporter's smarmy review praised the film, claiming that, at the very least, it had "brevity" on its side; the critic also acknowledged that Roy possessed "a degree of natural charm."

The film also featured Domingo Samudio, a.k.a. Sam the Sham, who possessed a cool, campy style all his own. Samudio was at the top of his game at the time, having busted into the Top Ten with his rowdy frat-boy rocker "Wooly Bully" in the summer of '65. The following year he hit the top of the charts howling at the beauty of a foxy "Li'l Red Riding Hood." Done up in his cape and turban, behind the wheel of a customized Packard hearse, Sam the Sham could often be found cruising the streets of Memphis with members of his band the Pharaohs in tow. But even a guest appearance by this groovy goateed King of Garage Rock couldn't loan this cinematic turkey an ounce of cred.

The *New York Times'* Renata Adler was surprisingly merciful in her review, deeming the film "an old-fashioned, good-natured bad movie to be seen at exam time or at a drive-in." Adler described Roy as having "a nice, unlikely face, something between Presley and Liberace . . . friendly, goofy and square." Unimpressed with Orbison's acting abilities, she wasn't exactly taken with his music either (making one wonder how familiar she was with Roy beyond "It's Over," which she briefly mentioned), calling him "a cooled-down Presley."

"Oh, it was terrible," Rodney Justo laughed, recalling the night Roy and the band went to the British premiere of *The Fastest Guitar Alive* in London. "They were riding on the stagecoach when the Indians began to circle around them and Sammy Jackson says, 'Here come the Indians,' and Roy's first line in the movie was 'And they're not sellin' blankets, either.' Maybe it would've attained cult status if it had been any worse! All the guys in the band were like, 'Hey, yeah . . . well, that's great, Roy!' But the minute we were away from him it was like, 'Oh, no!'"

"Once a year he would rent a small theater for a private showing of *The Fastest Guitar Alive*," Terry Widlake chuckled. "He knew how bad it was and would give everybody a scene-by-scene commentary. Roy had broken his leg on the set. In one scene he's seen backstage strumming his guitar with his toe. As he went to stand up a screen fell down on him and broke his leg! They had to stop the filming because he was in a cast, which he couldn't stand," Terry recalled. "He couldn't wait any longer for it to come off, so he told me to cut it open for him with a utility knife he used to build model airplanes with."

"Y'know, I don't even remember Roy being there," Harold Bradley said, recalling the soundtrack session for *The Fastest Guitar Alive*. "They flew some producer in from the West Coast who was tryin' to figure out what he wanted . . . a little flamenco guitar here and there."

Considering the catastrophe that had recently befallen the beautiful Claudette, it was a miracle that Roy was "there" at all. Perhaps spending his days memorizing lines and acting in a corny B-movie Western/comedy/whatever-it-was, was the best therapy Roy Orbison could've hoped for in the face of the devastation he was determined to live through.

No stranger to trouble and trauma himself, Keith Richards also admired Roy's "stoic personality," and marveled at Orbison's miraculous ability to "sail through anything, including his whole tragic life. . . . Nothing in his private life," the Stones' gnarly guitarist wrote in his autobiography, "went right for the Big O."

Provided with a second-rate director and script, clothes from another era, and a different name, Roy transformed into a womanizing, sharp-shooting vagabond, who suddenly existed in another time and place where wagon trains, Yankees, whooping Indians, beer halls, and flirty dancing girls with golden tresses were his biggest concern. If only for a few hours each day, Roy managed to escape the soul-crushing realities that lurked like a pair of thugs waiting to pummel him with each setting sun.

Since high school Orbison continually sought refuge from the "real world" at his local movie theater. Even before Claudette's death he was known to escape whenever possible to watch two or three films in a row. It wasn't unusual for Roy to sequester himself in a study or bedroom to watch a movie or quietly pore over some historical tome in lieu of socializing with the steady flow of houseguests.

"It's not like he was secretive, but he preferred to keep to himself," Bill Dees confided. "Roy hardly ever talked about himself. He liked to build model airplanes."

The soundtrack album to *The Fastest Guitar Alive* was the first record of Roy's to feature Bill Dees' name on its cover. This was a big deal for Bill, a breakthrough of sorts. Perhaps, at last, he'd finally get a shot at cutting his own record. But when he raised the issue, "Wesley looked me right in the eye and said, 'I don't want you to record.' Maybe he thought it might cause some kind of competition between Roy and me, I don't know," Bill said. Rose had already been through this dance before with both Rodney Justo and Joe Melson's records going nowhere, and saw no point in developing Orbison's sidemen's careers. But few of Roy's collaborators (beyond Bobby Goldsboro and Rodney Justo, who went on to become the original front man of the Atlanta Rhythm Section) managed to escape his orbit.

Roy, who initially considered the money that MGM offered him "so big it was scary," finally woke up and realized he'd signed a devil's bargain, a contract that called for an unheard-of three albums a year. Nobody could maintain that kind of output while keeping up a hectic tour schedule, not even the Beatles, who retired from the road in August 1966, after playing their final concert at San Francisco's Candlestick Park. The moptops had had enough of not being able to hear themselves over the locust horde of screaming fans. They proceeded to hole up in the studio, spending more time and money [much to their record company's chagrin] on one song than they'd previously spent on an entire album. Not that that would necessarily have been a winning recipe for Roy.

While the recording for Roy's next album, *Cry Softly, Lonely One*, had begun in March '66, the sessions had been suddenly derailed three months later by Claudette's death, and were once again put on hold while Roy tried his hand at acting, while simultaneously having to compose a set of new songs for *The Fastest Guitar's* soundtrack.

The album's title track, written by Joe Melson and Donald Gant, was a throwback to earlier Orbison songs, complete with another round of Joe's old-school "dum dum de do de dum dum" countermelodies.

Kicking off with a Byrds-style twelve-string guitar figure reminiscent of "Mr. Tambourine Man," "Communication Breakdown" alluded none too subtly to Orbison's marital problems with Claudette. Roy's voice effortlessly sailed above the pulsing bass and light, syncopated groove, as he blamed the failure of his latest heartache on the many pitfalls of his newly acquired good life. Another of the song's catchy guitar riffs was an oddly familiar little trill that echoed the Five Americans, a one-hit wonder band from Texas who soared to Number Five on the charts earlier that March with the insidious "Western Union Man." British session guitarist wunderkind Jimmy Page, who'd recently joined the Yardbirds, Roy's opening act on his 1967 tour of Australia, apparently dug the song so much he nicked the title for a hard-rocking wail of despair by Led Zeppelin.

Another of the album's more revealing moments comes with "Crawling Back," which delved into the dark side of codependency. Again, the Byrds' influence could be heard in the bright jingle-jangle of a twelve-string guitar. Although Wesley Rose admired Roy's tenacity and determination to rebuild his life, he felt that his client was damaging his career by dwelling on what he called "sick type of things." But Rose and many others missed the point. Rather than continue recording a slew of innocuous, country-flavored pop hits, Roy during his "dark period" recorded songs that bore the mark of his heroic struggle to work his way "out of the turmoil," as he later described the soul-numbing period that followed Claudette's death.

One man's pop ditty is another man's catharsis. What eventually became known as the school of confessional songwriting—a mode of self-absorbed expression practiced to perfection by navel-gazers from Leonard Cohen to John Lennon to James Taylor and Joni Mitchell, whose every verse directly reflected the changes and events in their personal lives—had its origins in Orbison's deeply personal songs. While offering nothing like the stark honesty of John Lennon's "Life as Art" songs that chronicled his relationship with Yoko Ono, Roy—along with Johnny and June Carter Cash, whose passion-fueled "Ring of Fire" was a metaphor for their smoldering, illicit love affair—was one of the first popular singers to strip himself emotionally bare in otherwise radio-friendly songs. While some might look at this sort of expression as therapy, or worse, narcissism, they not only misunderstand the heroic nature of battling one's own demons in public, but the bardic tradition of setting such trials and conflicts of the soul down in verse so that others might glean insight and understanding from them. Granted, Roy's battles of the heart were far from Poe's face-off with the raven in a lonely Baltimore garret, but the best of Orbison's work always had the ability to get under the skin of his devoted fans and slowly, methodically unnerve them.

One of *Cry Softly*'s finer moments came with the bluesy "Girl Like Mine." Driven by the elastic snap of a nylon-string guitar, the tune's sound and feel evoked Bobby Gentry's sultry summer hit "Ode to Billy Joe." But by the time the album was released a year later, in July 1967, Roy's old pals the Beatles had changed the rules of the game once more when they single-handedly transformed the LP into modern art with the release of their psychedelic opus, *Sergeant Pepper's Lonely Hearts Club Band*.

With a flood of new bands singing the praises of dope, free love, and revolution, *Cry Softly* seemed hopelessly old hat. And Roy, whose music had managed to remain timeless and free from whatever trend came down the pike, appeared on the album's cover oblivious, an anachronism with his pompadour blowing in the breeze as he steered his Excalibur convertible down the lost highway.

On March 5, 1967, Roy was back in England once again, playing at London's Finsbury Park, on a wildly diverse bill that featured a pack of rowdy mods known as the Small Faces, along with the veteran guitarist of the Yardbirds, Jeff Beck, and popsters Paul and Barry Ryan.

"That was Beck's new group with [with the young, unknown-at-the-time] Rod Stewart and Ron Wood on bass," Rodney Justo recalled. "But they got thrown off the tour after Jeff pulled 'a moody' and threw his guitar down during their set and walked offstage. The Faces, on the other hand, loved to party. They told us it was a tradition to do something wild on the last night of the tour. So we took Roy's guitar and tuned it up a half step before we went onstage. He started singing 'Only the Lonely' when he suddenly realized what was going on. He turned to look at us and grinned and whispered off-mic, 'You sons of bitches!'

Nonetheless, Chris Welch described the show in *Melody Maker* as "a right phantasmagorical experience," applauding the Small Faces, while he found Jeff Beck's new band underrehearsed yet "quite extraordinary." Roy, in the critic's opinion, predictably delivered "a much more gentlemanly performance."

British journalist/author Michael Gray, who first witnessed Orbison five years earlier in Liverpool, in 1962, felt he "could follow anyone, top any bill of teenage passion . . . quell[ing] in seconds a package-tour audience conditioned into screaming at spotty youths burping and bashing their guitars under lurid green lights." At the same time he praised Orbison's performance, Gray claimed Roy's withdrawn presence went beyond the normal level of shy. In Gray's estimation, Orbison was "more scared than I've ever seen anyone onstage look." Yet once he began to sing, the critic found himself entranced by "the sounds and feeling of his records, but with an extra, electric charge."

"Roy could be apprehensive at times with a new audience but he never had stage fright," Terry Widlake pointed out. "Quite the contrary. He enjoyed performing. Once, in Germany he had a kidney stone and went on despite doctor's orders." And in his brief time with the Candymen, Bobby Goldsboro never sensed Orbison was nervous about singing: "Roy actually looked forward to performing," he said. "He was always confident in his ability to hit the high notes."

Widlake first met Roy Orbison at the *New Musical Express* awards ceremony in March 1968. At the time, Widlake had been playing bass and singing backup vocals as a member of a London-based band called the Overlanders, who briefly topped the UK charts with a cover of the Beatles' "Michelle."

"My first impression of Roy was that he was a very mild-mannered person, extremely laid-back. He was standing at the bar drinking a cola. My friends had begged me to get his autograph," Terry chuckled. "But I had nothing for him to write on, so he signed his name on a one-pound note.

"They weren't just any run-of-the mill fans," Widlake recalled. "They were hard-core Orbison addicts! When Roy released a record they'd buy two copies—one which they proceeded to wear out and one they'd save for later. They actually timed the birth of their child to coincide with Roy's birthday. Fortunately, they called her Julie instead of Lana or Leah. If it had been a boy they would have surely named him Roy."

Within a year of meeting Roy, Terry received a call from Nick Firth, Acuff-Rose's London office rep at the time, asking him to organize a four-piece band to back Roy on what started out as a two-week tour of England.

"Clubland [as the UK music scene was known] had become big business at the time," Widlake explained. "It wasn't too expensive. Working-class people could afford to go. We usually played the same place every night for a week, converted old movie theaters that held about 1,000 to 1,500 people. It was like a variety show with jugglers and comedians for opening acts.

"Playing with Roy was an easy gig, but I was terrified," Terry laughed. "I had never played a show in my life where my knees turned to jelly beforehand. So in walked Roy with his booking agent Jerry Maxim, and he grabbed his guitar and said, 'Okay, let's try "Only the Lonely."' We played a little bit and he stopped and said, 'Okay, how about "In Dreams"?' 'That sounds good.' And that was it! He said, 'Just play it like the record and everything will be fine.'

"Roy was very lazy. He didn't like to rehearse. He didn't even warm up his voice. He just went out onstage and began to sing. He'd always hold back on the opening number, which was 'Only the Lonely.' Not just because he hadn't warmed up yet, but there was no one to adjust the levels, which were left to me to take care of. He'd look over at me and say, 'I don't think they can hear me, Terence.' Then he'd blast the auditorium with 'Crying.'

"The first gig on the tour was at the Conservative Hall in Finchley. The Iron Lady, Margaret Thatcher lived there," Terry recalled. "I wasn't only nervous because of Roy's fame—the press coverage of the show was ridiculous. . . . Louis Armstrong, who had a big hit at the time with 'Hello Dolly,' had just played the grand opening only a few months before. It seemed like the entire focal point of England's culture had become this hall in nowhere Yorkshire!"

Terry attributed Roy's massive popularity in England to "the operatic quality of his voice. His songs and singing resonated particularly with the Irish. He was immensely popular there, particularly in the worst of times. When we played at Ulster Hall in Belfast, the city had been under curfew. The docks were burning," Widlake recollected. "I remember going outside and the sky was red.

"We had played very few dates in the US at the time [in the late '60s]," Terry continued. "It was incredible. It seemed like after 'Pretty Woman' everybody had simply abandoned him."

It didn't happen like it will when they finally get around to making the movie of his life: The luminescent ghost of Claudette did not slip through a crack in his hotel window just before dawn to softly moan the boys' names in his ear. He didn't wake up in a cold sweat a moment later and reach for the phone in a telepathic panic to call Orbie Lee back in Tennessee to discover he was having yet another bad dream. Life is sloppier than that. We never see it coming and rarely, if ever, get the chance to find the words to neatly sum up the complicated emotions and reasons for everything we do in this life before the great director in the sky suddenly gets out the hook and unceremoniously sweeps us off the stage without a curtain call.

The boys had been down in the basement playing with fire, matches, or a lighter and some model airplane glue, when things suddenly got out of control. They'd most likely been setting toy soldiers and models of cars, tanks, and planes ablaze, making their imaginary battles seem all the more real. What red-blooded American boy hasn't done something like that?

It was just after 6:30 P.M. when three-year-old Wesley, the survivor, scrambled upstairs to alert his grandfather that his brothers, R. D. and Tony, had unleashed a raging inferno. Orbie Lee immediately dashed to the kitchen and filled whatever pots and pans he could and carried the water downstairs, hoping to douse the flames, but the blaze was way ahead of him. The heat was overwhelming as the smoke quickly enveloped him and the boys in a thick, gray, suffocating blanket as they strived for the door. Between the enormous draft the fire created and Braxton Dixon's modern "airtight construction," Orbie Lee couldn't get the damn door open. He finally pried it wide enough as four of them—Orb, Wesley, Nadine, and her sister Patty—slipped through when suddenly, according to Gallatin fire chief George Thompson, there was "an explosion in the basement which shook the burning residence," causing the door to slam shut while sucking R. D. and Tony back inside to their deaths.

The Orbisons' next-door neighbor on Hickory Lake, Johnny Cash, immediately came to the rescue toting a garden hose. At first he tried to subdue the flames, but he soon wound up phoning the boys down at the Gallatin Fire Department.

Roy had been in England at the time, playing a string of sold-out shows while juggling the long line of birds flocking to his swinging Mayfair bachelor pad. Sammy Davis Jr. happened to be in London as well, and had invited Orbison to sing at a benefit for the people of war-torn Biafra. They made an odd couple. Sammy gushed with personality, while beside him stood the sullen man in black. They sang duets of "Land of a Thousand Dances" and "Oh, Pretty Woman." Popping his fingers with a blinding fluorescent smile, Junior jumped up to the microphone to join Roy on his trademark tiger growl. It was one for the history books.

During this tour Roy met the beautiful chestnut-haired Barbara Anne Wellhöner Jakobs at a disco in Leeds. The first time they spoke, she insulted him. Nearly half his age, Barbara was not only clueless when it came to Orbison's music, she thought his blue jean jacket was tacky. Apparently Bob Dylan's rustic, ramblin'-boy look hadn't caught on yet with the kids back in Bielefeld, Germany.

Roy, once the target of small-town bullies, had become used to people fawning all over him. He found Barbara's sass intriguing. Bearing more than a small resemblance to Claudette, with her dark hair and eyes, she undoubtedly pushed Roy's buttons in a big way.

"When I first met Barbara, she was only seventeen," Terry Widlake recalled. "She could hardly speak a word of English."

If she was unfamiliar with Roy's music and didn't care for the way he dressed, then what attracted her to him in the first place? His stardom? Power? Years later Barbara explained that she found Roy "very different" from any man or musician she'd ever met. "There was something in Roy that was truthful and so honest." She'd found his "integrity" intoxicating.

On September 14, 1968, the night of the fire, Roy and his band had performed in Birmingham, UK. After the show he kissed his young German girlfriend good-bye, climbed into the limo with Bobby Blackburn, and headed for Brighton. They hadn't been at the hotel very long when Blackburn's phone rang. It was Wes Rose calling from the States with bad news. Bobby immediately called the front desk to send a doctor to Roy's room. Stunned, he waited for the physician to arrive before marching down the hall to inform Roy that two of his sons were dead. Blackburn wanted to make sure that if his old friend was going to collapse or become hysterical, there would be someone ready to hit him with a needle.

Roy was in bed, reading Churchill, when Bobby knocked on the door. Between the London fog and the sedatives, the ride to Heathrow was nothing but a blur. Roy gazed out the window into the black night, methodically chain-smoking every fag in the pack. Years later he told a reporter at the *Daily Sketch* he was "totally shattered."

Numb with tranquilizers, Orbison caught the next plane back to the States, arriving at Kennedy the following day, ghostly pale, rail thin, with his pompadour perfectly in place as the paparazzi's icy lightning bounced off his Ray-Bans. Connecting to his flight to Nashville, Orbison dragged himself, shell-shocked, through the airport like a rockabilly Frankenstein, accompanied by a TWA stewardess, who, despite the gravity of the situation, most likely couldn't help but feel giddy from all the attention she received standing in a celebrity's shadow.

In the days following the fire, gossip began to spread almost as quickly as the flames, and was nearly as fierce. The back-to-back disasters that had befallen Roy and his family sent tongues wagging and tabloid scribblers working overtime from coast to coast. While the floodgates of sympathy were thrown open, compassion was fleeting, eventually giving way to suspicion and brewing accusation that pointed toward Roy and his evil rock 'n' roll lifestyle. Orbison's latest tragedy undoubtedly provided a field day for those who keep score of the sins of others—first his beautiful wife Claudette and now two of his three sons, gone. Everybody knew Roy Orbison was a nice guy—the nicest: gentle, polite, thoughtful, and soft-spoken. But why in the world would the good Lord ever visit a series of wrathful, Job-like punishments down upon a man without good reason? People began to talk, of Claudette and the man who came to her house day after day while her husband was gone. And then, not long after her death, Roy was seen running around England in the company of a teenage German girl, playing his rock 'n' roll, and leaving his boys in the care of his elderly parents. In no time, hordes of tragedy-tourists would come cruising by, to rubberneck at the big black smudge where "the house that sin built" once stood.

"Mercy!" indeed.

Adorned with white doves, the two boys' caskets were buried at their mother's feet in the Woodlawn Memorial Cemetery. As they were laid to rest, a children's choir sang, buoying the boys' souls aloft toward heaven.

For most people, the level of misery that Roy Orbison endured is simply unfathomable. England's sardonic bard Richard Thompson unwittingly summed up Orbison's state of mind years later when he sang, "You just can't shake a man, the way that I've been shook" in his song "A Poisoned Heart and a Twisted Memory."

The fact that Roy was able to function at all after digging himself out from the rubble of his own personal blitzkrieg is a testament to his indomitable spirit. In such an overwhelming time of challenge and darkness, Orbison looked to the philosophy of his hero Winston Churchill, who, faced with the devastation of his beloved London by the Nazis, proclaimed, "When you're driving through hell, keep driving."

Remarkably, Roy seemed to bear no grudge over his overwhelming loss. Hard-hearted he was not. Twenty years later, in a television interview, Orbison would thank "a loving God and Jesus Christ," as well as the "good friends and kindred souls" who stood by him through the worst of his personal trials. Despite the soul-crushing one-two punch that pulverized him, Roy somehow managed to survive. Nor was he being flippant when he claimed to have "worked my way through" the devastating changes that life threw him without making it "the earth-shattering thing it was."

Following the boys' funeral, Roy took Chester and Gerry aside to assure them that no matter what, they would always be family and never to hesitate to ask if they ever needed anything. But this promise rang hollow once they boarded the plane back to Texas, and Roy turned the page on that chapter of his life. His in-laws could only serve as a grim reminder of the past and pain that he struggled so hard to shake.

"Roy could be totally taken by the sorrow, but at the same time he was very stoic," Buddy Buie claimed. "Maybe he didn't want to bother anyone with all that baggage. Once I asked him, 'How do you go home at night alone?' He said, 'You just have to.' I told him I didn't know if I had the wherewithal."

Guitarist Harold Bradley recalled briefly visiting his grief-stricken friend one night, holed up in a dark, lonely Nashville motel room. "Boy, that was really sad. It really shook me up. I had bought a lot of guitars for Roy. He'd call me and say, 'I want such and such. . . .' He got a Jose Ramirez classical guitar in Spain back in '62 and when I said, 'I want one,' he had Wesley get one for me. His Ramirez was either damaged or destroyed in the fire and he called and said, 'Harold, my guitar was burned, could you get me another one?' I told him I had been in Chicago with Chet Atkins and bought a second one. He said, 'I'll pay you for it. Could you bring it to me tomorrow night?' So after a session, I drove over to his motel and knocked on the door. He opened it. The room was pitch-black and there were empty food cartons and papers all around. He'd been in there for days. He didn't bother to turn the light on. I just gave him the guitar and he said, 'I'll have Wes Rose send you a check.' And I left. He was so sad, and it was upsetting to see him, because he had been alone in that room and had evidently been eating, for a few days. Speaking personally, I couldn't have persevered and lived through that."

Six months later, on March 25, 1969, Roy married Barbara Anne Wellhöner Jakobs. According to the Associated Press, who spread the story coast to coast, Barbara was a nineteen-year-old medical student who found being Roy's new "Pretty Woman" infinitely more exciting than studying bones and tissue. A couple years later, she let it slip that she was only seventeen at the time.

While the newlyweds made the news, Roy's surviving son, Wesley, was shuffled off to live with his grandparents before enrolling in military academy for the next few years, during which he saw his father sporadically, between tours and on holidays.

In the meantime, Roy had two new houses built on his Hickory Lake property, one for himself and Barbara, and a smaller cottage for his folks and Wesley. The Orbisons' new Hendersonville house was custom-built in the Bavarian style, albeit with a tiki room, an indoor waterfall, and vista windows that overlooked the lake. Each room was painted a different color—there were blue and green bedrooms and an orange hallway. Downstairs, the dining room floor was set in stone tile with custom furniture built to fit the V-shaped room. The walls and ceilings of the music room were covered in a thick purple carpet and bedecked with Roy's gold and platinum records and various awards.

The black smudge that scarred the ground would one day become a glorious orchard after Johnny Cash bought the tainted land from him. Yet everywhere he turned, Roy was confronted by his past.

Just six months earlier, in December 1968, Elvis had made a dramatic comeback with his first live performance in seven years. Leather clad and looking trim, he smirked at the cameras knowingly, as if to remind all those Beatles and Stones fans out in Television Land that he'd invented rock 'n' roll. But the excitement was short-lived. With the birth of the "Woodstock Nation," old-school rockers like Roy Orbison were dismissed as hopeless dinosaurs by the prevailing American counterculture.

One exception was Bob Dylan, who had retreated to Woodstock: He was nowhere near Max Yasgur's farm in August 1969. He was holed up in Music City, recording his country opus *Nashville Skyline*. Having reinvented himself as a country crooner, Bob, who claimed his newly marbleized voice just happened naturally after quitting cigarettes (although it sure sounded like his obsession with Hank Snow had gotten the best of him), soon came knock-knock-knockin' on Orbison's door. But Roy was touring Canada at the time, so Dylan ended up cutting "Girl from the North Country" and a handful of other unreleased gems at an informal session with Roy's next-door neighbor, Johnny Cash.

To Bob Dylan, Cash was neither rock 'n' roll star nor folk hero, but "a religious figure." Whether singing Shel Silverstein's kooky "A Boy Named Sue" or the Nine Inch Nails' solemn suicide ode "Hurt," Cash could ultimately make any song his own. With his resonant baritone, craggy face, and winning grin, he gave listeners no choice but to believe him.

While his career might have been on the wane, Roy's influence on the next generation of musicians ran deep. Gram Parsons, who originally joined the Byrds as "a jazz piano player," had spirited Roger McGuinn and company down to Nashville, where they recorded their country rock opus *Sweetheart of the Rodeo* with some of the city's best session men. Before overdosing on coke in a Joshua Tree motel room, Parsons had schooled Keith Richards with his encyclopedic knowledge and genuine love of country music, which led to the Stones guitarist writing "Sweet Virginia," "Far Away Eyes," and "Wild Horses" (a song long rumored to have been cowritten with Gram). If he hadn't written the songs himself (in his short career Parsons knocked out such classics as "Hickory Wind," "Sin City," and "Return of the Grievous Angel"), Parsons certainly knew where to find them. Gram was the first longhair to cover such Merle Haggard and Louvin Brothers songs as "The Christian Life" and "Cash on the Barrelhead." Parsons would discover in Washington, DC, a willowy, reedy-voiced folksinger named Emmylou Harris, with whom he torched a smoldering duet of the Bryants' "Love Hurts," a song that, although first recorded by the Everly Brothers, would forever bear Roy Orbison's mark.

Following Parson's untimely death, Emmylou followed her own path to country rock stardom. Her ethereal voice of pure blue longing would one day soon help breathe life into Roy's anemic career.

Many Moods was, understandably, the only album that Roy released in 1969. Both its title and the cover photo of Orbison grinning tepidly, looking "relaxed" in a cardigan sweater (was MGM hoping to court Perry Como fans?), blatantly spelled "easy listening."

Within was a set of ballads that included "Unchained Melody" and "More." The plan was clear. Though Roy was emotionally MIA, "the Voice" could prove itself once more on a set of standards without Orbison having to think too much about the task at hand. But, typical of his music, something darker lurked just below the surface. His rendition of "Try to Remember," a melancholy waltz from the perennial off-Broadway musical *The Fantasticks* and a favorite of such TV variety show singers as Julie Andrews and Ed Ames, might have seemed like an innocuous choice, but his performance is devastating. Roy's voice brims with emotion as he recalls a more sweet and peaceful time in his life that is gone forever. Orbison could not have been oblivious to the song's lyrics and the effect they would have on his fans who sympathized with the cruel fate his family had recently suffered. "Try to remember when life was so tender that no one wept except the willow," may not have seemed profound coming from another singer, but as his voice trembles and quavers when he sings, "Deep in December it's nice to remember the fire of September that made us mellow," it's enough to shred your heart. Did Roy purposely record this song as some sort of cathartic experience? September was the month that the Hendersonville tragedy took place. Was he purposely rubbing salt into the deep wound of his soul in hopes of healing himself?

A year later, in 1970, John Lennon would work out his personal demons in public by infusing the songs of his Plastic Ono Band album with the primal-scream-therapy technique he'd learned from Dr. Arthur Janov. Roy, of course, chose a more subtle, more dignified path, yet one that was just as transparent and powerful to anyone who bothered to notice.

Among the album's "many moods" of sorrow comes the occasional glimmer of hope and moment of redemption, as in Mickey Newbury's "Truly, Truly, True," where Roy sings, "For some the world may end, but for us it will begin again."

While Sam Cooke, Elvis, the Righteous Brothers, and Al Green have all put their personal stamp on "Unchained Melody," Roy delivers an Olympian performance of the song that features a surprisingly dissonant ending. The melodically lush "More" (Riz Ortolani and Nino Oliviero's theme from the controversial Italian documentary *Mondo Cane*) features lilting Neapolitan mandolins and a smart string arrangement. While both Nat King Cole and Frank Sinatra (the latter on his quintessential 1964 album, *It Might as Well Be Swing*, with the Count Basie Orchestra) phrase the tune in short, jazzy bursts, Orbison's glass-smooth delivery is a perfect vehicle for his pure emotional yearning. Oddly, Roy's "More" seemed to have more in common with Doris Day's 1964 version of the song.

The album also featured three Orbison/Dees cowrites, of which "Walk On" was the standout. A video of Roy singing in the studio was shot to accompany the song, which had been recorded in April '68 and previously released as a single. A strange soft-focus blurs his face, making his skin silvery and translucent as Vaseline. Orbison's eyes squint, barely visible behind hazy orange-tinted glasses. His hair, black and shiny, remains perfectly in place as every molecule in his body quickens toward the boiling point.

A doe-eyed babe in a white blouse suddenly appears in the studio while he sings, "We don't want the world to see us like we are." We never find out why or how their love failed or what they have to be so ashamed of. An illicit affair? Not the usual topic of an Orbison tune, but there seems to be an abundance of regret and guilt tearing them apart.

"Walk on to higher ground," Orbison pleads as the drums begin to pound like heavy artillery. His hand rolls into a fist and his eyes shut tight as his pale face vibrates with every note. "Don't forget me, if you ever loved me—walk on. . . ."

She finally gets the message and, with a toss of her silky shampooed tresses, turns and makes her exit. What a way to get dumped—from the opposite side of the glass in a sterile recording studio, while the engineer, who is also dressed in black and oddly resembles Roy, sits, staring straight ahead, ignoring the drama while he twiddles the knobs.

Another cowrite of Roy and Bill's, "Heartache," tells the tale of Roy's disembodied darling, who materializes each night, with her hair down ("I love it that way" Orbison moans), while he lies in bed "tossing, turning, trembling, burning." A deceptively cheerful pop ditty complete with Joe Melson "de-rum rum rum" backup vocals, "Ring of Fire"–style trumpets, a blizzard of strings, and a clangy reverb-soaked guitar, Roy delivers a lyric as eerie as anything found in the canon of American folk and country music from the Southern gothic murder ballad "Pretty Polly" to Lefty Frizzell's "Long Black Veil."

One of the great overlooked songs in Orbison's oeuvre, "Heartache," sadly went ignored in 1969. Although he recut it again in 1974, the song, much like Roy's ghost lover, would vanish forever without a trace.

"Coming after Claudette's death, people in England thought 'Too Soon To Know' was kind of naughty," Terry Widlake said. "But he'd actually recorded it before the accident. When I first heard 'Heartache' I was surprised, taken aback. I asked Roy, 'Do you think the public will go for this? Do you really want to portray yourself in this way?'"

Although Orbison had remarried and moved on with his life, the specter of Claudette never seemed very far off. Widlake recalled driving Roy to a gig in Bristol a few years following the tragedy, when Roy suggested they pull off the highway to take a back road. Upon seeing an old shack nestled under a small grove of pine trees, Roy instructed Terry to pull over. "It was a hut where they sold Indian trinkets," Widlake recollected. "We stopped inside the store, where they had various artifacts and souvenirs. I bought a small cedar jewelry box that I still have to this day. When we came out and got back in the car, Roy turned to me and said, 'This was the last place we stopped on our way back from Bristol before Claudette's accident.'"

"I was in France when I heard a song on the radio by Gilbert Bécaud in a bolero style and thought if Roy did it, it would be enormous," Fred Foster said, recalling a tune he thought was destined to be an Orbison classic. "I tracked down the lady who published it but she had just sold the rights to it thirty minutes before I got there. She sold it for $2,500. I told her I would've bought it for $10,000. I hired Mitchell Parish, who wrote 'Blue Tango' and 'Stardust,' to translate it into English, and then I played it for Roy. I said, 'Here's a monster!' He said, 'I don't hear it. I don't like it.' I waited a week and played it for him again. Everyone I brought it to turned it down. Eventually Herb Alpert did it. The song was called 'What Now My Love?' It would have been perfect for Roy!"

"Gilbert was a genius," Foster emphasized. "In the original version of the song, the love of his life leaves him and he's haunted by the memory, wandering empty streets, through the fog. The imagery is powerful. Then he actually sees her again on the street and says, 'If you looked at me with love, that would be great. If you looked at me with hate, okay, I understand, but to look at me with indifference, I cannot deal with that!' But Mitchell Parish missed that in his translation, which was the heart of the song."

"Et Maintenant" (the song's original title in French) as sung by Gilbert is powerful stuff. Hammering the piano keys, Bécaud delivers the lyric as if every word burned his tongue with bitter fire. The dynamic continually builds on a rolling snare until the singer erupts with a volcano of emotion. In comparison, the Orbison arrangement (undoubtedly inspired by Frank Sinatra's perky big-band arrangement) is oddly bouncy, considering the lyric is essentially a suicide note.

Foster's frustration is understandable. He was right and he knew it. If he'd had the chance to produce Roy singing "What Now My Love?" years before everyone from Sinatra to Elvis to Sonny and Cher had their way with it, there's little doubt that Roy would have had another hit on his hands during his stint at Monument. But as it did Bécaud's ex-lover, indifference apparently got the best of him.

Roy with his lethal weapon on the set of *The Fastest Guitar Alive*. (Metro-Goldwyn-Mayer/ Getty Images)

B-movie poster boy, 1967. (Courtesy Everett Collection)

Top: Roy Kelton Jr., Barbara, and Roy, circa 1972. (Photoshot/Getty Images)

Right: Roy on tour in the seventies. (Trevor Dallen/Getty Images)

Alan Mayes' cartoon, *The Adventures of the Big O*. (Courtesy of Alan Mayes)

Roy on tour in Australia. (From the collection of Terry Widlake)

RIGHT: Pickin' and almost grinnin'. (Getty Images)

BOTTOM: Neil Diamond, Terry Widlake, and Roy Orbison at the Sydney Opera House, March 1974. (From the collection of Terry Widlake)

Carl Perkins, Roy, Johnny Cash, and Jerry Lee Lewis singing for "The King" on *The Johnny Cash Christmas Special*, November 30, 1977. (Photofest/CBS)

Rockin' the Cocoanut Grove for *A Black and White Night*, Roy, with Bruce Springsteen and Elvis Costello, September 30, 1987. (Photofest/HBO-Cinemax)

A band of half-brothers—the Traveling Wilburys. From left to right—Lefty (Roy), Otis (Jeff Lynne), Lucky (Bob Dylan), Charlie T. (Tom Petty), and Nelson (George Harrison). (Photofest)

Roy gets his well-deserved star on the Hollywood Walk of Fame, January 29, 2010. Back row—T Bone Burnett, Jeff Lynne, Joe Walsh, Dan Aykroyd, David Lynch, Chris Isaak, and Dwight Yoakam. Front row—Wesley, Alex, Barbara, Roy Jr., and Phil Everly. (Jason LaVeris/FilmMagic/Getty Images)

NINE

GREETINGS FROM JERICHO PARKWAY

E verything in Roy's life at this time, as he later admitted, was "a bit hazy." And to make matters worse, his label, MGM, as he explained in his typically gentlemanly fashion, "wasn't really viable."

More famous for its classic films, Metro-Goldwyn-Mayer as a record company was a strange affair. Formed in 1946, MGM Records built its initial reputation on releasing soundtracks to such musicals as *The Wizard of Oz*, *Gigi*, and *Singin' in the Rain*. A catalog of classical recordings would bring the label an air of prestige before Frank Walker, the company's president, signed Hank Williams in 1947. Soon after, MGM found itself a leading purveyor of country music. The label's roster eventually expanded to include Mel Tillis and Roy's old pal Conway Twitty (whom producer Jim Vienneau had initially turned down).

With the British Invasion of the early '60s, the label suddenly had a slew of chart-topping hits from the Animals and Petula Clark, while its subsidiary, Verve Records, originally a hip jazz imprint, added Greenwich Village folkies Richie Havens and Laura Nyro to a growing batch of eclectic groups that included the Blues Project and the Velvet Underground, as well as "the Ugliest Rock Band in the World": the Mothers of Invention. But though the label enjoyed success, MGM seemed to lack clear vision. The imprint lived up to its motto, "Music to suit every taste," and in its struggle to please fans of every stripe (and paisley), MGM Records became a sort of sonic junk shop, in which Orbison wound up getting lost. Or perhaps the label was just ahead of its time with its "throw it at the wall and see if it sticks" approach to marketing, which eventually became the standard modus operandi of the record business in the '90s.

But during Mike Curb's stint as president of MGM, the record company seemed more concerned with its artists' drug habits and lack of morals than with selling their music. Curb's self-righteous campaign led to the label dropping nearly twenty bands, including the Velvet Underground and the Mothers of Invention (led by the notoriously straight-edge Frank Zappa), who he believed existed to "promote and exploit hard drugs through music."

Of course this had little to do with Roy Orbison, who, when it came to the typical excesses of the rock 'n' roll lifestyle, was either a true non-conformist or a hopeless failure, depending on your point of view. As a boy, Roy's father, Orbie Lee had steered him clear for any taste for alcohol. Seeing his dad with a glass of bourbon in his hand one day, Roy asked what he was drinking. "And he told me, and I said 'Can I have some?' And he said sure. So I slugged back a big shot of whiskey and I think I was sick for about six days. So that turned me off of drink forever. I still don't drink."

George Jones or Keith Richards he wasn't. Wild tales of debauchery are few and far between in the Orbison story. While an anonymous source claimed to have seen Roy "higher than a Georgia pine" upon occasion, whether wired on diet pills (which might explain the extreme fluctuation in his weight over the years) or relaxing with a whiff of reefer, Terry Widlake disputed any such rumor: "Roy liked to sleep and watch TV. He wasn't a drinker or pill popper. He told me once that in the early days he'd been on a terrible, grueling bus tour with Johnny Cash and couldn't take it anymore. They'd always arrive with just enough time to change into their stage outfits and get up onstage and sing. One night Roy told Johnny he didn't have the strength to play his set. Cash told him, 'Here, take this,' and handed him a pill. After a little while Roy got to feeling pretty good and was ready to do the show when suddenly somebody came on the bus to tell him the concert had been canceled. So he just lay there, wired the whole night, unable to get to sleep."

Bobby Goldsboro, who played guitar and sang with Orbison in the Candymen, concurred with Terry: "Roy didn't allow drinking or drugs. I don't think anybody in the band had even *heard* of drugs." On the other hand, Buddy Buie hinted at Roy taking "the occasional diet pill to keep goin.' But," as he pointed out, "marijuana hadn't even been invented yet in our world!"

"He went into a different world after I left," Widlake said, recalling a time in the mid-'70s in Eugene, Oregon, when he was confronted by the local sheriff about clouds of marijuana smoke pouring from the tour van door. "Roy had decided he wanted the Price brothers, who had a band called Squeedro Heejee, the name inspired by a TV commercial they'd seen for a hydro squeegee, to be his backup band [When I smelled the smoke] I said, 'Are you sure it's not bloody aftershave?' They used to wear an awful amount of cologne," Terry laughed. "It seemed strange, but I was naive about such things, and besides, Oregon had been the first state to legalize pot. But as the sheriff said, they preferred you smoke it once you left the city limits. Roy never smoked marijuana in my presence, but they were getting into it in the back of the bus while I was up front driving."

Meanwhile Fred Foster, who never had much respect for Wesley Rose in the first place, could only watch as Roy was lured away from the support and success he'd had at Monument by big promises and big money. Foster's role as Roy's producer was quite similar to Jerry Wexler's working with Aretha Franklin in her halcyon days at Atlantic Records (1967–79). Like Franklin, who thrived under Wexler's guidance, Roy had found his voice at Monument. Once Aretha left Atlantic and moved on to "bigger and better" things at Clive Davis' new label Arista in 1980, her music was never the same. Roy's experience of leaving Monument for MGM was remarkably similar. Lacking direction, the feel—that elusive, intangible quality essential to making great music—was gone. Franklin's records, no matter how well produced, arranged, or recorded, lacked the very thing her name had become synonymous with: soul. Orbison's records became similarly lackluster, once Wes Rose edged Fred Foster out of the producer's chair.

Buddy Buie put it succinctly: "Roy wouldn't have been the Roy he was without Fred Foster."

"Nothing jelled after he left Monument," Harold Bradley lamented. "At MGM he didn't have Fred there to guide him. The people there weren't too sure about Roy's dreams and vision of how he wanted his records to sound. It was just never the same after that, the togetherness. . . . I made all those moves with him. I went through the MGM thing, and the last session I cut with him was for Mercury. Roy would come in and say, 'Here, play this, this is how Fred Foster told me to do it.' And he'd play an open ringing D chord like he used on 'Crying' instead of those closed, dance-band chords I used."

Fred had no qualms about letting his old friend—and anyone else within earshot—know just how he felt about Orbison's latest album, *Hank Williams the Roy Orbison Way*. He considered it a travesty, plain and simple, "a bad career move."

Outside of a handful of scruffy, long-haired "outlaw" pickers and singers, as the new generation of Texas cowboy singers led by Willie Nelson and Waylon Jennings had become known, Hank's legend had been languishing for years in some lonesome valley until Roy Orbison eventually took up his old hero's mantle. As the album title's rustic typeface boldly announced, this was a collection of Hank's music, done up à la Orbison. Anybody thinking Roy was going to follow Hank down the "Lost Highway," paying homage with a postnasal twang and an acoustic guitar with a whining fiddle and weepy pedal steel guitar, was in for a shock from the moment they dropped the needle on that slab of black vinyl.

The record's cover portrayed Roy clad in black, in stark contrast to Hank's trademark white suits. Beside Orbison was a roughly collaged image of Williams, looking pale and ethereal, like a phantom genie in a cowboy hat who'd just popped out of a bottle to see what condition his condition was in. With his black hair now combed down in a Beatle bowl, and donning his obligatory shades, Roy sat behind a desk with his hands folded, perhaps in meditation, communing with Hank's spirit or maybe in prayer, begging forgiveness for the trespasses he and his producer Jim Vienneau had committed.

Initially Roy admitted he'd been on the fence about Hank Williams, claiming his music was "too Tin Pan Alley–ish" for his taste. "I liked him well enough," Roy told Nick Kent, "but didn't reckon him as the genius I now perceive him to be—the guiding light of us all, in a way."

Often jarring, occasionally brilliant, Jim Hall's rococo arrangements bordered on the surreal at times, as Hall took enormous liberties with the holy hymns of the Father of Country Music. While Hank's outfits once glittered with rhinestones, his music remained stark and economical no matter what success or excess came his way. There was never a note wasted on Williams' records. Hank's voice was penny-plain, and every solo, whether played on pedal steel guitar or on fiddle, had been ironed out to match the sharp creases of his polyester pants. But Roy and his posse had gone and Elvisized ol' Hank! They fattened up those rail-thin melodies with an all-you-can-hear smorgasbord of Nash-Vegas production. The ghost of Luke the Drifter was free on bail and running amok in Sin City. "Hey Good Lookin,'" now featured a clutch of punchy horns and a badass bass line. Yet no matter how over-the-top the arrangements were, Orbison remained the album's star. Not too surprisingly, Roy's take on Hank's "Cold Cold Heart" dripped with unabashed regret, while icy vibraphones, shimmering strings, and a pack of backup singers who sounded like they got lost on their way to an Andy Williams Christmas special oohed and ahhed like the winter wind on valium. The real surprise came with the sounds of a Coral electric sitar (a favorite of psychedelic bands just a few years earlier) snaking around the lyrics in lieu of the traditional pedal steel guitar. Built on the gentle lope of a Fats Domino–inspired gospel groove, the lyric to "You Win Again" continued to fuel Orbison's Losers' Hall of Fame persona. While the lush arrangement of "I Can't Help It if I'm Still in Love with You," was too warm and fuzzy to send anybody reaching for the razor blades, there's little doubt that Roy could have kept the folks at the suicide hotline working overtime with this one had Fred Foster been sitting behind the console. Instead of infusing the song with his usual dose of paranoia, Orbison turns Hank's floor-walking nightmare of pain and regret into a fond, nostalgic look in the rearview mirror. A very groovy Al Kooper–style organ break lightens things up for a moment until Roy's voice scales the heights of the song's bridge with a double shot of pure yearning. As he sings, "Heaven only knows how much I miss you," one has to wonder if Claudette's memory didn't continue to haunt him even after he married Barbara. And with its excessive production bordering on parody, Hank's tale of "Kaw-Liga," the lonesome cigar store wooden Indian, was a light-year from the records Roy once adored growing up in Wink.

Love it or hate it, the album was without a doubt the oddest and most original offering in Orbison's catalog to date. Its kitschy aesthetic was decades ahead of its time and would have made a splash in the late '80s with hipsters who revered Les Baxter's exotic soundtracks and Juan Esquivel's retro bachelor pad music. But in 1970, it simply went ignored, and Hank's music would languish for another year until his pale, raspy-throated ghost was suddenly resuscitated by *The Last Picture Show*, Peter Bogdanovich's bleak portrait of a West Texas town.

Whether the album was conceived as a loving tribute to Hank with the intention of furthering his legacy through new interpretations of his music, or as a calculated business deal by Wesley Rose (Acuff-Rose owned the Hank Williams catalog), Fred Foster was right when he called it an exercise in futility—but not for the reason he had in mind. *Hank Williams the Roy Orbison Way* was nowhere to be found in the summer of 1970. Few of the sidemen who played on the record even recalled making it, while most of Orbison's fans never heard it until it was rereleased in 2009 as part of a twofer CD package along with a Don Gibson tribute album.

Hank had also been on Dylan's mind at the time as well. Having retired from the stage following a disastrous tour of England and a near-fatal motorcycle accident in the spring of 1966, Bob made his comeback three years later at the Isle of Wight Festival, clad in white from head to toe, with his hurricane hair curiously tamed and parted on the side, looking more than a little like Hank Williams.

Roy's homage to Hank was years ahead of its time. By the end of the 1960s the Rolling Stones' bad trip that had begun with *Their Satanic*

Majesties Request started to wear off and they returned once more to playing roots music, recording covers of Robert Johnson and Mississippi Fred McDowell songs that cut to the bone. Having moved from Woodstock to Malibu, the Band by 1973 had begun to lose their fastball. Between the balmy weather and the laid-back L.A. lifestyle, this pack of backwoods Canadians (and their Arkansas drummer) had lost touch with guitarist/songwriter Robbie Robertson's poetic vision, which briefly reunited the disenfranchised citizens of the Woodstock Nation with the America they dreamed of. As Robertson's inspiration waned and members of the group grappled with various addictions, the Band temporarily found their sense of direction once more, digging into their repertoire from their early days as a struggling bar band before they'd crossed paths with Dylan. The ensuing album, *Moondog Matinee*, featured a smattering of great Elvis, Chuck Berry, and Fats Domino covers. Two years later, John Lennon would pay off a debt he owed to music publisher Morris Levy for having found a little too much inspiration in Chuck Berry's "You Can't Catch Me." In return for brazenly pilfering Berry's "flattop" for the Beatles' "Come Together," Lennon recorded an album of rock 'n' roll oldies produced by Phil Spector that not too surprisingly included a couple of Chuck's tunes (owned by Levy) along with classics by Buddy Holly, Little Richard, and Gene Vincent.

Recorded live at the Batley Variety Club in Yorkshire and released on London Records (the Stones' label, which distributed all of Roy's American albums in England), *The Big O* was unfortunately also nowhere to be found in the States in 1970.

The album featured Orbison's touring band the Art Movement, who brought him a more stripped-down, rootsy sound that would've undoubtedly resonated with a younger rock crowd if they'd had the chance to hear it. From the opening twang of J. D. Loudermilk's lowdown bluesy "Break My Mind," the record had a warm sound and genuine feel that was missing from his MGM sides. A surprise cover of the Beach Boys' "Help Me Rhonda" (who better than Roy could sing a line like "help me get her out of my heart?") showed Orbison stretching beyond his typecast image of the man forever traumatized by heartache, uncertain if he'll ever love again, all to the buoyant bounce of a Brian Wilson melody. Smothered with overdubbed strings and marred by the obligatory doo-wop backup vocals that made Orbison's early records so cool, "Only You," was just another typical '50s-style heartbreak number that only helped bolster Roy's anachronistic image.

Once again Roy's songwriting was sadly nowhere to be found, except for a remake of his old Sun standard "Go! Go! Go!"—or "Down the Line," as it became known after Jerry Lee hammered his personal stamp into it. Recorded in England and intended as a British-only release, *The Big O* was a Whitman's sampler of Roy's favorite American music, covering a lot of bases, from the country pine of the Louvin Brothers, to Motown and Stax numbers. Roy's take on Berry Gordy's "Money (That's What I Want)" kicked off by tipping its hat to the Beatles (by way of the Isley Brothers) with a "Twist and Shout" buildup before busting into the infectious hook that made it a standard for everyone from the Fab Four to British avant-rockers the Flying Lizards.

Roy, who always called England his second home, claimed he felt freer there, an ocean away from the emotional anchors of his past, and these sessions clearly prove it. During an outtake of the Louvin Brothers' "When I Stop Dreaming," Orbison, hoping to inspire his sidemen to play in the laid-back style of the Nashville cats he'd grown accustomed to, advised them to "just forget we're recording and just pick, pick, and grin, okay?"

The album also included a number by bassist Terry Widlake. A year before Widlake crossed paths with Roy, his band the Overlanders—now dubbed the Art Movement—had scored a Top Thirty hit with his "Loving Touch." Roy now made the song his own on *The Big O*. Built on a Stax soul–style bass hook, "Loving Touch" was a '60s-type pop confection with happy-go-lucky lyrics about falling love at "a wave of her hand." It was more typical of hits by the Association or the 5th Dimension than something one expected from Roy, but it showed Orbison trying to move beyond the lonely, dark corner he'd painted himself into as an artist (if his fans and management would allow him to).

"We [the Art Movement] had only been with him for a short time at that point," Terry Widlake said. "The album wasn't planned at all. Ron Randall, who was the head of Acuff-Rose in London, wanted to do it. It was his pet project."

After backing Roy for a 1969 tour of the UK and Canada, the Art Movement joined Orbison on a total of ten world tours, including extended jaunts to Asia and Australia. While members came and went, Terry stuck with Roy for the next decade. An electrifying concert from Melbourne in October 1972 captured Orbison (clad in a white polyester suit, with lank black hair) along with the Art Movement, breaking a sweat on Wilson Pickett's warhorse "Land of a Thousand Dances," which they'd previously recorded on *The Big O*. Roy seemed an unlikely candidate to call out a shopping list of dance crazes from the Pony to the Chicken to the Alligator and the Mashed Potato, but it was plain to see he was enjoying himself.

"Roy picked the song," Terry explained. "He wanted to do something different in the set. We'd played a show at the Playboy Club in London with Sammy Davis Jr. and they did 'Land of a Thousand Dances' together and we kept on playing it ever since."

Evoking the grinning, grooving ghost of Buddy Holly, Roy would also sing the Johnson Brothers' "Casting My Spell on You," as the Art Movement laid down a solid, romping Bo Diddley bomp-a-domp rhythm.

While few people rarely equate Roy Orbison's seemingly morose persona with "party music," he performed songs such as "Let the Good Times Roll," a standard played in every barroom in the American South, for years.

The Big O's last track was by far the strangest of the lot, but with Sammy King's "Penny Arcade" Roy found himself back on top of the British charts once more. Breaking into a surreal strut, the song—with its comical horns, gooey wah-wah guitar, and plinky glockenspiel, all laid over an old-timey banjo rhythm—sounded like something out of *Willie Wonka and the Chocolate Factory*. Whether under the influence of England's trad jazzer Acker Bilk or lost in London's heady psychedelic fog, Orbison seemed to have momentarily fallen down the rabbit hole of antiquity. Meanwhile "Penny Arcade" shot to Number One in Australia and New Zealand. After rumors began to circulate that Roy had bought the song off Sammy King on the cheap, the songwriter cleared the Big O's name in an interview with the Yorkshire *Evening Post*, claiming he was "the perfect gentleman and very polite. . . ." But, as King pointed out, "I can't say it made my fortune. It was the prestige which mattered."

In recent years "Penny Arcade" has become the beloved theme song of the Glasgow Rangers, a Scottish football team. Perhaps a stadium full of rabid sports fans madly chanting its lyrics would have helped explain the tune's enormous appeal to most Americans, who simply scratched their heads, wondering what Roy would throw at them next.

Sammy King admitted to feeling "a strange mixture of excitement and anxiety" on his way to meet Roy at the Batley Variety Club, where he was performing with his band. Nervous about asking Orbison to listen to a demo of his latest songs, King instead found Orbison generous and gracious.

"His quick smile and soft 'hello' put me at ease straightaway," Sammy recalled. "After a few formalities I mustered the courage to ask him if he would listen to a song or two and maybe give me a few tips."

As Roy and the band were about take the stage, Orbison gently apologized for not having time to give King his attention, and suggested they meet at a nearby restaurant after the show. Sammy claimed he was "floored" by Orbison's invitation.

After dinner, King set up the tape recorder when suddenly he "became aware of seats being set up around us. Having fully expected Roy to sit in a quiet corner and listen through headphones, [I now realized] that this wouldn't be the case. My humble efforts were going to come under the scrutiny of Roy's band, his entourage, [and] his wife, manager, and friends too!"

Preparing himself for the worst, Sammy played the first track for Roy, a slow ballad called "After Tonight," which he hoped might suit Orbison's style. "I thought it might meet with his approval but my hopes were dashed when his wife Barbara said straightaway that it 'wasn't really Roy.'" With the next song, "I Got Nothing," Sammy got just that—nothing.

"I sensed that my audience was beginning to lose interest, but to his credit, after it had finished Roy asked if there was anything else on the tape. I nodded and he said, 'Just leave it running,' and he listened to the remaining four tracks."

The final tune, "Penny Arcade," "was an up-tempo bouncy type song I was intending to enter for the Eurovision Song Contest and not the type of song I could see him taking any interest in at all," King said. "I would never have played it to him in a million years."

Doubtful his "work had created much interest," Sammy rewound the tape and was beginning to pack up his things when Orbison approached him. Expecting a few songwriting tips and patronizing comments at best, King was surprised when Roy asked for a copy of the tape. "He said he was going back to Nashville soon and [said] he would like Wesley Rose to hear it. Unbelievably, within six months I got word that 'Penny Arcade' was to be Roy Orbison's next single.

"Many years later I learned that Roy himself insisted on recording it, against everyone's advice," Sammy said. Since his early days at Sun and RCA, Orbison had allowed himself to be manipulated by his producers to record material that was both substandard and ultimately hurtful to his career. But now Orbison followed *his* instincts, ignoring whatever disparaging comments flew over the song.

"When they're right, you can tell," Roy said, explaining his intuitive process for choosing what new material to sing.

"He believed the song had a magical quality to it that no one else, including me, could see. He was right, too. It got Roy's career back on track. 'Penny Arcade' is actually more popular today then it ever has been. It's [been] forty-three years since Roy recorded it, and I have been assured by the young fans of Glasgow Rangers Football Club that it will be handed down and sung by the generations to come," King said proudly. "And all this is thanks to Roy, who was the only one to see the magic of the song. He really did know his stuff!"

If "Penny Arcade" had been a stretch for Orbison's American fans, there was nothing in his catalog that could have prepared them for Bobby Bond's "Southbound Jericho Parkway," a piece of musical theatrical schmaltz second only to Jimmy Webb's "MacArthur Park." The rambling story of Mr. Henry Johnson, whose life is falling apart at the dreams, begins with Roy singing over a cello and the exotic twang of an electric sitar. This seven-minute convoluted tour de force, produced by Don Gant and performed by the Neon Philharmonic, shifts tempos and gears repeatedly as the song's protagonist finally reaches his ultimate destination by driving his Lincoln Continental into a wall. The saga continues as news travels to his friends and relatives, who respond to the tragic suicide of "a good, clean man."

Orbison's fans were used to all sorts of subtle sadomasochistic sentiments and macabre scenes laced throughout his songs over the years, but this mini opera went beyond his usual dramas, and was more akin to the Who's rock operas, with their heady lyrics, or David Bowie's epic *Ziggy Stardust*. Renegade musician/author Tupper Saussy's rococo arrangement ebbs and flows until the song suddenly ends and Roy sighs, "And time went past," leaving you wondering what in the world you just heard. Amazingly enough, "Southbound Jericho Parkway" made it past Roy's gatekeepers and was chosen to round out *Roy Orbison's Greatest Songs*, yet another *Best of* compilation, released by MGM in February 1970. It remains the consummate oddball track in a career peppered with oddball tracks, but at least it was one that Roy believed in.

David McKinley was working as an assistant engineer at Woodland Sound in Nashville in 1971 when Roy booked the studio to put the finishing touches on his new album, *Memphis*.

"Everybody in Nashville showed up at the session to play, and they just sat around, waiting in the lobby," McKinley recalled. "He'd hired a ton of musicians. There were two drummers—in fact, there were two of everything! I thought, Oh my God, what is this? But he was only there to overdub some vocals and a few percussion tracks. I got the feeling it was an obligatory album to fulfill his contract at MGM. I don't even remember seeing it in the stores after it came out."

Therein lies the trouble and tragedy of Roy's lost years at MGM, a deadly combo of his management's insistence that he churn out new material regardless of quality while at the same time receiving little or no interest or support from his record company and, ultimately, the public.

McKinley, who deeply respected Orbison as an artist and singer, found his process of getting into and shaping a song rather surprising: "Atmosphere was very important to him. First he cleared everybody out of the control room who didn't need to be there, and then he had us turn off all the lights, even on the music stands. Then he'd begin to run through the songs, listening to the tracks, gathering it all in. Roy would prepare by mumbling and muttering the words. It was almost comical. At first his intonation would be way off, but then he'd begin to zero in. I'd never worked with anyone who did that before. Maybe they'd noodle around with the melody or phrasing, but Roy had another, different perspective."

Like everyone who knew Orbison in the wake of the devastating tragedies he faced, David McKinley found him withdrawn, "gentle and melancholy," he recalled. "Roy was extremely polite, even syrupy at times. His [speaking] voice was soft and breathy. Yet he wanted things done in a certain way. So you'd better get the headphone mix and the lighting just the way he wants it."

Following a tour of the UK where Orbison and Otis Redding crossed paths with each other night after night, performing at the same venues, the two singers wound up sitting together on the same plane flying back to the States. At one point, rumors began to fly over the possibility of Roy and Otis Redding cutting a record together. While Roy had nothing on Redding in the fire and funk department, he did heartbroken and lonely as well as, if not better than, anybody. It was even money as to who could sing with more pain per square inch and then skulk off wearing the sorry crown of "Mr. Pitiful." But all talk and plans for the project, tentatively titled *The Big O*, were dashed after the Georgia dynamo went down in a small plane over Madison, Wisconsin, in December 1967.

Roy did, however, make his own less-than-successful trip to Otis' old stomping ground a few years later. Released in November 1972, *Memphis* was a mixed bag that ranged from the soulful to the ridiculous.

Propelled by a choppy snarling wah-wah guitar vamp, "Run Baby Run" revealed the influence of Stax Records, home to Otis, Sam & Dave, and Wilson Pickett, among other giants. The song, another "she mistreats him but he doesn't care cause he's so desperate he'll do anything for her love"–style lyric originally written by Roy's old partner Joe Melson and Don Gant for the Newbeats (who opened shows for Orbison on tours of the UK years ago), was tailored to Roy's persona. This was white soul music, an oxymoron until the mid-'60s, when "blue-eyed soul" artists such as the Rascals, Van Morrison, and Dusty Springfield made the music their own and punched their way to the top of the charts with more depth and grit than any 1950s cover artist before them had to offer.

The opening cut, a cover of Chuck Berry's "Memphis, Tennessee," was not the strongest track on the record—Orbison's voice sounds oddly thin, and Chuck's punch line about the girl he's desperately trying to reach on a long-distance call being just six years old fell flat. Perhaps if Roy had taken the song back to his days at Sun (as the album's title implied) and played it with a rootsy feel, sung it with a dash of slapback on his voice, and picked his own lead guitar, the track would've shined instead of sounding like more business as usual.

There's an old joke in the music biz that fit Orbison's MGM records like a custom-made Nudie suit—"If it's worth producing, it's worth overproducing." But no matter what sort of schlock Roy's arrangers and producers foisted upon him, from a chorus of keening *Star Trek* sirens to layers upon layers of schmaltzy violins, "the Voice" would still transcend their sonic trespass.

Memphis clearly bore the excesses of its day. Vapid lyrics, saccharine flutes, and the perky rhythm of Joe Melson's "I'm the Man on Susie's Mind" foreshadowed the coming disco craze. Jim Hall's cloyingly sweet arrangement brought to mind another saying commonly heard around the American South—"Too much sugar for just one dime." But, as with every Orbison album on MGM, there were always a few great tracks if one was willing to wade through the dross. Built off a righteous gospel piano vamp, "Take Care of Your Woman" revealed the influence of Ray Charles. Fred Foster regularly looked to Ray as the benchmark to compare Orbison's recordings during his stint at Monument. Over the years, Roy and Ray covered much of the same ground. Orbison first cut Don Gibson's "I Can't Stop Loving You" on *Lonely and Blue* in 1961, a year before Charles' quintessential version. Whenever Roy needed to rouse his crowd from the melancholy spell he cast over them, he'd reach for Ray's "What I'd Say" to bump the energy up a notch.

Perhaps because he felt "I Can't Stop Loving You" had become the exclusive domain of Ray Charles, Orbison had purposely steered clear of it on his recent tribute to Don Gibson. But his uninspired remake on *Memphis* brought nothing new to the table, causing some of his fans to wonder whether Roy was lacking ideas or just paying more rent in the Acuff-Rose tower of song.

Side two opened with one of the album's best tracks. Propelled by a chunky electric rhythm guitar, "Run the Engines Up High" recalled the revved-up trucker's anthem "Six Days on the Road." Roy's vocals, framed by a smoking fuzz guitar riff, soared, as the singer momentarily freed himself (along with his fans) from the murky, debilitating emotions that routinely dogged him.

Sung over an earthy gospel vamp, Orbison's rendition of "Ain't No Big Thing" took the song to a deeper emotional place than Elvis' version, which featured a twangy Dobro and a loping country beat. But the next track, Roy's take of the classic Sonny Curtis number "I Fought the Law," lacked all trace of real conviction. Orbison came off as neither desperate nor dangerous. A bit of slide guitar and wailing harmonica gave the song a roots-rock feel but still couldn't manage to cut through a corny arrangement trivialized by a hoary batch of backup singers singing a Joe Melson–style countermelody. Once an integral component of Roy's early hits, the light 'n' fluffy "ya-ta-ya-ta-ya-ya" vocal riff now sounded ridiculously out of place.

Although the musicianship on Roy's records was generally bulletproof, there was little or no continuity between the tracks. And if there had been any original concept behind the album's title, it was apparently tossed out the window with the last pair of songs, which were strong enough to have appeared on any Orbison record.

"Three Bells," famous in France as "Les Trios Cloches," had been a showstopper in the repertoire of the country's legendary chanteuse Edith Piaf. Whether sung by Orbison or Piaf, the tear-jerking ballad of Jimmy Brown was certain to unlock a floodgate of emotions.

"Danny Boy," the album's final track, was simply staggering. Written by British lawyer Frederic Weatherly, who nicked the melody from an old fiddle tune called "Londonderry Air," "Danny Boy" has been played and sung in every neighborhood pub on earth and covered by everybody from Bing Crosby to jazz pianist Keith Jarrett. Roy's rendition is emotionally pulverizing. Like a Method actor drawing from personal experience, Orbison dug deep, undoubtedly dredging up the memory of his sons' tragic deaths as he delivered a volcanic performance.

And therein lay the frustration of being an Orbison fan, knowing "the Voice" was always there, capable at any moment of shattering your heart, no matter how they tried to drown his performance in a sea of schmaltz.

"After the divorce, he'd thrown himself into touring," Barbara Orbison told *Mojo* magazine years later. "He always said he felt safest onstage— that's where he could keep up that part of him that wanted to crumble." But by the time Roy set out on his extensive/exhaustive four-month world tour in September 1972, he was no longer battling those phantoms of his past. He had remarried, had a new family, and appeared to have moved on.

The grueling schedule of 125 shows over 105 consecutive nights might have won him a place in the *Guinness Book of Records* (the extensive trek covered most of Europe, Hong Kong, Korea, and Japan before Orbison returned once again to Australia, with a side trip to Taiwan and the Philippines), but it took a serious toll on his health. Beyond fulfilling his role as a breadwinning itinerant musician who looked after his family and kept his name and music before the public, Roy was driving himself into the ground at a rapid rate. Yet he soldiered on, maintaining his standing as a living legend, despite the ravages of an aggravating ulcer and a relentless nicotine habit. "This business takes years off your life," Roy once said, knowing well the price he paid for fame.

Released in 1973, *Milestones* was an ad hoc collection of current pop hits, including Roy's rendition of the Bee Gees' "Words" (also recorded by Elvis), Neil Diamond's classic "Sweet Caroline" (another Elvis fave), Cindy Walker's "You Don't Know Me," and Dobie Gray's eternal rock anthem "Drift Away."

The album's single, "Blue Rain (Coming Down)," featured a cascading harp and shimmering vibes and flutes, as Roy's voice, seething with heartache, vaults to the heavens.

As Orbison's songs build slowly, methodically, to their carefully designed climax, they evoke a feeling of deep yearning, what poet Anne Sexton called that "awful rowing toward God." No matter how many times you've heard Roy sing "Blue Rain," you still find yourself wondering if he really *can*, if he really *will* hit that high note. Few singers in the history of pop created that level of sheer intensity. It's like watching a ski jumper who makes it look easy as he gracefully, seemingly effortlessly, flies through the air with no trace of doubt on his face. Meanwhile, the crowd waits anxiously, wondering if he will land in one piece.

No matter how great Roy's songs were, what ideas or riffs the revolving door of writers, studio musicians, and band members loaned to his music, it was "the Voice" that ultimately resonated with people and sold millions of records. As one fan recently commented on YouTube: "Hearing Roy Orbison always gives me a Big O."

But by this point no one was surprised by the tepid reviews, dismal sales, and public apathy toward *Milestones*, and after twelve albums in eight years, Roy was finally freed from his contract with MGM.

That same year, Wink's one-time gridiron hero Grady Lee Orbison died. His life, a tangled trail of failed marriages and dead-end blue-collar jobs, had been coming apart for quite some time.

"Grady had been living in a trailer park in Hendersonville. He was a great, crazy guy, a real roughneck, very fond of drink," Terry Widlake recalled. "Pappaw, as the family called Orbie Lee, once told me about how Grady used to get drunk back in Wink and drive his car up onto the railroad tracks to help guide him home. He finally wound up crashing into a telephone pole."

Grady Lee was laid to rest beside Claudette and the boys. Both Roy and Orbie elected to stay home and skip the funeral, having recently had more than their fair share of sorrow. Barbara, who handled all the arrangements at the Phillips-Robinson Funeral Home, allegedly joked with the mortician that by now the Orbisons deserved a discount.

Perhaps Roy and Grady Lee had more in common with Mr. Johnson, the tragic hero of "Southbound Jericho Parkway," than anyone realized. While his big brother had finally lost control, Roy still managed to steer clear of telephone poles and brick walls for the time being, although career-wise it seemed like either might be his destination.

No matter what trends Roy halfheartedly delved into, in hopes of staying relevant in a rapidly changing scene, his attempts were either treated with embarrassment by MGM or just failed miserably on their own. Whether by ineptitude or design, his record company sadly might've sold more copies of his latest album if they'd been buried under a rock. Like Brian Wilson, Roy Orbison apparently "wasn't made for these times."

"As the '60s turned into the '70s I didn't hear a whole lot I could relate to," Roy later told Nick Kent, "so I kind of stood there like a tree, where the winds blow and the seasons change and you're still there and you bloom again. With time."

TEN

DOWN THUNDER ROAD
AND BACK

With the release of *Born to Run*, rock 'n' roll had a new boss. If anyone was in doubt, they didn't have to look very far to find the scruffy-bearded beatific King of the Gypsies slyly grinning on the covers of both *Newsweek* and *Time* on the same week. With his mush-mouthed poetry, low-slung Telecaster, and black leather jacket, Bruce Springsteen returned a desperately needed sense of urgency to rock at a time when sexual ambiguity, outrageous costumes, and sterile production values ruled the day. The Boss' sonic hot rod was a chop-shop special artfully welded together with equal parts from Bob Dylan's, Phil Spector's, and Roy Orbison's junkyards. Like a white-hot lighthouse beam cutting through the fog of memory, Bruce's shout-out to Roy "singin' for the lonely" in "Thunder Road" not only caught people's ears, it rang the bell of collective memory, sparking visions of the ghostly dude with the dark shades and big voice.

For nearly a decade, Orbison had been sidelined, lurking in the shadows of America's cultural landscape, lost in a twilight zone of oldies radio programming and neon-lit burger-joint jukeboxes. Rock 'n' roll's glory days were long gone, razed by Dylan, the British Invasion, LSD, and the Vietnam War. And Springsteen, who now conjured hope for the bewildered true believers of the American dream, honored his hero, the champion of lonely hearts, Roy Orbison, by tossing a beer can into a still pond and roaring off into the night in his burned-out Chevy as the ripples slowly began to spread.

Terry Widlake recalled the European editor of *Time* magazine phoning Roy at London's Mayfair Hotel to ask his thoughts about Bruce Springsteen. Bruce, who considered Orbison a mentor, once drove all the way from the Jersey Shore down to Nashville to open a show for him back in the late '60s. Springsteen's first impression of his hero bordered on the otherworldly, as if he'd seen an apparition before his very eyes: "He had a feeling about him where it seemed like if you went up to him and tried to touch him, your hand would go through him. It seemed like he'd fallen from another planet. He had that purity when he sang . . . and he always had that loneliness, and that distance."

Orbison, on the other hand, was confused. Looking quizzically at Terry, Roy gently begged, "Who the hell is Bruce Springsteen?" He didn't know the Boss from a sack of salt. Apparently the European editor was fuming over the fact that *Time*'s cover had been bought and paid for by Springsteen's management in a brazen publicity push, the likes of which had only been previously lavished upon Elvis Presley, the Beatles, and, more recently, David Bowie (in his Ziggy Stardust guise), around whom a P. T. Barnum/cross-gender circus erupted in advance of his American debut at Carnegie Hall.

Meanwhile, Orbison's career had gone from bad to worse after signing with Mercury Records, a label whose identity problem dwarfed MGM's catalog of hits and mistakes. The new album's title, *I'm Still in Love with You*, sounded like pandering of the worst kind.

Perhaps the most interesting aspect of the album was its cover, which depicted Roy driving one of his beloved British sports cars, an MG convertible, with the top down. A strange cloud (looking like a gryphon or a hellhound baring fangs, ready to take a bite out of his perfect pompadour) hovered over his head. Was it meant to forecast yet more rain for the man famous for "Crying" his heart out since 1961? Or perhaps it was supposed to symbolize the disembodied spirit of Claudette, who, although dead eight years, still followed the poor guy around, inspiring yet more songs with titles such as "Heartache," "It's Lonely," and "Hung Up on You." Although married to Barbara, with two young sons and a beautiful new home, Roy, if he hoped stay in the game, was forever doomed to play "A Man of Constant Sorrow" (as the old folk song goes). Mourning evidently was good for business.

With *I'm Still in Love with You*, Roy still claimed to still carry the torch for his faithful fans, but the feeling ultimately went unrequited, and Roy's latest once more slipped quietly under the radar, unnoticed.

The Caruso of Country had apparently lost his thunder. Roy Orbison was clearly stuck in a rut, spinning his shiny spoke wheels, chewing on what had already been chewed.

According to *Crawdaddy*'s Greg Mitchell, who interviewed Orbison in 1974, Roy seemed to be taking the decline badly. While Mitchell saw Orbison as "more of a curiosity than a legend," *Melody Maker*'s Michael Gray considered Roy a fixture from a bygone era, "fated to remain Mr. 1960." Regardless of if or when his much-anticipated comeback would ever happen, Orbison's British fans continued to cue up outside club doors, no matter how small the venue.

"I'm glad that he was the highest-paid cabaret artist in the UK last year," Gray claimed, but "it is a sad place to see an artist who was indeed, albeit briefly, one of the humbler giants in our music."

Meanwhile, Roy crossed the Pacific once again for another tour of Australia, where his records routinely turned gold and platinum. In America he found whatever work he could, singing to the dwindling pack of true believers who made up his crowd at nightclubs, shopping malls, and car shows. Aside from the eternally ebullient Bruce Springsteen, few seemed to remember Orbison or care about him. Nonetheless, Roy kept up a hectic tour pace through 1975, until he no longer saw the point anymore.

Just when he finally decided to hang up his rock 'n' roll shoes, Fred Foster lured his old friend back into the studio again, for the first time in nearly three years since releasing *I'm Still in Love with You*. Signing a one-shot deal with Monument, Orbison cut the misguided and mis-named *Regeneration* in 1976.

The first inkling that things were askew was the record's playlist. Once again, of the album's ten songs, none of them had been written by Roy. There seemed to be an abundance of bad ideas from the get-go, from the feeble attempt to update Orbison's sound with a disco beat, to the cover of Tony Joe White's "I'm a Southern Man," a song that managed to reinforce every tired old redneck stereotype at a time when the South appeared to be experiencing a rebirth and a new progressive era under the Carter presidency. With its swampy conga groove, punchy soul horn arrangement, and wah-wah guitars, "Under Suspicion" sounded as if Roy and Fred had momentarily fallen under the funky spell of Curtis "Superfly" Mayfield. Perhaps Wesley Rose had a point years before when he accused Fred Foster of making "pop shit nigger records."

With Fred Rose's "Blues in My Mind," Roy, over a gently plucked nylon-string guitar and lush string arrangement, laments over a lost love that has driven him to the brink of madness. "I Don't Really Love You" once again casts Orbison in the role of the brokenhearted loser desperately trying to save another hopeless relationship from crashing and burning. By the 1970s, the tasteful production that enhanced Roy's earlier Monument sides had become excessive to the point of absurdity. Whatever nuances Kris Kristofferson had in mind when writing "Something They Can't Take Away" were obliterated by a string arrangement and a chorus of cloyingly sweet and syrupy oohs and aahs.

It is particularly telling that there is very little of the brilliance of Roy's earlier Monument recordings to be found on *Regeneration*. The atmosphere that made those records so unique and powerful in the first place was long gone, strangled either by the sonic sterility that obsessive overdubbing brings, or by the fact that Orbison had gotten up to bat with an entirely new, untried team. Bob Moore's absence makes one wonder just how much input he had in the creation of Roy's original masterpieces in the first place.

Perhaps the only spark from *Regeneration* that managed to stand the test of time is David Wright's retina-frying album cover art, which portrayed Roy's disembodied head (looking suspiciously like that of Elvis) floating on a swirling red and purple background bright enough to induce an acid flashback or epileptic seizure.

Regeneration was unanimously panned by the critics, and Monument never bothered to rerelease it on CD after vinyl was put out to pasture in the late '80s. The only excuse Monument could manage to muster was that the album was cut in haste. With few interested in anything other than Roy's past, Foster released his old friend from his contract with no strings attached.

Roy Orbison, as far as the American public was concerned, had seen better days: He was just another old-timer from a bygone era who'd lost his fastball.

Back on the road again in 1977, Roy was booked to play the Old Waldorf in San Francisco. Upon arriving, Terry Widlake was immediately put off by the club owner's smug attitude. Not only did he show little respect for Roy, but it seemed like he was completely unfamiliar with his music.

The San Francisco music scene in the '60s was comprised of a small, clubby bunch of hippie jam bands that included the Grateful Dead, Jefferson Airplane, and Big Brother and the Holding Company. Roy Orbison's dark rhapsodies stood in stark contrast to their organic/orgasmic electric extrapolations. His pale complexion, jet-black hair, and monochromatic clothes were the antithesis of their tie-dyed pajamas, free-form dancing, and live-for-today lifestyle. Although hardly "establishment," Orbison clearly had nothing to do with the counterculture. Ironically, Roy's unique voice and appearance made him the true iconoclast amongst that crowd. Yet nothing—not his fame, individuality, or gentle manner—could buy him one ounce of respect from the proprietor and his crew.

"Being a legend is a great thing," Roy once said. "But it doesn't tune your guitar or change your tire."

"We didn't even have a proper dressing room. They weren't real walls, just a couple of dividers," Widlake groused. Roy and his band were scheduled to play two shows that night. After the band packed the house on the first set, the manager returned singing a different tune. Wheeling in a cart filled with champagne, whiskey, beer, and wine, he announced that all drinks were on the house. Not only was the turnout better than he'd imagined, it was *who* was in the crowd that really won him over. "Bette Midler, Boz Scaggs, and all of the Eagles were there . . . really, anyone who was in showbiz," Terry remembered.

Thanks to a stellar set at the Old Waldorf, Orbison was soon opening arena shows for the Eagles, whose nightmarish epic "Hotel California" had soared to Number One in February 1977 and continues to haunt oldies radio to this day. Roy's stock was suddenly on the rise once again.

Beginning in 1974, Linda Ronstadt had taken the charts by storm with a series of vintage American rock 'n' roll covers, from Betty Everett's "You're No Good" (her first Number One) to the Everly Brothers' "When Will I Be Loved" (Number Two) and Buddy Holly's "That'll Be the Day" (Number Eleven). Besides respectable renditions of Patsy Cline and Hank Williams songs, the doe-eyed Latina also belted out Motown hits by Martha and the Vandellas and Smokey Robinson.

With her 1977 release *Simple Dreams*, Linda mined Buddy Holly's songbook for another smash with an edgy cover of "It's So Easy," which shot to Number Five. But it was her passionate delivery of Roy's "Blue Bayou" that inspired a *Rolling Stone* reviewer to liken her to jazz singer Billie Holiday in his glowing review. Ronstadt wasn't merely posing, trying on Orbison's shade of lonesome like a new dress or eyeliner; she connected with the song on a deep level, evoking the pain and isolation that Roy experienced in his youth when he yearned to escape the Wink wastelands. Linda sang "Blue Bayou" like she meant it, and the song soared to Number Three, selling nearly ten million copies.

Ronstadt finally met the man at a party thrown by Emmylou Harris, celebrating the stellar success of her cover of "Blue Bayou." Mesmerized by Roy, she tried to catch a glimpse of the enigmatic eyes behind his famous Ray-Bans but wasn't as persuasive as Marianne Faithfull had been years before, when she unmasked the mystery man for a photo shoot and then peered coyly over the famed frames. "It was kinda like looking at Darth Vader," Ronstadt said, "except Roy was so nice."

Orbison then found himself accosted by a raving, scraggly-haired hippie who recalled his B-sides better than he could. It was Neil Young, one of rock's greatest chroniclers of human loneliness. Neil had previously met Orbison years before in Winnipeg, in 1962, when Roy, according to Young, was "at the top of his game." Although Neil thought Orbison's band "kicked ass," it was the singer's enigmatic image, his "aloofness [that] influenced me profoundly," Neil told Nick Kent. Not only did Neil play a white Gretsch Falcon (rimmed with gold sparkle filigree), a favorite guitar of Orbison's back in the '50s, and not only did his 1974 release *On the Beach* featured a small snapshot of Roy on its cover, but Young once aptly described his song "Don't Cry" as "Roy Orbison meets heavy metal."

By August 1977, Elvis had left the auditorium, but not before lavishing some well-deserved praise upon Roy one night at the Las Vegas Hilton. Pointing his old labelmate out in the crowd, the King, in a moment of genuine humility and respect, told his devoted fans that Roy Orbison was "the greatest singer in the world." Roy reportedly cried like a baby upon hearing the news of Elvis' death.

Bobby Goldsboro confirmed Presley's passion for the Big O after flying with the King to Los Angeles in the '70s: "The plane stopped in Memphis and Elvis and his entourage got on. Later his piano player David Briggs came over and said, 'Elvis wants to meet you.' Then Elvis came up and sat with me all the way to L.A. All he wanted to talk about was Orbison! He was in awe of Roy's voice."

While getting his props from Elvis, Orbison also gleaned attention of a more dubious kind from the guerilla comedy troupe from *Saturday Night Live*. John Belushi's famous parody of Joe Cocker's spastic delivery of "A Little Help from My Friends" on *SNL* in October 1975, led him to satirize Roy's image two years later in a skit called "Great Moments in Rock 'n' Roll." The bit began with Laraine Newman recalling her days as a Pamela Des Barres–like groupie complete with colorful caftan and headband. She confessed she was "ready to do anything" to get her hands on Orbison's famous shades, and then, with a wry grin, showed off the much-coveted prize mounted on a wooden plaque. Bill Murray, as Roy's sleazeball good-ol'-boy manager, clad in a loud polyester shirt and checked jacket, begs Belushi to get rid of her. She pleads with Roy that they've been together for a week and she hardly knows anything about him beyond what the rest of the world already knows—that "he always stood perfectly still when he sang and he always wore dark glasses." Meanwhile, Belushi as Roy stands center stage looking like a cross between North Korea's recently appointed Supreme Leader Kim Jong-un and Peter Boyle in *Young Frankenstein*.

Speaking and acting more like Elvis, in a hopped-up, speedy, macho twang that was altogether unlike Orbison, Belushi blows her off by handing over his coveted shades; then, dazed by daylight, he teeters around until grabbing another pair as the band then breaks into a thoroughly mundane cover of "Oh, Pretty Woman." Halfway through the song, the lock-kneed Belushi takes a board-stiff pratfall as Murray rushes to grab the mic stand and hold it while the prostrated fading star continues to sing. Belushi manages to get back on his feet, where he stays until the end of the song. While the *SNL* audience loved it, it was, in a word, merciless. A less stoic, more thin-skinned artist who hadn't been steeled by a life such as Roy's might've reached for the revolver.

Roy returned to Television Land again on November 30, 1977, when *The Johnny Cash Christmas Special* featured Sam Phillips' boys reuniting to sing the praises of their fallen friend Elvis. Standing shoulder to shoulder like a lineup of aging comic-book superheroes, Jerry Lee, Carl Perkins, Roy, and the show's host traded verses on Sister Rosetta Tharpe's righteous "This Train Is Bound for Glory." The King, as Cash reminded the studio audience, "loved gospel songs." The irony of this bunch preaching the straight and narrow wasn't lost on Johnny, who cracked a knowing smirk while Jerry Lee, the biggest hell-raiser of the lot, looking like a malicious maître d' in white dinner jacket and bow tie, warned the "jokers" and "cigar smokers" amongst the crowd that, unless they repented, they'd never set foot on "God's train."

The song, driven by a chugging harmonica, played by *Hee-Haw*'s house-band director and former Roy sideman Charlie McCoy, featured a violin section (those weren't fiddles!), which modulated, in order to accommodate "the Voice," just moments before Roy made his grand entrance.

There was no way this crew was going home without trotting out a few of their greatest hits. Jerry Lee mercilessly slammed "Whole Lotta Shakin' Going On," Perkins dusted off his "Blue Suede Shoes" once more, and Roy predictably delivered yet another solid take of "Oh, Pretty Woman." Clad in black with a blinged-out white custom Telecaster, Orbison proved he still had decent guitar chops with a bit of fancy cross-picking, while the strings and keyboards added flourishes of sonic filigree.

A few weeks later Roy took the stage again, at the Memphis Liberty Bowl on December 19, 1977, to reprise Leiber and Stoller's "Hound Dog" during a schmaltz-laden halftime show dedicated to Elvis that was received with just short of the kind of enthusiasm reserved for the Second Coming.

Following the fur-draped opera diva Marguerite Piazza, Orbison, in contrast to the King, stood, as always, stock-still as he sang. His washed-out face revealed a bemused smile as "the Voice" effortlessly galvanized a football stadium emblazoned with an enormous guitar and a hound dog comprised of white-uniformed marching-band cadets.

Anemic and exhausted, Roy collapsed following the performance.

If the resounding chorus of "His truth is marching on," punctuated with a round of fireworks igniting the sky above a roaring stadium filled with teary-eyed, patriotic flag-wavers was almost enough to kill him, his doctor warned Roy, then he had better cut out all the stress and cigarettes or he'd soon be singing with the King, on a double bill, in that extraplush luxury lounge in the sky.

"He was always in terrible shape," Terry Widlake confided. "He loved junk food, particularly candy bars. There were always wrappers by the side of the bed in his hotel room." The unholy trinity of grease, sugar, and nicotine, compounded with his lazy ways, would catch up with Orbison by his early forties.

Following the holidays, Roy was rushed to Nashville's Saint Thomas Hospital, where he underwent a triple bypass on January 18, 1978. It turned out he'd been on the verge of a colossal coronary. Moments before succumbing to the anesthesia, Orbison joked with the surgeon, asking him to leave a big scar zigzagging across his chest that he could show off onstage.

While walking the lonesome valley of mortality, Roy received what he considered the "most thrilling fan letter ever," from the family of a girl named Michelle, who had been raped and thrown from a train on her way to Hertfordshire, England. Her desperate folks hoped that Roy might record a few words or a song for Michelle that might somehow magically rouse her from her coma. Apparently, she came to after responding to the tape he sent.

"All I did was invite her to a concert the next time I came to England," Orbison told *NME*'s Penny Reel in 1980. "Then a couple of weeks later she rang me on the phone from hospital, and she was very lucid and said thank you for sending the tape."

Roy met Michelle on his next British tour, and recalled her coming to "at least one of the concerts. . . . I sympathized with her a great deal [as] I was not in good shape. I think it was only six weeks after having open-heart surgery at the time."

On the mend, Orbison signed with Elektra/Asylum Records that October. Not surprisingly, Roy found himself odd man out amongst Asylum's stable of singer-songwriters, comprised of members of L.A.'s "Avocado Mafia"—Jackson Browne, Joni Mitchell, Linda Ronstadt, and the Eagles, all of whom were big fans of his music. But his ensuing album, *Laminar Flow*, released in July 1979—its title was inspired by some obscure aeronautics term—was another disappointing, ill-conceived affair.

The cover shot portrayed Roy with a thin, creepy grin, stylin' in a silky black shirt open wide to show off that new shiny zipper of a scar—which the Asylum art department unanimously voted to airbrush into obscurity, taking with it whatever edge the album might possibly have had. Very little of the record bore repeated listening beyond "Hound Dog Man," a gentle, affectionate tribute to Presley. It was one of only three songs that Roy had a hand in writing on the album.

Laminar Flow holds the dubious honor of having been the "whitest" album ever recorded at Muscle Shoals, the legendary Alabama studio where everyone from Aretha Franklin to the Rolling Stones cut some of their most soulful sides. Even Roy's most devoted fans, the Brits, thought it stunk. *Mojo* magazine, England's monthly rock bible, trashed *Laminar Flow*, calling it "among the feeblest [albums that Roy] ever recorded."

Like a man possessed, Roy wasted no time getting back on the road again as soon as possible. "I was workin' ninety days later to make sure that I could work," he said (referring to his recent open-heart surgery) in a television interview.

But Orbison's live shows at this time didn't fare much better than his latest sonic flop. "I'll tell you what hurt me to my heart," Buddy Buie confessed. "When I went to see him in a club in Atlanta and he was playing disco. It was a travesty! It just took my breath away."

Like everyone else manipulated into following the prevailing trends of disco and punk—no matter how ridiculous they appeared, donning absurd clothes and cutting lousy records in their desperate attempts to stay current—Roy would've been better off sticking to his guns. Under the sway of hopelessly unsophisticated market forces, namely record company knuckleheads who knew nothing about music, as well as his clueless management whose only interest in Orbison was in the revenue he generated from their songbook catalog, Roy was bullied into pumping out pabulum and chasing vapid fads, which unsurprisingly yielded zero in terms of artistic merit or cash flow.

While largely regulated to the oldies circuit, Orbison surprisingly found himself embraced by a slew of neo-rockabilly proto-hipsters, from Robert Gordon to the Stray Cats, and outliers like the Cramps. Roy's influence soon spread beyond a small circle of cool oddballs to include everybody from Lou Reed, who sang the praises of Roy's Spartan rockabilly guitar riffs, to Iggy Pop, who emulated Orbison when moaning the occasional ballad in a disaffected baritone, to slacker singer-songwriters like Beck and King Missile's John S. Hall, whose "Loser" and "Wuss" seemed to pick up where Roy's pathetic "Chicken-Hearted" left off.

Roy's sullen presence and charcoal aura would also inspire a micro wave of oddball art, by everyone from Marvel Comics' Stan Lee, who allegedly based Spider-Man's archenemy, supervillain Doctor Octopus, on Orbison's singular image; to Roy's onetime bandmate Alan Mayes, who concocted a comic strip titled *The Adventures of the Big O*, inspired by his travels with Roy; to Orbison's bassist/road manager Terry Widlake, who continues to work on a novella, written in the first person, from Roy's point of view. But the most bizarre of all these artists (aside from the Cramps' Lux Interior, who had an uncanny knack of channeling Roy in panties and heels) has to be Ulrich Haarbürste, who has a kinky obsession with wrapping Orbison up in cling film (better known in America as sandwich wrap). He has actually written a novel about it and maintains a web page, on which he warns unsuspecting viewers that his warped tales are not meant "for those of a nervous disposition or children under the age of twenty-five."

Haarbürste's surreal writing (his tales often feature a sidekick terrapin by the name of Jetta) has inspired additional contributions of fan fiction from a variety of authors who offer twisted fantasies about Roy in short stories and haikus. A common theme that runs through these strange tales centers around Orbison's lack of a coat, which inevitably leads to the author, hoping to protect his hero from the elements, lovingly wrapping him up in cling film to keep him safe and secure wherever he suddenly and mysteriously appears on his never-ending world tour, be it Oslo or Antarctica.

Probed by an interviewer from *Vice* magazine as to whether his obsession was "a sexual thing," the demented Düsseldorfer replied, "I do not know, but it is certainly a beautiful thing. I think we are too eager to reduce everything to sex. It is very, very sensual though."

Thankfully, along with the weirdos, some of his greatest fans were now in the position to pay Roy back for all the beauty and inspiration his music had given them, by awarding him plum gigs in the limelight.

In March 1980, Roy was enlisted to play a series of eight stadium shows as the opening act for the Eagles in San Francisco and L.A., a booster shot that helped kick-start his anemic career.

Orbison claimed to have "a lot of fun," on the brief tour, which exposed his music to a new generation, who unexpectedly found themselves gob-smacked by a pudgy, middle-aged man dressed in black, effortlessly singing emotionally devastating songs that haunted their heads and hearts for weeks to come. For the first time in years, Roy felt optimistic about the future. "Things are moving at a very good pace,"

Orbison proclaimed. "I got this feeling around '54, I got this feeling around '59, and I get this feeling now that what I want to do is going to happen." (Hopeful as he was, Roy would have to wait another five or six years before he was back in the fast lane again.)

"We played more shows in San Diego and L.A. and were invited to a big Hollywood party," Terry Widlake recalled. "Barbara was beside herself. That's when a light seemed to go off in her head. She suddenly realized the potential for a rebirth of Roy's career in America. Not long after that, they moved to California."

Roy's duet with Emmylou Harris was recorded that same year: "That Lovin' You Feelin' Again," produced by her then husband Brian Ahern, would earn Roy his first Grammy, oddly enough as a country artist. A lilting pop ditty, "That Lovin' You Feelin' Again" was one of the better tracks on the soundtrack to *Roadie*, a thoroughly stupid and forgettable film starring Meat Loaf and Art Carney ("Norton" had clearly hit rock bottom in this role as Meat's disapproving father), with cameos by everyone from Roy, to Hank Williams Jr., to Ramblin' Jack Elliott, Debbie Harry, and Alice Cooper. Roy himself returned to the silver screen untriumphantly during a cat fight in some sweaty, smoke-filled Lone Star honky-tonk when Hank Jr. yanked him up onstage to quell the out-of-control crowd with a rousing round of "The Eyes of Texas." It's almost funny.

But in a more lasting tribute, Emmylou, who first became famous for her harmony vocals with the doomed angel of country rock, Gram Parsons, adored Roy to the point that she claimed she could never sell her house after its walls resonated with his voice one night when Orbison sang for a party at her L.A. home.

The following year, Don McLean (whose song "American Pie" forever enshrined contemporaries Buddy Holly, Ritchie Valens, and the Big Bopper) topped the UK charts with his cover of "Crying." While Orbison's original version of the song was a deeply tragic ballad of a broken man, easily reduced to tears of regret over an epic heart-break that continues to haunt him, McLean, in his accompanying video, sat beside a glowing fireplace, gently picking his guitar, the epitome of the '70s soft, sensitive male searching for the perfect love. This dose of "peaceful easy feeling" was enough to send a polite citizen headfirst into a raging punk rock mosh pit.

Perhaps the most unlikely bearer of Orbison's mantle was Van Halen, who reached Number Twelve in 1982 after shredding "Oh, Pretty Woman." If David Lynch's bizarre take on "In Dreams" in *Blue Velvet* was enough to unnerve Roy, Van Halen's twisted video for "Oh, Pretty Woman" was certain to have him flat on his back, on a hundred-dollar-an-hour psychiatrist's couch, staring up at the ceiling through his Ray-Bans, wondering what else his art could possibly inspire.

Combining the best (or worst, depending on your point of view) of California B-movie kings Roger Corman, Russ Meyer, and Ed Wood, the minidrama opens in some desert town, as two midgets (perhaps "little people" would be the more politically correct term here, but let's keep it in the spirit in which the video was made) clad in hot-pink jumpsuits gleefully taunt and recklessly grope a hapless babe whose arms are bound above her head, while she kicks her long, shapely legs wildly in hopes of landing a gold high heel in one of their nasty faces.

Meanwhile, VH front man David Lee Roth—in the guise of the Hunchback of Notre Dame—watches the whole ordeal unfold on television back in his grungy lair. Resembling a demented Michael Caine, Roth alerts his buddies, a sword-wielding samurai warrior, a coconut-eating Tarzan, a squinting Clint Eastwood gunslinger (played by Eddie Van Halen), and a dashing, rouge-cheeked Napoleon aristocrat (David Lee, again, in a double role) who arrives in a shiny white limousine and struts around, undoubtedly certain that he's prettier than the distressed "Pretty Woman" they've all been summoned to rescue.

And, if that (along with Eddie's scorching guitar work) wasn't enough to scramble your brain, the gnarly pair busy torturing the lovely Esmeralda suddenly, inexplicably don full Sioux war bonnets. (Undoubtedly the phone was ringing off the hook with calls from lawyers representing a nation of furious Native Americans.) Yet the big show-down never takes place. The distressed damsel's debauchers instantly step back, defenseless at the sight of the mismatched superposse. An unexpected twist comes in the video's final moments when the "Pretty Woman" is set free and suddenly flings off her wig to reveal her true identity . . . and we discover that *she* is a *he*.

Voilà!

MTV immediately banned the video. Apparently drag queens were neither their nor their sponsors' idea of acceptable entertainment. Yet the whole thing was so far over the top that the Orbison Empire would have been hard-pressed to drum up a serious lawsuit against Van Halen, and anyway, no jury would've voted to convict them if Eddie and David Lee copped an insanity plea. But in the wake of outrageous '70s glam rock queens such as David Bowie as Ziggy Stardust, and Tim Curry as Frank-N-Furter in eternal cult flick fave *The Rocky Horror Picture Show*, one had to wonder what the big deal was all about.

Spending sixty-five weeks at the top of the charts, Van Halen's 1982 album *Diver Down* (which included their take on "Oh, Pretty Woman") sold in the neighborhood of four million copies in the US alone. Pushed by Warner Brothers to cut a cover song with mass appeal, Eddie Van Halen chose to shred Roy's classic rocker. Despite the song's enormous success, Eddie complained to *Guitar Player*'s Jas Obrecht that he'd rather "bomb with one of my own songs than [have] a hit with someone else's."

BULGARIAN HOLIDAY

S uddenly Roy Orbison began showing up when and wherever you least expected him. No one would have guessed he'd make an appearance on the hip late-night comedy show *SCTV* on July 17, 1981, playing himself on "Mel's Rock Pile 20th Anniversary Special."

"One of the things I wish people knew about Roy was how funny he could be," Bobby Goldsboro pointed out. "He rarely spoke onstage and didn't do too many interviews, but he was hilarious! We would do off-beat impressions and break each other up. We used to laugh constantly."

George Harrison later revealed that his half brother "Lefty Wilbury," as Roy became known, not only had a delightfully dry sense of humor, but he'd memorized most of Monty Python's absurd routines. George adored the brilliant British comedy troupe to the point that he mort-gaged his palatial estate, Friar Park, in order to produce their biblical farce, *Life of Brian*. Harrison's love and respect for Roy's voice and classic early songs, coupled with his and Roy's shared passion for Monty Python's surreal humor, led the former Beatle to ask Orbison to join the Traveling Wilburys.

The *SCTV* skit, a farce on PBS pledge weeks, was hosted by the Brillo-haired Mel, played by Eugene Levy as an impossible nerd, com-plete with horn-rimmed glasses and a polyester suit. Flummoxed, standing beside his hero, Mel faints repeatedly while his groovy crowd, which includes Rick Moranis and Dave Thomas done up in bad plaid jackets, enthusiastically dances to yet another airtight rendition of "Oh, Pretty Woman." Roy, the straight man's straight man, valiantly endures Levy's goofball ribbing as Mel, after managing to pull himself together, asks if he lifted the idea to wear sunglasses from the Blues Brothers (undoubtedly visions of Belushi came bounding back into Orbison's brain)—and why he never made a killing in the pork sausage business like Jimmy Dean. Orbison's second song, "Working for the Man" was the real treat of the show, smooth and tight as the silver blousy shirts and black vests worn by his backup band.

Orbison was back in America's living rooms again, with a guest appearance on the *Dukes of Hazzard*, serenading the buxom Daisy Duke with "Oh, Pretty Woman" in March 1981. Dressed in black, Roy lightly flicked the strings of his Ovation guitar as he loosely lip-synched along to his smash hit for the umpteenth time, while the locals cavorted and howled. Orbison looked remarkably human in contrast to the carefully coiffed Hollywood hillbillies who fawned over him, who looked like they'd been sculpted out of butter and stashed in the refrigerator for safekeeping. Daisy turns her down eyes and feigns a full-blooded blush as Roy sings the line "lovely as can be" (punctuated by another round of hellacious rebel yells). With her cutoff shorts, tight blouse, and cascading lion's mane of hair, Daisy (a knockoff of Daisy Mae Scragg from Al Capp's *Li'l Abner* comic strip) sits beside Roy atop a bar, coyly shimmying her shoulders and slapping her suntanned thighs along to the rhythm, while Sheriff Rosco Coltrane and the stogie-chomping Boss Hogg prove true every cliché about middle-aged white men trying to boogie. Orbison gives Daisy his famous throaty growl and she melts instantly, throwing her arms around him. As the song ends, Roy is suddenly besieged by the citizens in Hazzard, who all want a piece of him, from Daisy, who lands a big wet one on his thin, grinning lips; to Bo and Luke, the show's hillbilly hot-rod heroes, who want to buy him a brew; to the sheriff, who hands him a trumped-up ticket, which Boss Hogg then tears up, only to hand him another. Orbison once more tepidly delivers his lines. Apparently, he had plenty of reasons to get out of Hazzard as fast as possible.

The People's Republic of Bulgaria, the USSR's closest ally in the Eastern Bloc, seemed an unlikely place to find a mad throng of devoted Roy Orbison fans, but longtime ruling autocrat Todor Zhivkov and his notoriously liberal daughter, Lyudmila, in particular, had a taste for Western culture despite the nationalistic atmosphere that permeated their country. With the "Bulgarian Thaw" of the late 1950s, outlawed books, music, and art briefly saw the light of day before another wave of thickheaded ideology once more dampened the dance.

Ultimately, Roy's old pals the Beatles had done more in their giddy, cheerful way to liberate the repressive atmosphere suffocating Russia than all the years of political bravura and carefully measured peace talks. It was the great forbidden decadent desires that the West had to offer—Detroit dream cars with big fins, air conditioners, and radios that blasted the ragged anthems of liberty; rock 'n' roll; and Hollywood films—that would ultimately punch a hole through the Iron Curtain.

Bulgaria was the first Communist country to do business with Coca-Cola, which in 1965 began to bottle and sell their sugar-charged swill with a Cyrillic label. Bulgaria would eventually enjoy a more permissive atmosphere, inspired in part by their neighbors in Czechoslovakia, who first welcomed Beat poet Allen Ginsberg as a cultural ambassador before suddenly deporting him in 1967. Social satirist/guitar god Frank Zappa would also be celebrated in Prague by playwright/president Vaclav Havel in 1990.

With his performing career having reached a stalemate in America, Roy leapt at the chance, strange as it might have been, to perform with a full symphony orchestra in Sofia, Bulgaria, in June 1982. He was the first American pop star to be invited by the Bulgarian government to headline the Golden Orpheus Festival. Orbison played a sixty-minute set (which was later televised) to a crowd comprised of VIPs and visiting dignitaries from twenty foreign countries.

Conductor Tim Goodwin worked frantically right up to showtime, reworking Anita Kerr's arrangements of Roy's tunes into a full-blown orchestral extravaganza. Orbison began the set, as usual, with "Crying."

"The strings were playing and the band had built up, and sure enough, the hair on the back of my neck just all started standing up," Goodwin recalled, stunned by the power of Roy's voice. "It was an incredible physical sensation."

Unfortunately, Orbison didn't get to see too much of the city beyond the stage and his hotel room as he was mobbed by a horde of fans on the streets of Sofia. No one, least of all Roy, expected this level of adulation. But these were culturally famished people, for whom the lyrics of "Running Scared" held a more poignant meaning than they did for his Western fans. Somehow Orbison spoke their language. The average oppressed Bulgarian could relate to him, seeing himself in a paranoid dramatic ballad that celebrated the triumph of the underdog.

Goodwin described an atmosphere of giddy liberation spreading through the crowd who, he recalled, were so overjoyed they began "throwing babies in the air." And although the audience spoke very little or no English, they somehow "sang along" to their favorite Orbison songs, having memorized his lyrics phonetically.

Roy's brief visit apparently had an enormous impact on whatever pop music industry existed in Bulgaria at the time. Mariana Traycheva and Todor Traychev, whose music was considered "dangerously Western" by the socialist government, would later emigrate to America, where they would be free to sing their strange glitzy brand of country music without Communist consternation. Not surprisingly Traychev sang dressed in black with his eyes obscured behind a pair of aviator shades. After his high, lonesome Bulgarian pine failed to conquer Nashville, Todor returned to Sofia in 1994, not to pursue his music career but as a tripe king, importing his countrymen's favorite delicacy from "the decadent West."

Back home again, Roy appeared on *Austin City Limits* on August 5, 1982, playing another solid but predictable set of hits with the only surprise being a prayerlike reading of "Hound Dog Man," in honor of his "old friend" Elvis.

Later that month Roy would put "Oh, Pretty Woman" out on the street for a jeans commercial, recording a thirty-second version of his signature song, substituting the word *Sasson* for *pretty*. As a perky blonde in skintight dungarees goes strutting by, she gets the eye from every guy in town, from the testosterone-charged high school football team on a yellow bus to an old man in a hat playing checkers. The sight of her literally knocks over a bow-tied, Beatle-coiffed mailman. Inevitably, she goes sashaying past Roy's long black limo, where he sits peering out the window, holding his guitar. "Mercy!" he says, taken aback. It works every time, like Johnny Cash introducing himself with that cocky grin. But Cash never "Walked the Line" for Hush Puppies.

The odyssey of Claudette's anthem has taken more than a few curious turns over the years, from Bill Dees' spontaneous utterance of "Pretty women don't need any money," to 2 Live Crew's rap parody of Roy's trademark song in 1989. The Miami hip-hoppers' take on "Pretty Woman" seemed too goofy at first to actually offend anybody. But after the track exploded, selling in the neighborhood of a quarter of a million copies, Acuff-Rose soon came knocking.

Built off Orbison's trademark riff, the lyric—delivered in a knuckle-headed chant over a fat drumbeat and accented by rhythmic record scratching—morphs from "pretty woman" to a "big hairy woman" who "looks like [the Addams Family's] Cousin Itt" to a "bald-headed woman" in the final verse. The case went all the way to the Supreme Court, who, in March 1992, upheld 2 Live Crew's right to have their way with Orbison's dream girl.

No matter, the "Pretty Woman," bruised but proud, picked herself up and walked on, making her next appearance on late-night infomercials with Barbara Orbison, who, in a thick German accent, hawked her new perfume by the same name.

Between Van Halen's appropriation of the tune and his endless TV guest appearances lip-synching the played-to-death oldie, Roy inevitably seemed, at least to a younger generation, not much more than a one-hit wonder—he was just the "'Pretty Woman' guy," who apparently never recorded another song in his life. Add to that a movie released in 1990 by the same name, starring Julia Roberts in the role of Vivian, a leather-booted Hollywood hooker and Richard Gere as a cutthroat yuppie businessman, two physically radiant people who "both screw people for money."

Unlike the song's protagonist, Gere's character, Edward, works from a position of power—he's suave, plays chess, and has a chauffeur. The movie is basically a '90s version of *My Fair Lady*: Edward takes Vivian out to dinner and the opera and buys her everything she could possibly desire, all the while believing that one day soon those aggravating "ain'ts" will miraculously vanish from her vernacular and she'll blossom into the respectable woman that he knows dwells deep inside.

While movies usually allow for a greater plot development than a two-and-a half-minute song does, *Pretty Woman* ends the same way as Orbison's most popular tune. When all hope seems lost, she changes her mind at the last minute and comes walking back to the guy, charmed and intrigued, whether the hero is a dashing dude like Richard Gere or the lonely, nearsighted Roy Orbison, standing on a street corner, recklessly eyeballing every girl in sight.

TWELVE

CALIFORNIA BLUE

I t happened like clockwork. Once Roy was out of the woods with his health problems, it was Barbara's turn. She'd been suffering for quite some time from the debilitating effects of agoraphobia (an irrational and overwhelming fear of going out in public). Somebody had to deal with the details of their everyday lives—get the kids off to school and look after her. Roy took this latest setback in stride, seeing it as a second chance to make up for his shortcomings as an absentee father with his first family. After three dismal albums in a row and an exhausting life on the road, it seemed like the smartest career move he could make at this point was to drop the ball and stay home. Thanks to Van Halen's cover of "Oh, Pretty Woman," Orbison now had a sizeable cash cushion that allowed him to pass up the degrading steady stream of gigs at car shows and discotheques.

Throughout his "lost years" Roy maintained a fierce conviction regarding his place in the rock 'n' roll pantheon. Author Ellis Amburn believed Orbison's pride caused him to ultimately "[blind] himself to the truth" about his career. Although constantly described by his peers and fans as "gentle," and "humble," Roy was unable to let go of his hard-won fame, which he'd doggedly worked to preserve at the cost of his health and eventually his life.

Since the failed promise of *Regeneration*, Roy was routinely confronted by the press, wondering when his "glory days" would return. In his typically reserved manner, Orbison always did his best to evade reporters' comments and questions on the subject of a comeback. As far as he was concerned, he'd "arrived" years ago, long before many of those pesky journalists were born, and although he'd been cast into the fickle abyss of disposable pop stars following the meteoric success of "Oh, Pretty Woman," Roy would struggle over the next twenty years to maintain his stature as one of the original founding fathers of rock 'n' roll, even if it meant playing at car shows or shilling "the Voice" for blue jean commercials.

Yet according to Barbara, Roy was hardly sitting around wondering what to do with himself during his "forgotten years." "He designed houses, he collected cars, he bought model airplanes. He was a student of history. He loved to travel. His world was very complete despite his not being a musician. You could have been on an overseas flight between New York and London for eight hours sitting next to him, and he would have talked to you about writing, about his kids, your kids, politics, football. . . . He would never have said, 'I'm a singer-songwriter.'"

With Roy at home, taking good care of her, Barbara quickly regained her health and confidence, and with the Van Halen money rolling in, she was soon back in fighting form. Barbara would instigate a lawsuit against Wesley Rose in 1982, pushing Roy to take a stand against his old friend and manager to collect back royalties owed him from Acuff-Rose.

"Everybody was afraid of her," Bill Dees said. "She was always suing somebody. They tried to get me involved in that lawsuit with Wes, but I'd gone over to the man's house, played Ping-Pong, and swam in his pool. I wasn't going to sue him!"

"Wesley had a big heart and was an honest man," Bob Moore said on his friend's behalf. "He was a fun guy, a kind guy who gave a lot of struggling musicians a break and a room to write in his building. I never heard from one writer over the years who said they were ever cheated by him."

So what was the $50 million lawsuit all about? It seemed deeply out of character with Roy's mild-mannered personality.

"Roy knew that Wes was cheating him and he finally took him to court," Fred Foster put it simply. (Acuff-Rose eventually returned the favor, posthumously suing the Orbison estate for more than a million dollars plus royalties when Roy failed to deliver ten contracted songs for which he'd been paid $70,000 in advance.)

"Roy was a different person by the time Barbara came along," Bob Moore pointed out. "Not a bad person, but different after all the tragedy and everything he'd been through."

British writer Barney Hoskyns described Barbara Orbison as "a tireless and astute businesswoman" and found himself humbled by the disc-bedecked walls of the four-story Nashville offices of Still Working Music, which remain a virtual shrine to her husband to this day.

Barbara would take Tammy Wynette's sentiment "Stand by Your Man" to a whole new level, avenging anyone who ever wronged her husband, including the man he'd named one of his sons after—Wesley Rose. The deal Rose had cut for Roy with MGM was a recipe for disaster. No one could deliver three albums a year while maintaining a hectic international touring schedule, not even prolific songwriters like Dylan or the Beatles, whose crazed conveyor belt of fame had them churning out two LPs a year along with a fistful of singles, an annual Christmas message, two feature-length films, and whatever videos had to be shot to accompany their latest hit. Something had to give. Sadly, it was the level of artistry he'd achieved at Monument Records.

"The albums were all made very hurriedly, partly due to the fact that Roy was on the lazy side," Terry Widlake explained. "The days would go ticking by. He always seemed to be in breach of contract."

Roy Orbison was never actually in the "Class of '55." He was a substitute. Orbison and the Teen Kings didn't arrive in Memphis until the following spring, when they recorded "Ooby Dooby" at Sun Studio in March 1956. As far as Roy was concerned the project's clever title was a misnomer.

But on September 19, 1985, there he was, back in Memphis, working on a putative tribute to Sun Records called *Class of '55*, along with his old labelmates Johnny Cash, Jerry Lee Lewis, and Carl Perkins. At that point, the King was either eight years dead or, according to the more imaginative supermarket tabloids of the day, driving a Mister Softee truck around the Upper Peninsula of Michigan, giving free ice cream away to all the kids. Whatever you chose to believe, Roy had been brought in once more to fill Elvis' 11Ds.

At the helm the of the project was producer/songwriter Chips Moman, who'd recently completed an album with the Highwaymen, an all-star posse comprised of Johnny Cash, Willie Nelson, Kris Kristofferson, and Waylon Jennings.

Orbison's contribution to the album was nominal at best. He didn't play guitar on a single track, and of the album's ten songs, he took the lead vocal only once, on his own "Coming Home" (cowritten with Will Jennings and J. D. Souther), which opened the album's flip side.

Trading verses with Cash, Perkins, and Lewis over the big, bowlegged beat of Waylon Jenning's "Waymore's Blues," Roy was predictably given the song's most maudlin lyric: "If you wanna get to heaven you got to d-i-e." Although it's unclear what he contributed to the song, Orbison was also given an equal share of the writing credits on "We Remember the King," Cash's reverential homage to Elvis.

Among the album's many guest stars were June Carter Cash, Rockpile's guitarist Dave Edmunds, Marty Stuart, and Rick Nelson, (his last recording session and the only record for which he received a Grammy). John Fogerty, Creedence Clearwater Revival's raspy-throated, guitar-twangin' front man (perhaps the truest disciple of the Sun style, and who's been known to rock a pretty mean "Ooby Dooby") led the record's standout track, "Big Train (from Memphis)." But Orbison was merely another passenger on that eight-minute pile-driving express.

Filmed by Dick Clark's crew, the sessions portrayed Roy, the quintessential loner, as happy to be one of the guys. There was plenty of joshin' around the microphone, with Jerry Lee freely ad-libbing lyrics, but according to Perkins' autobiography, Orbison "seemed frightfully introverted." In truth, Roy was routinely late each day and only hung around the studio if he was needed, preferring the solitude of his tour bus to the company of his old buddies.

Orbison's attitude is understandable considering that Perkins later confessed there were more than a couple of occasions when he "could've killed Jerry Lee just as easy as [he] could have walked by him." Lewis, as far as Carl was concerned was "wilder than a guinea hen," constantly trying to upstage his fellow bandmates. Cash, Perkins, and Orbison had all moved on with their lives since their early days at Sun. While enjoying their tenure as the elder statesmen of rock 'n' roll, they all walked the straight and narrow line of sobriety, whether thanks to their iron-willed women or the firm hand of the Jewish carpenter. But the Killer never forsook the rock 'n' roll lifestyle, not for a goddamn minute. The others could only collectively shake their heads and roll their eyes during a press conference at the Peabody Hotel as Jerry Lee spilled his stash of pills all over the floor in front of a reporter from *Rolling Stone*.

Unlike Cash, who was known as a man's man, Roy was never truly one of the boys, whereas Jerry Lee was nearly feral, like one of Kerouac's mad ones, "who are mad to live, mad to be saved, desirous of everything at the same time, the ones who never yawn." Orbison was the guy who, try as he might, never fit in. While his older brother Grady Lee, the town rowdy, worked out his aggression on the gridiron as the star guard of the Wink Wildcats, Roy claimed he was "totally anonymous, even at home."

"Roy was not a happy camper. He seemed to have a lot of weight on his shoulders," New York "radio personality" (he detests the term DJ) "Cousin" Brucie Morrow said. Morrow recalled meeting Orbison in the mid-'80s at an all-star rock 'n' roll revival show he emceed in Keene, New Hampshire, that included Chuck Berry, James Brown, Carl Perkins, and Johnny Rivers. "The bus pulled up to the fairgrounds, he walked out, looked at us, and just turned around and got back on the bus again. It was clear that he didn't want to be involved socially. He was a private guy, but the second he got onstage he was warm and welcoming. Offstage I felt like I was looking at a different person."

Roy Orbison innately understood the difference between loneliness and solitude. He sought solitude, even relished it. It's where he found clarity, whether writing, reading, or building model airplanes. Yet he found his image as the eternal loner ironic. Between his family, friends, and fans Orbison's life was filled with more people than he had time for. "I don't think I've been more lonely than anyone else" he once said in response to a question about "Only the Lonely."

Three days later, on September 22, Orbison performed at the first Farm Aid benefit in Champaign, Illinois. Organized by Willie Nelson, Neil Young, and John Mellencamp, the concert was initially sparked by a comment Dylan made during his notoriously ragged Live Aid set—while Bob (backed by a pair of stoned Stones) was happy to loan his clout to the world hunger crisis, he thought it would be "great if we did something for our own farmers right here in America." And so now here they were.

The wildly diverse roster, which included everyone from John Denver to Loretta Lynn to Lou Reed, drew a crowd of 80,000 and raised $7 million. Although Orbison was hardly a champion of grassroots politics, the sentiment behind this cause had been planted years ago, back in his childhood, when he heard about his parents' desperate days, when they first migrated from Oklahoma to Texas in search of work.

That October Roy and Barbara and the boys moved to Malibu. Relocating to California "lifted all of those old feelings about Hendersonville," Barbara told *Mojo* magazine. "The change," she claimed, "was really good to [Roy] emotionally. It reminded him of Texas, those cold mornings and cold nights. He used the fireplace, he loved the sunsets. He loved driving a convertible every day. I don't think anybody in Hendersonville ever saw Roy, whereas in Malibu he went everywhere—to the grocery, to have breakfast, to the beach."

According to Terry Widlake, "it had always been Barbara's big dream to live at Malibu Beach"—not just for its natural beauty, but to mix with Hollywood's elite social strata.

It wasn't long before the Orbisons, according to Malcolm Boyes, the smarmy guest host of *Lifestyles of the Rich and Famous*, "moved right out of the shadows and into the spotlight." With "Oh, Pretty Woman" pumping in the background, we are privy to tag along with Boyes on his special assignment to find out how Roy, the "multimillionaire survivor," spends his money.

"The Orbisons are no country bumpkins," Boyes crowed. "All those decades of gold discs have allowed them to decorate their new home in priceless antiques." The same old stories linked Roy's legend to those of Elvis and the Fab Four. We are treated to a moment of family frolic, with Roy, Barbara, and the kids playing catch around the pool while the ghosts of Claudette and Roy's two dead sons are dredged up once more. Meanwhile, back in Nashville, nearly a continent away, Roy's mother, Nadine, and his abandoned son, Wesley, watched his new family happily whack a tennis ball back and forth in the California sunshine. *Lifestyles* shows Orbison ("a fine figure of a man," as Mick Jagger once quipped) pumping weights (with the help of his trainer). Even his workout suit is black. "And now Roy is looking forward to rocking into a ripe old age," Malcolm Boyes predicted.

Having promised "Wild Hearts Run Out of Time," (a song he'd cowritten with Roy) to director Nicolas Roeg for his new film *Insignificance*, Will Jennings suddenly found himself in a pickle. Jennings had booked two sessions, one to track Roy and the band, and another to mix and master it. On the third day he planned to fly to London and deliver the goods to Roeg. But Roy, who was under the weather with a sore throat, unexpectedly called Jennings and told him to go ahead and record the song and he'd be in the next day to lay down his vocal. Not having actually heard Roy sing the song yet, Will was becoming a nervous wreck, worried if Orbison would even show up. Relieved when Roy finally appeared at the studio, Jennings began to freak out over what he later described as the "noise coming out" from the vocal booth. The unnerving caterwauling turned out to be Roy, finding his way into the song, experimenting with the melody, bending and molding it to make it his own. It was his method, no matter how strange it may have sounded. Will looked at his coproducer, David Briggs, and wondered, "What if he can't sing anymore?" But in short order "the Voice" "internalized the song," as Jennings described Roy's quirky process, in shaping another emotionally wrenching performance. His fears quelled and his faith restored in the legend, Will finished "Wild Hearts Run Out of Time" and delivered it to Roeg on schedule.

Sneaking into a local movie theater in Malibu to watch *Blue Velvet*, Roy claimed he was "aghast, truly shocked" as a ghostly Dean Stockwell, in a frilly shirt and garish paisley smoking jacket, dangles a cigarette holder while lip-synching "In Dreams." The unnerving scene barely lasts a minute and a half before Dennis Hopper's psycho hooligan Frank Booth, overcome by a myriad of conflicting emotions evoked by the song, ejects the record, bringing Stockwell's strange charade to a sudden end. It wasn't until he saw the film a second time, years later, that Roy could appreciate Lynch's bizarre and innovative use of his "candy-colored clown." Perplexed as he was, Orbison had to admit he admired the film's "otherworldly quality."

With "In Dreams" haunting the psyche of movie fans around the globe, Roy signed with Virgin Records in 1987, ending an eight-year exile without a contract. T Bone Burnett was brought on to produce *In Dreams: The Greatest Hits*, which, according to Roy, was recorded "concert style, with no overdubs" at L.A.'s Oceanways Studio. The session auspiciously fell on April 23, Roy's his fifty-first birthday. But Roy needed another *Super, Very Best of, Golden, Greatest, All Time, Essential Hits* collection in his discography like he needed another carton of cigarettes.

Beyond the initial four Monument releases, Orbison's career was plagued by a serious lack of continuity from record to record that was enough to put off the most devoted fan. Yet this double-album redux actually made sense, as the Fred Foster–produced sessions had long been out of print. But as decent as the new versions of his old classics were, they couldn't stand up to the originals.

To promote his new record, Roy played for a VIP invitation-only guest audience in Nashville—incredibly, the first time he ever performed there. It's hard to fathom how a legend of Roy Orbison's caliber never performed in Music City—let alone Chicago, until 1979, and finally in Los Angeles, in the '80s—but there are more than a few holes in the logic of his career that can't be explained.

As his brand of mood and brood was now considered potential magic for any new Hollywood soundtrack, Roy recorded the maudlin

"Life Fades Away" to accompany Robert Downey Jr.'s overdose scene in *Less Than Zero*. Although a fine song, like Downey's character it ultimately stiffed, doing little for Roy's career other than providing a nice paycheck.

Nonplussed by John Belushi's cutting satire of him a few years earlier, Roy finally appeared on *Saturday Night Live* on May 23, 1987, performing three songs ("Crying," "Oh, Pretty Woman," and "In Dreams") instead of the usual two, at the request of the show's producer, Lorne Michaels. Guest host Dennis Hopper introduced Roy, whose every note and hair was predictably in place.

Orbison was back on the road again that August for three weeks, zig-zagging across the country with his band, playing dates from California to New York, making a quick jog around New England, and then heading back to the West Coast, to Eugene, Oregon.

On September 30, Barbara organized a tribute to Roy at the Cocoanut Grove in L.A.'s historic Ambassador Hotel. The Grove was no arbitrary choice: The joint had serious history. Since the '20s it had been a favorite haunt of Hollywood legends, from Chaplin and Valentino to Dietrich, Hepburn, Tracy, and Grant. The club had been a regular gig for Sinatra, Garland, and Liberace, as well as such legendary jazz figures as Dizzy Gillespie, Benny Goodman, and Nat King Cole. But in the first week of June 1968, the decades-long party suddenly came to a tragic end when Bobby Kennedy was gunned down in the kitchen after celebrating his victory in the California primary.

"I was fascinated with the place," singer Syd Straw recalled. "I lived just around the corner from the Ambassador. It was a perfect room for that concert, very posh, with all those cool people. It was a gorgeous show, but that was the last exciting moment for the hotel." (After years of decline, the Ambassador was finally razed in 2005.)

A Black and White Night, as the show was dubbed for its high-contrast, cool noir style, was directed by Tony Mitchell as a television special for Cinemax. Roy fronted Elvis' legendary TCB (Taking Care of Business) band, which featured legendary guitar-slinger James Burton, looking slick in a white dinner jacket, picking his trademark paisley Telecaster, along with pianist Glen D. Hardin, Jerry Scheff on acoustic bass, and drummer Ronnie Tutt.

A stellar cast of guest stars had been rounded up by producer/musical director T Bone Burnett to back up Roy, including Bruce Springsteen, Elvis Costello, and Tom Waits.

As Roy recalled, "Nobody brought attitude problems with them." In lieu of artistic temperaments, Orbison found an ebullient atmosphere of camaraderie and "real professionalism." Costello concurred, claiming everyone was "very down-to-earth." k.d. lang, who sang backup vocals along with Bonnie Raitt, Jennifer Warnes, J. D. Souther, and Jackson Browne, remarked that "every ounce of ego was checked at the door. It was definitely a show of respect and love for Roy."

Respect quickly turned to awe for many of the performers who played with Orbison that night. "Roy was one of the sweetest, most incredibly gracious legends I've ever met," gushed the redheaded blues goddess Bonnie Raitt. "There was simply no voice like his, and the beauty and soul that imbues every song and performance will stand among the greatest always. It was a thrill and an honor to be able to perform with him and get to know him a bit during the filming of the historic *Black and White Night* show."

Elvis Costello was surprised how "Roy sang very, very quietly throughout the rehearsals. He had obviously learned to save his voice." Never having heard Orbison sing live before, Costello began to wonder if Roy "had the power that the records suggested. I couldn't make out if he was holding back or that's just the way he sang. It wasn't until we got on the set until he really let fly." In the heat of the moment, Elvis found Roy's full-bore operatic attack "really frightening."

"I had a couple of nerve-racking moments," Costello later confessed, referring to the solo acoustic guitar introduction he played on "Running Scared." Although everybody involved was familiar with Orbison's classic songs, they soon realized the compositions were full of what Elton John's lyricist Bernie Taupin deemed "radical left turns"—unexpected chord structures and odd meters. Basic song charts had been passed around for the guest artists to follow. Elvis recalled the humbling experience of sitting with Springsteen in the cramped dressing room before the show, "frantically trying to learn these songs.

"You couldn't jam on Roy's songs; you have to know them. They're very complex. Therefore it became very necessary that there be a band that could play them," Costello pointed out. Nonetheless, Elvis relished his "groovy job" as the auxiliary member of the TCB band, playing some rhythm guitar, adding a dash of organ, and wailing a bit of "'Love Me Do'–type harmonica" on "Down the Line."

Orbison's live show varied little over the years. "The Voice" was always dependable, the set list all but carved in granite, and although he had good solid road bands, the TCB all-stars managed to breathe new life into the old warhorses on that September evening. It seemed as if all the decades of touring had been one long dress rehearsal leading up to this brief moment in time.

The show's emcee, T Bone Burnett, had previously sparked Dylan's born-again phase during the Rolling Thunder tour in 1976, and produced Elvis Costello's roots-rock milestone *King of America*, pairing the younger Elvis with Presley's TCB band and members of Los Lobos.

"Is everybody loose?" Burnett goaded the crowd. "I love Roy Orbison. I'm very respectful of the man, but you don't need to be *too* respectful."

"It was a very curated crowd," Syd Straw laughed, referring to the hand-picked VIP audience of actors, musicians, and industry types that included Leonard Cohen, Billy Idol, Sandra Bernhard, Dennis Quaid, Harry Dean Stanton, Kris Kristofferson, and Steve Jones of the Sex Pistols. Elvis Costello described the scene as "a slightly spoiled Los Angeles business crowd" who "got a little bit touchy toward the end," when the show began to run over four hours. Thankfully, very few left, out of respect for Roy.

Standing center stage, Orbison, as usual, barely moved a muscle. He looked like a benevolent vampire in a black buckskin jacket, with a Maltese cross dangling at his throat, his pale face glowing in the harsh white spotlight as he gently strummed his black Gibson 335.

The audience spontaneously erupted in applause as his effortless falsetto scaled the dizzying heights of passion in "Only the Lonely." James Burton's guitar gently wept to the lazy sway of "Blue Bayou" as the backup vocals soothed the crowd like a cool breeze on a humid summer day. Jerry Scheff's upright bass and Ronnie Tutt's fat snare laid down a steady-rockin' groove on "Dream Baby," as Bonnie Raitt, Jennifer Warnes, and k.d. lang cooed, "How long must I dream?"

Punctuating the song with his snarling Telecaster, Springsteen edged toward center stage to share the mic with Roy. Suddenly, Bruce seized the moment, cueing the band to hit it once more, amping the dynamic of the song's ending.

"I think [Springsteen] was really anxious that he didn't upstage Roy by accident. He was very respectful." Elvis Costello pointed out that Bruce, in the wake of the enormous success of "Born in the USA" carried "the burden of people expecting him to be the big rock star of the time."

Raul Malo, front man of the Mavericks, marveled at how Roy "did everything wrong [health-wise]. Before he'd go onstage he'd have a Pepsi and a cigarette, which goes against everything that we know nowadays you should do as a singer."

"Roy was a vocal superhero," Syd Straw exclaimed. "He had this otherworldliness. He was an unearthly singer that bounced it back up to the sky from where it came. I loved the harmony singers, but I was just chompin' at the bit to get up there and sing with him," Syd confessed.

A great shaper of air in her own right, Straw had been an early choice to harmonize on the duet version of "Crying" with Roy. "I had just been signed to Virgin Records at the time [her debut, *Surprise*, was released in 1989]. They took me to some studio in a groovy shack in the Hollywood hills to do this demo. I sang along with [a tape of] Roy, which was a lot of fun, and I was extremely excited, but the powers that be passed on it. They said I was 'too country.'"

No stranger to the song, Syd had sung "Crying" since the late '70s, when she worked with MTV diva Pat Benatar, who eventually cut her own version years later, in 1991. "I was wistfully envious of the whole situation," Syd admitted, referring to the record company's decision to go with k.d. lang. "I guess my consolation prize was being invited to the *Black and White Night*."

Initially, lang had her doubts about singing "Crying," feeling it wouldn't work well as a duet and might stand better as a solo performance or with "either Roy singing or me singing. But then I started to wake up and go, 'It's Roy Orbison that you'll be singing with, you goon.'"

The duet was cut in Boston with Don and David Was producing, and k. d. recalled recording the song with Roy as "an overwhelming experience." Sharing the same microphone, their faces momentarily brushed against each other. "His cheeks were so, so soft, and yet his body was providing this enormous sound," lang marveled. "He may look meek, [but] he used his body to get that projection."

The new arrangement of the song revealed a Tex-Mex influence with Steve Gibson's nylon-string guitar flourishes adding a Latin flavor while Terry McMillan's prairie harmonica wailed, as Orbison's and lang's voices intertwined like flower vines, ascending to the song's climax.

"Everything I did with Roy brought baskets of horseshoes," lang later said. "He was like a Midas to my career."

"Grateful" as Orbison said he was to have "captured this moment on film," *A Black and White Night* nearly met with disaster when a 6.1 earthquake hit the following morning in Whittier, just south of L.A., killing six people and injuring another hundred. The tapes went missing, until they were eventually discovered under a fallen chandelier.

Two weeks after the filming of his television special, Roy was once again reunited with his old pal Carl Perkins, when they performed together at the Valley Forge Music Fair on October 15. It seemed like the time had come to reconnect with some of the people in his past, and maybe mend an old fence or two. He even called Joe Melson to see if any creative spark still existed between them. Melson, whose personal ambition and mixed emotions over his partner's success had led to their falling out, had previously given up on the idea of ever writing with Roy again, claiming that crafting songs specifically for Orbison's voice and persona "doesn't work." "It takes forever and is no good anyway," he complained to *Melody Maker* in 1977. While they managed to put aside whatever grievances stood between them long enough to take another shot at cowriting, nothing they came up with appeared on any of Roy's subsequent albums.

THIRTEEN

IN BOB'S GARAGE

It seemed like kismet, a bit of spontaneous magic that Nelson Wilbury (a.k.a. George Harrison) would later attribute to the effects of a full moon. The story of how Harrison, Bob Dylan, Tom Petty, Jeff Lynne, and Roy Orbison converged to form the Traveling Wilburys has reached mythical proportions with each retelling over the years. But it's ultimately about how a bunch of (famous) friends got together to play some good music without making grandiose plans or being pressured by their respective record companies to concoct a commercial hit.

Unlike the ill-fated Blind Faith, the Wilburys was no superhype supergroup. Sure, everybody involved had stellar credentials and plenty of platinum records, as well as the lawsuits and divorces that always seem to go hand in hand with tremendous success. But by this point they were all a bit older, wiser, and gentler, and whatever issues of status or artistic differences might have existed between them were now only so much water under the bridge. But as Dylan once sang in "Sweetheart Like You," "You have to be an important person to be in here, honey."

In the spring of 1988, ex-ELO front man Jeff Lynne was producing George Harrison's latest album, *Cloud Nine*, when he got a call from Roy Orbison inviting him over to his house in Malibu to kick around a couple ideas for his first studio album in over a decade. In the meantime, Harrison, needing one more track for the B-side for his new single "This Is Love," was on his way to a songwriting session with Lynne, when he stopped by Tom Petty's place to pick up a loaner guitar and asked him to come along. When they arrived, much to their surprise, they found Roy Orbison waiting for them. Sitting around in circle, strumming guitars, everybody tossed a couple of scraps into the sonic stew, and George soon left with a hook or two that might do the trick.

Knowing it would be a few days before he could book a studio in L.A., Harrison called his old pal Bob Dylan, who had a reel-to-reel and a couple microphones set up in his Santa Monica garage.

The next day the four musicians converged at Dylan's house to finish up and record their half-written song. While Bob prepared a barbecue for his friends, Harrison suddenly found the much-needed chorus to his new tune stenciled on a cardboard box lying about in Bob's garage.

A tender but wary look back at the ex-Beatle's life and career, "Handle with Care" would become the perfect vehicle for all five musicians despite their distinctly different styles.

As Harrison later told the press, "Everybody was there and I thought, I'm not gonna just sing it myself, I've got Roy Orbison standing there. And then as it progressed, I started doing the vocals and I just thought I might as well push it a bit and get Tom and Bob to sing the bridge."

Embroidering the song with his weeping slide guitar, Harrison sang the verses while Dylan and Petty jumped in with their ramshackle harmonies until Orbison's voice comes cutting through on "the lonely bit" that Jeff and George wrote specifically for him. "I'm so tired of being lonely . . ." Roy moaned like a disembodied ghost.

For the first time in years, if ever, Orbison, surrounded by this rogues' gallery of superstars, finally felt free enough to confess to the world he was sick of being typecast as "lonely" and that, as the lyrics told, he had "some love to give" beyond singing the same old hits the same old way night after night.

Roy's career had run up against that brick wall where his early hits had become a curse as much as they'd been a blessing. No matter how brilliant Brian Wilson's latest pop masterpiece might be, the crowds always came to hear "Barbara Ann" and "Help Me Rhonda." Roy found himself in a similar jail of his fans' making.

Years later, Barbara Orbison told Barney Hoskyns: "He would have said, 'I'm sitting in front of you here, you can see I have a suntan, I'm skinny, I have dogs running around, kids, I have a great-looking wife. And yet the world has given me this place in rock 'n' roll of the sad, lonely, pale, pudgy man.' Roy was so sick and tired of holding that place." But according to Terry Widlake, "Roy was fine with that. He was just happy that people still cared for his music."

In a rare glimmer of record company wisdom and insight, the boys in Warner Brothers' A&R department deemed "Handle with Care" "too good" to be the flip side of George's new single. In a moment of inspiration, Harrison thought the only thing to do was to form a band, knock off a few more songs, and make an album. Petty and Lynne loved the idea. Dylan was in if everybody else was. That left Roy.

Having driven down to Anaheim to catch Orbison's show, Petty, Lynne, and Harrison barged into his dressing room like a pack of awestruck fans and "begged" Roy to join the band. From there, all the pieces quickly began to fall into place. Dave Stewart (of Eurythmics fame) offered them his home studio, as George, according to Petty, "liked recording in houses better than studios," where they could hang out and swap lyrics and riffs while cooking up more songs and barbecue. Everybody involved agreed it was best to keep the whole ordeal very hush-hush. Better the record companies and media remained in the dark while the music had a chance to flourish.

Released in October 1988, *The Traveling Wilburys Volume One* was nothing if not a good time. Derek Taylor, the Beatles' former press wiz who also worked his linguistic magic for the Byrds in their early days, was brought in to create a bio that stoked the band's mysterious history. According to "Professor Tiny Hampton of Please Yourself University," one "Dr. Arthur Noseputty" believed the band was "closely related to the Strangling Dingleberries, which is not a group but a disease." If this bit of madness wasn't enough, Monty Python's Michael Palin was invited to write the album's absurdist liner notes (under the nom deplume of Hugh Jampton), comparing the band's evolution to that of penguins "taking to ledges." The Wilburys, according to anthro-non-apologist Dr. Jampton, were originally "a stationary people" who began to evolve by taking "short walks." "The further the Wilburys traveled, the more adventurous their music became." Ultimately, he proclaimed their songs possessed "the power to stave off madness."

The origin of the Wilburys' handle, Harrison told an MTV interviewer with drop-dead candor, came directly by appointment of Prince Philip after he and Jeff Lynne played a royal command performance for HRH the Duke of Edinburgh. "Is it true?" she begged earnestly. "Of course, would we lie to you?" George replied, as his "half brothers" giggled nervously, fidgeting about in their chairs.

"Everybody picked their name," Petty told author Paul Zollo, "because we didn't want it to sound like 'Crosby, Stills Nash and Young,' like a bunch of lawyers." Harrison, the Wilburys' prime instigator, knew the zany camaraderie of the Beatles' early days could never be duplicated. That kind of spirit can't be forced or faked (even by the Monkees). But as a devoted gardener, he understood it could be nurtured. Judging by the grin on their faces, everybody appeared to be having a blast as they posed for a group promo shot, brandishing shiny new guitars like a pack of pirates who'd just pilfered the Gretsch factory.

"Being in this group where we were sort of equal contributors, all of a sudden, was a great relief," Tom Petty confessed. "And I think everyone really enjoyed that."

Everybody's respect for Roy was obvious. Drummer Jim Keltner recalled the rest of the band watching in awe, "with their mouths open" as Orbison sang. "This enormous voice was coming out with all this emotion, and yet he was standing perfectly still, and it looked like maybe he was just talking to himself. It was just totally effortless for him." While Harrison claimed "the Voice" gave him "goose bumps," Petty joked about getting "Roy's autograph every day."

Orbison's sole songwriting offering on *Volume 1* was "Not Alone Anymore," although he also recorded an original ballad called "The Winged Serpent" based on "The Sick Rose" by the eighteenth-century visionary poet William Blake. For whatever reason, the song never made the final cut, nor did it appear on any of Roy's subsequent posthumous albums, and remains a lonely angel, floating in the ether of the Orbison myth.

After years in exile, wandering the lonely valleys of the American pop-culture wasteland, it seemed that Roy Orbison had finally arrived. He'd suddenly become the touchstone for rockers of every stripe and style, from Don McLean to Van Halen to Tom Waits, to his fellow Wilburys to U2.

"It was like Bono was with the president. He just worshiped Roy," Keltner claimed. "Roy inspired that from people," Will Jennings concurred. "He had a royal quality, a princely quality."

"I was so happy for Roy, that he was finally getting the respect he deserved. He'd become iconic by the end of his life" Rodney Justo said. "Man, I remember playing shows with him where his name was listed as Ray Auberson!"

FOURTEEN

GOING OUT ON A HIGH NOTE

The seeds to "She's a Mystery to Me" were planted mysteriously one night in Bono's brain as he slept with the soundtrack to David Lynch's *Blue Velvet* set on repeat. Upon awakening, the lead singer of U2 discovered the words and melody to a new song echoing in his skull. Assuming it was something he'd picked it up off the disc, Bono listened back to the entire album to find the tune had actually been inspired by a night of what he later described as "disturbed sleep."

Later that day, he played his new song for his bandmates, between raving about the "genius" of Roy Orbison. Bono claimed he'd been somehow "haunted" by Roy's presence and was certain he'd written the song for him. Then, as Bono told Michka Assayas, "a very strange thing happened"—a security guard at their show that night appeared to inform him that Roy Orbison was waiting at the door. Suddenly, Roy was standing before him, applauding the band, telling everyone how much he enjoyed their show and asking U2's flabbergasted front man if by some chance he had a song that might suit his style for a new record.

The album's original title, *The Underside of Pop Romance*, would soon be abandoned for *Mystery Girl*, the hero of Bono's ethereal anthem. For U2's bard, recording with Roy was an "extraordinary" experience. Bono marveled at how effortlessly Orbison emoted his lyrics, barely moving his lips as he sang. Yet, the Irish singer observed, it was "all there" in the playback.

Released February 7, 1989, *Mystery Girl* quickly sold in the neighborhood of two million copies. Along with Bono's contribution, it included Elvis Costello's song "The Comedians," which he claimed had originally been inspired by "In Dreams." Asked by producer T Bone Burnett to write a tune for Orbison's new album, Costello had reworked an old number he'd previously abandoned that, although bearing the stamp of his often complex (and sometimes convoluted) style, closely resembled Roy's songs from the Monument days. The lyric, which portrays a wistful loser who, trapped atop a Ferris wheel, manages to find humor in watching his lover walk away with another man, fits perfectly into Orbison's scrapbook of heartache.

The album's smash hit, "You Got It," was the first collaboration between Roy, Jeff Lynne, and Tom Petty. Written during Christmas '87, before the sudden, unexpected emergence of the Traveling Wilburys, the song was apparently inspired when Jeff and Roy were standing around in Petty's driveway, admiring Tom's brand-new Corvette. After checking out the engine, the three musicians were momentarily stumped over how to get the hood back down. When Tom finally figured it out, one of them (presumably Roy) remarked, "You got it!"

Another highlight from *Mystery Girl* is the no-nonsense groove of "All I Can Do Is Dream You," an update of "Dream Baby" that features Rick Vito's snarling lead guitar over the relentless thwack of Mike Curry's snare. "California Blue," another song that found its inspiration in Orbison's earlier work, is an airy, lightly strummed ballad, buoyed by the crisp click of claves and Lynne's cascading synth lines. Like "Blue Bayou," the lyrics yearned for better times to come.

While Steve Cropper's Telecaster and the Memphis horns give Wesley Orbison's first song, "The Only One," some genuine soul flavor, Bill Dees and Roy's final collaboration, "Windsurfer," which (driven by a grungy Hawaiian style slide guitar) tells the story of a brokenhearted beach bum, sounds like a lost treasure from Brian Wilson's songbook.

"I had written a song called 'Awesome Love' that Roy liked," Buddy Buie said, recalling a track that slipped through the cracks. "He called me and said he'd like to come down [to Alabama] and 'put his two cents in.' I hadn't seen him in a long time. His tour bus dropped him off at my place and he put his signature on it. But in the end the producers passed it up. They said it was 'too Valley.' As Roy was leavin' he handed me a black shirt and a pair of his jeans to get rid of. They smelled like smoke and he didn't want Barbara to know he was at it again."

Back on top of the world, and in the thick of a hectic schedule, constantly juggling recording dates, tours, and video and photo shoots, Roy casually remarked, "The devil is chasing me." Whether or not it was a premonition, Orbison seemed to intuitively know that he didn't have long. Although his half brother Nelson Wilbury (George Harrison) sang "Beware of Maya," which warned of the pitfalls of the material world, Roy had once again become consumed with ambition to rebuild his legacy, in hopes of making up for all the lost years he'd spent simmering on America's back burner.

On November 18, 1988, Orbison was regaled at the Diamond Awards Festival in Antwerp, Belgium, where he played a short set that included the only live (actually lip-synched) performance of "You Got It" (mimed timpani included). From there he met Barbara in Paris briefly for their "second honeymoon."

Returning to the States, Roy was soon back on the road again, performing for younger crowds who'd recently discovered him thanks to the success of the Traveling Wilburys. But many of his new fans were disappointed that "Not Alone Anymore" hadn't made it into his set list of oldies. Claiming he had no time to rehearse new material, Orbison promised to revamp his show for the following tour. After a handful of dates on the East Coast, Roy gave what turned out to be his final performance at the Front Row Theater in Highland Heights, Ohio. Predictably, there were no surprises. As usual, the band cranked out the hits like a well-oiled machine while "the Voice," as Will Jennings later testified, "was as good as it ever was." Right up until the day he died.

"We spent the whole day together" Fred Foster said, recalling the last time he saw Roy, two weeks before Orbison's death. "He was signed to

Virgin at the time, getting it together. Barbara was producing the record. He stayed out of it," Fred said.

Respectful of his friend, Foster chose to "stay out of it" himself. There was no question Fred had been Orbison's greatest producer. Aside from the muddle of *Regeneration*, Fred's instincts had been spot-on when it came to Roy's music, and now he had to bite his tongue over Barbara's heavy-handed control of the singer's career. She had no background in music, and although she fiercely guarded her husband's legacy and privacy, Barbara constantly candy-coated Roy's quirky, dark side. Her management—from supervising in the studio to producing best-of compilations or overseeing various video projects—made her husband's image and music come off as lightweight and two-dimensional.

"Roy wasn't one for physical exertion," Fred continued. "When it came time for me to go, he said, 'I'll walk you out.' I thought that was kind of strange. I got into my car and rolled down the window and he asked me, 'Could we do it again?' I said, 'Sure.' He said, 'Fantastic! We'll do it! I'm goin' to Ohio for four one-nighters and then I'll be at my mom's for Christmas. Barbara is goin' to Germany.' 'Sounds like a winner!' I said. Then he said, 'Good-bye,' which shocked me, because Roy *never* said good-bye. He always said, 'So long . . .'"

The last time Jim Keltner saw Roy, Orbison had been on a diet and "had lost a bunch of weight and was looking real trim." Keltner thought Orbison, with his lank black hair pulled back into a ponytail, resembled a benevolent samurai.

Roy Orbison's last night on earth, Tuesday, December 6, 1988, was spent at his mother's house. He'd spent the afternoon flying remote-controlled model airplanes with Wesley and Benny Birchfield, his tour bus driver (a bluegrass musician best known for his high-lonesome harmonies with the Osborne Brothers), who was married to Roy's old friend country singer Jean Shepard, the widow of Hawkshaw Hawkins.

After dinner with Benny and Jean, Roy quietly ignored a series of sudden, sharp pains in his chest, dismissing it as indigestion or perhaps a few pangs triggered by his family reunion. There was plenty to be stressed out about, coming off the grind of his latest tour while gearing up for yet another trip to England, to promote the Wilburys' album.

Returning to Hendersonville had always been a mixed blessing for Roy. No matter how far he'd come, the ghosts of the past were never far off. And although he adored his mother, Nadine, better known as "Mammaw" (for whom he'd recorded a number of tributes over the years, including the lilting waltz "Mama," in 1962, as well as her favorite song, Stephen Foster's ethereal "Beautiful Dreamer"), there had been a number of issues that still remained unaddressed between father and son. With Barbara away in Germany visiting her family, it seemed like a good time and place to try and patch up whatever old wounds lingered. (Neil McKay's play *Take the Night*, produced and aired by BBC radio in March 2009, would later offer insight into the dynamic of Roy and Wesley's relationship.)

"Mammaw told me they lay on the bed and just talked for hours. Roy was trying to reconcile with Wes for not having been a close father," Terry Widlake explained. "Wes wasn't a problem child. The poor kid was simply left out. After Claudette died, Roy did not take him back into the fold. Wesley was displaced. Mammaw and Pappaw brought him up. They were his real parents. Then Roy and Barbara got married and built their new house. He'd want to go and stay with his father but Barbara would tell him, "I'm sorry, Wesley, we have plans.""

According to Widlake, Wesley's new stepmother "wanted nothing to do with Claudette or whatever she spawned." Terry recalled seeing the boy crying at a car show in Chicago when Barbara "didn't allow him to hold his daddy's hand. That was a side of Roy I was surprised by and didn't understand. Barbara controlled him in many ways," Terry said. "Years later, Wesley was living in a car. He'd stop by and I'd offer him a meal and invite him to stay with us. But he never did. If anybody had a reason to be driven to drugs, it was Wesley."

Like his estranged father, Wesley, too, tried to take life's hard knocks with a sense of equanimity and forgiveness. "There were times when Daddy wasn't himself," his troubled son admitted to Ellis Amburn. "[But] he came to his senses at the end."

Back home, the pain returned, repeatedly stabbing Roy in the chest. Wesley, who had run out to the store to pick up some snacks and soda, returned to find his father in the bathroom. It seemed like he'd been in there too long. He went over and knocked on the door. There was no answer. He shook the handle. Nothing, only silence. The door was locked. A moment later he broke it down, to find his father slumped on the floor, lifeless. Together, Nadine and Wesley waited in tears as the ambulance arrived to rush Roy's spent body to the Hendersonville hospital, where he was pronounced dead just a few minutes before midnight. He was fifty-two.

Tom Petty, a.k.a. "Charlie T. Wilbury," informed of his "half brother" Lefty Wilbury's sudden passing by a phone call from Nelson, later recalled in *Living in the Material World*, Martin Scorcese's documentary of Harrison's life, how he was taken aback by George's caustic quip, "Aren't you glad it wasn't you?"

A diligent student of the Bhagavad-Gita, Harrison believed the human soul inhabits the body for a brief time only to reincarnate again, after picking up a new "vehicle," which carries us along on our next "earthly mission." Although George infused many of his best songs, like "Love You To" and "Within You, Without You" with Eastern philosophy, he was also known for his wicked sense of humor.

Searching for the words to honor his departed friend, a somewhat glib George Harrison assured the press that Roy would "be cool in his astral body."

In no time, the media descended upon the band's surviving members, wanting to know who the new fifth Wilbury would be. Despite both Roger McGuinn and Del Shannon recently dropping by, Petty immediately quelled any brewing suspicions. The chair (as it appeared in the video for "End of the Line," which the band released following Roy's death) would remain forever empty.

"We never intended to replace Roy," Tom told Paul Zollo. It was never a consideration. There was only one Roy Orbison. In honor of their departed brother and true to the group's quirky humor, their follow-up album was dubbed *Volume 3*, a not-so-subtle statement that something, or someone, was clearly missing.

FIFTEEN

BEYOND THE END:
A WIDOW'S WALK

Chaos often follows in death's wake. At first no one could reach Barbara in Germany with the news of Roy's sudden death. There were pressing questions that needed answering. What were they to do with the body? Was Roy going to be buried or cremated? When and where would the funeral be? In Nashville or L.A.? Somebody had to make the call.

Jean Shepard had grown tired of waiting and organized a wake five days later at the College Heights Baptist Church in Gallatin, the local house of worship for Johnny Cash, Kris Kristofferson, and other country stars. As far as Jean was concerned, Roy Orbison belonged to the people, so everybody was welcome: family (both Wes and Roy's little brother, Sammy Keith, attended), friends, and fans. According to Sammy, the phone at the house never stopped ringing. How so many people got the number, he never could figure out.

In the meantime, Roy's remains were flown to Los Angeles. Barbara's high-profile gathering to celebrate her late husband was an altogether different affair. A tribute concert was quickly organized at the Wiltern Theatre on December 11, which featured the Stray Cats, who backed up Don Henley, Tom Petty, Graham Nash, Bonnie Raitt, and Will Jennings, who honored his friend by reciting Lord Byron's melancholic meditation on separation, "We'll Go No More A-Roving." Wesley didn't bother to fly out. The Fradys, needless to say, were not invited.

Roy was buried on December 15 in the elite Westwood Cemetery, also the final resting place of Marilyn Monroe, Dean Martin, and Natalie Wood. Much to the consternation of his fans, Orbison lies (to this day) in an unmarked grave (just a few yards away from Frank Zappa, who was also buried incognito without a tombstone).

"It was a terrible day, raining torrentially," recalled Will Jennings, who acted as one of Roy's pallbearers. "It was just so sad."

Meanwhile, Orbison's posthumous career ascended to unimagined new heights. With *Mystery Girl* and *The Traveling Wilburys Volume 1* simultaneously topping the charts, Roy was once again a member of an extremely elite club. Apart from Michael Jackson, and Elvis, Roy Orbison was the only pop star to have two albums in the Top Five of the *Billboard* charts at the same time.

Even in death, the great equalizer, Roy continued to endure comparisons to his old friend/nemesis Elvis Presley. Oddly enough, it was Barbara who felt compelled to measure the experience of her husband's recent passing with the sad, lonely demise of the King: "You couldn't even compare Roy's death with Elvis," she pointed out, calling Presley's demise "a death in darkness" while her husband was still vital, "very much involved in daily living."

"So many people adored Elvis," she said. "But I don't think he ever could feel it." In Roy's case, his widow claimed, he was not only "fortunate" because of all the admiration and support he received from his fans and fellow musicians, but "he could feel the love."

No matter how obnoxiously Jerry Lee Lewis may protest, Elvis will always be rock 'n' roll's once and future king. Despite his phenomenal voice and the great songs he'd written, Roy Orbison knew he'd never wear that crown. Thankfully, no one until now has been tasteless enough to point out another similarity that both men shared—they both vanished into God's grace while sitting on "the throne." "Right at the end of his life, Roy was asked why he was working so much," Barbara said. "He said, 'I have found out in life that it's not the goal—the next Grammy or the next Number One. It's the journey.'"

But the journey all too often has a way of killing the traveler. The rock 'n' roll highway is littered with roadkill. And Roy Orbison, like so many before him, whether victims of habit or by accident, died too young.

Although Barbara Orbison spent much of 1990 involved in charity work, organizing a benefit concert to establish a residence for mentally handicapped homeless people in Los Angeles, there was still plenty of unfinished business of her husband's to attend to. Released in October 1992, *King of Hearts* was a posthumous hodgepodge of singles and various unfinished tracks and demos tweaked by a handful of high-profile producers, from Don and David Was and Chips Moman to Robbie Robertson. Included in the mix were Roy and k.d. lang's stunning duet of "Crying" and Will Jennings' "Wild Hearts," and "I Drove All Night." The second song was originally written for Roy, who first cut it back in 1987; Cyndi Lauper hit the charts with "I Drove All Night" two years later, in the spring of '89. Remixed by his "half brother" Otis Wilbury, a.k.a. Jeff Lynne, Orbison's version of "I Drove All Night" grazed the Top Ten in the UK and brought Roy a posthumous Grammy.

The album's title was a curious choice: It was a good choice, as Roy was a great chronicler of the intricacies of human relationships; but at the same time, the King of Hearts is known as the suicide king—the monarch of love, so driven by passion that he winds up jamming a sword through his skull.

In December 1991, Barbara's friend Cassie Brosnan died from ovarian cancer, leaving behind her husband, Pierce Brosnan, best known for playing James Bond, and three young children. A year later, Barbara and "007" were seen together at the third annual Fire & Ice Ball, a benefit for women's cancer research held at the Beverly Hilton Hotel. According to Peter Carrick's biography of Brosnan, they'd been brought together briefly by their "shared sense of loss."

Even with Roy gone, tragedy continued to hound the Orbison clan. In the early morning of November 2, 1993, a fire broke out in Topanga Canyon. Driven by high winds, the flames quickly grew out of control, scorching over a thousand acres in the first hour. A 30,000-foot column of smoke billowed from the inferno, turning the California sky into a vision of hell. As it had nearly once a decade over the last forty years (1956, 1970, and 1985), the fire swept down to the beach in Malibu, where it continued to rage for the next three days, despite the efforts of more than 700 fire fighters. By the time it was all over, there were three dead and $500 million in damages. Among the 268 houses that burned was the Orbisons' new home.

Not two months later, on January 17, 1994, at 4:30 A.M., the worst earthquake in over twenty years hit Los Angeles, a 6.9 on the Richter scale, killing fifty-seven, injuring 9,000, and taking down parking garages and freeway overpasses in the Northridge suburb of L.A. Barbara Orbison's Santa Monica office was among the buildings destroyed in the disaster. With her home in cinders and her business in shambles, she returned once again to Nashville's Music Row to keep the Orbison empire—Still Working Music—alive.

John Morthland, in his 1998 *Texas Monthly* article on Roy's posthumous career, would chalk the Orbisons' recent loss up to more "bad luck." But considering the constant calamity they routinely faced over the years, "luck," in whatever shape or form, trivialized such monumental challenges. There seemed to be another force beyond everyday happenstance at play that shaped the events in Roy's and his family's life.

Orbison's odyssey often appears mythical, like something from the pages of an old fairy tale, complete with a side of spooky numerology: The ugly duckling with the golden voice became a world-famous singer only to be quickly forgotten by a fickle public. His young, beautiful wife was killed on the sixth day of June (the sixth month) of 1966. Two sons and two houses would eventually be incinerated. And the last and perhaps strangest event of all came with Barbara's death. After battling pancreatic cancer for the better part of 2011, she passed away on December 6, exactly twenty-three years to the day of her husband's death. Beyond the odds and uncanny poetry of a couple dying on the same day is the added coincidence that Roy was born on the twenty-third of April. Beneath his mild-mannered persona, there seemed to be a mystic channeling the spirits.

Contrary to his morose image, Roy Orbison claimed to have lived most of his life "in a state of genuine contentment." "You have to be forgiving," he told Nick Kent in December 1988. "You have to also acknowledge the love people give to you. You've got to let the sorrows of the past go."

The source of his "strength and balance," Roy revealed, was "a working relationship between me and Jesus Christ." Although he confessed to having "drifted away" from the Church of Christ he sporadically attended growing up in Texas (after all, the local congregation had condemned dancing, and Roy's band played for dances), in his later years Orbison returned to the fold once more.

While Roy had no "pure statement" to offer regarding his beliefs, he claimed he tried to "live by the rules of morality" and with "a certain faithfulness in all things." "Your mind," Roy emphasized, "is created by a higher power, and common sense will often tell you what to do."

As he was typically soft-spoken and reserved in interviews, friends and fans were surprised by Orbison's recent comments about his spiritual views in the press. Never one for in-depth philosophizing, he told Nick Kent, "God has his plans and I've got mine," and left it at that.

k.d. lang never claimed to be a close friend of Roy's, but her intuition was spot-on when she sized him up as "a Buddha." "He seemed to break through [the tragic events in his life] and become very spiritual and very analytical and philosophical about it. . . . He'd lived his emotional life through his music, and that had left him very peaceful and calm."

But one still can't help but wonder what might have been. Orbison claimed to have recently "rededicated" his life to Jesus, a more subtle way of saying he was born again. While his old Sun labelmates, Elvis, Cash, and Perkins all recorded their fair share of gospel music, Jerry Lee, the most conflicted of the bunch and in most need of a little insurance for his journey across the River of Jordan, was known to delve into "that old-time religion" on occasion. Yet Orbison stuck with the secular over the sacred. While loaning his voice to Coca-Cola and Sasson Jeans, Roy remained reticent about recording an album that openly praised his Lord.

Perhaps following *Mystery Girl* Roy was preparing to delve into the mystery itself. But it wasn't to be. Orbison, whose life, at times, seemed to mirror that of Job's from the Old Testament, certainly endured enough hardship to qualify as a instrument of the infinite. While the tragedies he suffered didn't cause him to go crazy with drugs, alcohol, rage, or religion, chances were, Roy, no matter how infused he'd recently become with the Holy Spirit, would never have worn his spirituality on his sleeve. It just wasn't "the Orbison way."

"God," as John Lennon sang on his first solo album, 1970's *Plastic Ono Band*, "is a concept by which we measure our pain." While Lennon bitterly denounced holy books and spiritual and political leaders as well as Elvis, Dylan, and his former bandmates, Orbison transcended that pain, not by denying it but by living with it, accepting it, and finally growing through it. Two of his half brothers in the Wilburys had previously gone down their own spiritual path, much to the bewilderment of their fans. In 1979, Dylan surprised the world when he became a born-again Christian. While his album *Slow Train Coming* grabbed people's ears with a funky gospel groove, Bob wound up alienating most of his crowd when preaching fire and brimstone at his concerts with the same vitriol that once fueled his early "finger-pointing" songs like "Positively 4th Street."

George Harrison, under Lord Krishna's spell, would also become a bit heavy-handed when trying to enlighten friends and fans about the spiritual path. Known around Apple, the Beatles' headquarters, as "His Lectureship," the "Quiet Beatle" admonished his audience to free themselves by "chanting the names of the Lord" rather than getting high and boogieing.

If Orbison had recorded a gospel album, he undoubtedly would've allowed "the Voice" do all the work while remaining quiet about his personal views. Ultimately, the songs of gorgeous melancholy that reflected the haunted inner landscape of Roy's soul were born of memory, imagination, and dreams. As he told journalist Kristina Adolfsson days before his death, "my life is a never-ending dream."

SELECTED
DISCOGRAPHY

Roy Orbison at the Rock House
Sun 1260—originally released 1961
A good collection (but not necessarily the best) of Roy's singles cut during his stint at Sun Records.

Lonely and Blue
Monument M 4002—originally released 1961
Featuring "Only the Lonely" and two gems by Don Gibson, "I Can't Stop Loving You" and "(I'd Be) a Legend in My Time."

Crying
Monument M 4007—originally released 1962
Featuring "Crying," "Running Scared," and "Nightlife," along with Roy's smoldering take of Boudleaux Bryant's "Love Hurts."

Roy Orbison's Greatest Hits
Monument M 4009—originally released August 1, 1962
The first of (too) many *Greatest Hits* and *Best Of*s. But this one features some great tracks not included on his first two Monument releases, such as "Candy Man," "Dream Baby," and "Uptown."

In Dreams
Monument MLP 8003—originally released July 1963
Another fine Monument moment featuring "In Dreams," "Shahdaroba," "Blue Bayou," and "(They Call You) Gigolette."

Early Orbison
Monument MLP 8023—originally released October 1, 1964
A collection of previously released tracks. Essential for "Pretty One" alone.

More of Roy Orbison's Greatest Hits
Monument MLP 8024—originally released July 1, 1964
Various classic singles not included on any previous album, including the epochal "It's Over," the dark and foreboding "Falling," and the mystical "Leah."

Orbisongs
Monument MLP 8035—originally released 1965
"Oh, Pretty Woman" and various other tracks, including "Let the Good Times Roll," which Roy performed regularly in concert for years, and the lovely "Yo Te Amo Maria."
This album marks the end of Orbison's time at Monument Records.

There Is Only One Roy Orbison
MGM E 4308—originally released July 1, 1965
The Big O's debut on MGM held little greatness beyond "Ride Away," his freewheeling motorcycle opus.

The Orbison Way
MGM E 4322—originally released January 1966
Includes the beautifully twisted "Crawling Back" and one of Roy's best (and most underrated rockers), "Breaking Up Is Breaking My Heart."

The Classic Roy Orbison
MGM E 4379—originally released July 1966
Worth it alone for the cover shot of Roy deep in Southern goth mode. Includes the fabulous forgotten track "Pantomime" as well as "Twinkle Toes."

Roy Orbison Sings Don Gibson
MGM E 4322—originally released January 1967
Roy pays tribute to the great songwriter Don Gibson. Standouts include the bouncy bowlegged "Big Hearted Me" and the deliciously cryptic "Too Soon to Know."

The Fastest Guitar Alive
MGM E 4475—originally released June 1967
The soundtrack album to Roy's cinematic flop. Includes the kitschy "Medicine Man," the campy gunslinger ballad "Pistolero," and "There Won't Be Many Coming Home," a melancholy metaphor for the Vietnam War.

Cry Softly, Lonely One
MGM E 4514—originally released October 1967
His third album of 1967! By now Roy was beginning to spread himself thin. Memorable tracks include "She," "Communication Breakdown," and the title cut.

Roy Orbison's Many Moods
MGM E 4636—originally released May 1969
At first glance this appears to be an easy-listening record. The cover shot portrays Roy in a cardigan sweater with a pleasant grin, but the "many moods" are actually few and unsurprisingly melancholic, for the most part, as the Big O turns in chilling performances of "Walk On" and "Try to Remember."

The Big O
London HAU 8406—originally released 1970
This record was released only in the UK and finds Roy backed by his British touring band the Art Movement. Roy's American fans missed out on a real gem with this one. A collection of some of Orbison's favorite tunes, the playlist includes a smattering of covers, of everything from the Beach Boys' "Help Me Rhonda," to the Louvin Brothers' "When I Stop Dreaming," to Chris Kenner's eternal frat-house rocker "Land of a Thousand Dances," which Roy regularly performed in concert. The record has a refreshingly rootsy sound and includes Sammy King's "Penny Arcade," a bit of British music hall that had Orbison's American fans scratching their heads in wonder.

Hank Williams the Roy Orbison Way
MGM SE 4683—originally released August 1970
Not at all what you might expect. More Lee Hazlewood than *Grand Ole Opry*. A strange and wonderful record. "Kaw-Liga" and "Hey Good Lookin'" must be heard to be believed.

Roy Orbison Sings
MGM SE 4835—originally released May 1972
Yes he does. Beautifully and tenderly. But unfortunately there's not much here worth remembering.

Memphis
MGM SE 486—originally released November 1972
The last two tracks, "The Three Bells" (an old favorite of French chanteuse Edith Piaf) and a knockout delivery of "Danny Boy," take the cake on a record where both Roy and his backup band sound, for the most part, like they're just going through the motions.

Milestones
MGM SE 4934—originally released September 24, 1973
A milestone only in that Roy was finally freed from his contract with MGM after releasing a series of turkeys, although it is interesting to hear him cover Neil Diamond's "Sweet Caroline," and "Otis Redding's "I've Been Loving

You Too Long (to Stop Now)." "Blue Rain (Coming Down)" is the keeper of the set.

I'm Still in Love with You
Mercury SRMI 1045—originally released 1975
Out of the frying pan, into the fire.

Regeneration
Monument MG7600—originally released 1977
Despite a grooving rhythm section, the long-awaited reunion of Roy with Fred Foster, producer of Orbison's classic early hits, just didn't pay off. The trouble lay in a shoddy repertoire. Roy's contribution as a songwriter was negligible, and very few of the tunes he and Foster chose to record were tailor-fit to the Orbison persona.

Laminar Flow
Asylum 6E 198—originally released 1979
Roy under the evil influence of disco, complete with a scary cover snap of the Big O clad in black satin. There's nowhere to go but up from here. "Hound Dog Man," his tribute to his old friend Elvis, is worth a spin.

Class of '55
America/Smash 830-002-1 M-1—originally released May 26, 1986
Back with his old pals Johnny Cash, Carl Perkins, and Jerry Lee Lewis, with Chips Moman at the board. But beyond his fifteen seconds of fame on Waylon Jennings' "Waymore's Blues," Roy gets lost in the shuffle. His one contribution to the album, "Coming Home," is good stuff.

In Dreams: The Greatest Hits
Virgin 90604-1—originally released 1987
Redux. T Bone Burnett–produced versions of the old classics. A solid job and, as the Monument catalog was currently out of print, a good way to keep Roy's music in the public's ears.

Traveling Wilburys Vol. 1
Wilbury 9 25796-1—originally released October 18, 1988
Big fun with George Harrison, Bob Dylan, Tom Petty, and Jeff Lynne. Roy Orbison was back, reestablishing his place in the rock 'n' roll pantheon with six words—"I'm so tired of being lonely!"—in the bridge to the hit single "Handle with Care" His sole song on the record, "Not Alone Anymore," was an instant classic.

Mystery Girl
Virgin 7 91058-1—originally released February 7, 1989
What a cruel joke fate dealt Roy while in the midst of making the comeback we'd all hoped for when he suddenly died of a heart attack on December 6, 1988. Orbison never lived to see this album's release, nor the fantastic success it garnered. Roy was once more in fine form here, collaborating with everyone from Bono and Elvis Costello to his old partner Bill Dees and his "lost" son Wesley.

A Black and White Night
Virgin 91295-2—originally released November 23, 1989
The soundtrack to the excellent made-for-TV special by the same name. Produced by T Bone Burnett.

King of Hearts
Virgin 86520—originally released October 20, 1992
The last go-round. A good album as far as posthumous releases go, compiled from old singles and various sonic scraps. Includes "Heartbreak Radio," "We'll Take the Night," "I Drove All Night," and Roy's duet with k.d. lang on "Crying."

BIBLIOGRAPHY

BOOKS

Amburn, Ellis. *Dark Star: The Roy Orbison Story*. New York: Knightsbridge Publishing, 1990.

Assayas, Michael. *Bono*. New York: Riverhead Books, 2006.

Bowman, David. *This Must Be the Place: The Adventures of Talking Heads in the 20th Century*. New York: Harper Collins, 2001.

Coleman, Ray. *Lennon*. New York: McGraw Hill, 1985.

Dawidoff, Nicholas. *In the Country of the Country*. New York: Vintage, 1998.

Emery, Ralph. *The View from Nashville*. New York: Quill, 1998.

Escott, Colin, and Hawkins, Martin. *Sun Records: The Brief History of the Legendary Label*. New York, London: Quick Fox, 1980.

Faithfull, Marianne, with Dalton, David. *Faithfull: An Autobiography*. New York: Cooper Square Press, 2000.

Goldrosen, John. *The Buddy Holly Story*. New York: Quick Fox, 1975.

Harrington, Joe. *Sonic Cool: The Life & Death of Rock 'n' Roll*. Milwaukee, WI: Hal Leonard, 2002.

Helm, Levon with Davis, Stephen. *This Wheel's on Fire*. New York: Quill, 1993.

Kennedy, Rick, and McNutt, Randy. *Little Labels: Big Sound*. Bloomington and Indianapolis: Indiana University Press, 1999.

Lehman, Peter. *Roy Orbison: The Invention of an Alternative Rock Masculinity*. Philadelphia, Temple University Press, 2003.

Marsh, Dave. *The Heart of Rock and Soul: The 1001 Greatest Singles Ever Made*. New York: Da Capo Press, 1999.

Marcus, Greil. *Mystery Train*. New York: Plume, 2008.

McDonough, Jimmy. *Shakey: Neil Young's Biography*. New York: Anchor Books, 2003.

Padel, Ruth. *I'm a Man*. London: Faber & Faber, 2000.

Patoski, Joe Nick. *Willie Nelson: An Epic Life*. New York: Little, Brown and Company, 2009

Perkins, Carl, and McGee, David. *Go Cat Go*. New York: Hyperion, 1996.

Starr, Victoria. *All You Get Is Me*. New York: St. Martins, 1995.

Wyman, Bill, with Coleman, Ray. *Stone Alone*. New York: Viking, 1990.

PERIODICALS

Hoskyns, Barney. "The Lonely Blue Dream of Roy Orbison." *Mojo*, January 1999.

Jopling, Norman. "Roy Orbison: An Unexpected U.S. Hit For Roy." *Record Mirror*, September 14, 1963.

Reel, Penny. "Roy Orbison." *New Musical Express*, December 20, 1980.

Sandall, Robert. "It's Over: Roy Orbison." *Q*, February 1989.

"Totally Shattered." *The Daily Sketch*. April 17, 1970.

TELEVISION/VIDEO/YOUTUBE

"Elvis Costello Talks About Roy Orbison." YouTube video. Posted by "harton-mitch," April 24, 2011.

Interview from *In Dreams: The Roy Orbison Story*. Orbison Productions, 1999. Directed by Mark Hall, written by Maryse Rouillard. Made-for-TV documentary, 1:30.

Interview with the Traveling Wilburys (George Harrison, Jeff Lynne, Tom Petty, and Roy Orbison). YouTube video, from an interview broadcast by MTV on October 28, 1988. Posted by "vitorbastos123," January 25, 2012. http://www.youtube.com/watch?v=KTDKbQFda3c.

INTERNET SOURCES

"Bill Frady Fights Back!!!!!!" http://www.geocities.ws/mart118/misc/frady2.html.

Michael Fremer. "Mr. Natural: Recording Engineer Bill Porter, Parts 1& 2." *Analog Planet*. Posted May 1, 2009. http://www.analogplanet.com/content/mr-natural-recording-engineer-bill-porter-part-i-0.

www.RoyOrbison.com

DVDS

Roy Orbison: Live at Austin City Limits. Directed by Gary Menotti. Chatsworth, CA: Image Entertainment, 2003. DVD, 64 min.

Roy Orbison, A Black and White Night. Directed by Tony Mitchell. Cinemax television special aired January 3, 1988. Chatsworth, CA: Image Entertainment, 1999. DVD, 64 min.

ACKNOWLEDGMENTS

Thanks to everyone I interviewed, for their time, memories, and insights:

Harold Bradley, Buddy Buie, Charlie Calello, Cowboy Jack Clement, Bill Dees, Fred Foster, Ronnie Gant, Jimmie Dale Gilmore, Bobby Goldsboro, Carolyn Hester, Sammy King, Al Kooper, Dave Marsh, Charlie McCoy, David McKinley, Bill Moody, Bob Moore, Kittra Moore, "Cousin" Brucie Morrow, Bonnie Raitt, Syd Straw, Richard Thompson, and Terry Widlake.

Big thanks to my editor Mike Edison for his Roman-candle enthusiasm, Buddha patience, and bulldog belief in this project; to my more-than-wife, Marilyn Cvitanic; and to my friends who helped me along on this journey, reading early drafts and listening to my endless rants about Roy—Cheryl Pawelski, John Lomax III, Oliver Trager, Estelle DeBates, Dominic Ording, Linda Roy, Jeff Greene, Oliver Cvitanic, and the guys at Mercer Street Books.

R.I.P. Barbara Orbison and Bill Dees.

INDEX